Taunton's

BASEMENTS COMPLETE

EXPERT ADVICE FROM START TO FINISH

STEVE CORY

The Taunton Press

The Taunton Press, Inc.
63 South Main Street, PO Box 5506
Newtown, CT 06470-5506
e-mail: tp@taunton.com

Editor: Carolyn Mandarano
Copy editor: Nina Rynd Whitnah
Indexer: Cathy Goddard
Jacket/Cover design: Kim Adis
Interior design: Kim Adis
Layout: Sandra Mahlstedt and Susan Lampe-Wilson
Illustrator: Mario Ferro

Photographers: Steve Cory, except p. 5: Stephanie Montanari of Redstart Construction, Inc.; p. 6: Just Basements, www.justbasementsottawa.ca (left) and Tech Lighting (right); p. 7: Just Basements, www.justbasements ottawa.ca; p. 8: courtesy of Armstrong Flooring, Inc. (top) and Just Basements, www.justbasementsottawa.ca (bottom); p. 9: Dreamstime (top and bottom right) and Just Basements, www.justbasementsottawa.ca (bottom left); p. 10: Just Basements, www.justbasementsottawa.ca; p. 11: Just Basements, www.justbasementsottawa.ca (top, center, and bottom left), courtesy of Armstrong Flooring, Inc. (top right), and Krause Construction, LLC, Denver, Colo. (bottom right); p. 12: courtesy of IKEA (top left), Dreamstime (top right), and courtesy of Armstrong Flooring, Inc. (bottom); p. 13: Dreamstime (left), Shutterstock (top right), and design: Suzanne Martin, LLS, build: Michael Martin, Luxury Renovations (bottom right); p. 14: courtesy of IKEA (top and bottom left) and courtesy of Armstrong Flooring, Inc. (bottom right); p. 15: courtesy of IKEA (top); p. 16: SFA Saniflo, Inc., manufacturer of macerating and grinding toilet system (top), Just Basements, www.justbasementsottawa.ca (bottom left), and courtesy of IKEA (bottom right); p. 17: Kohler Co. (top left), courtesy of IKEA (bottom left), Stephanie Montanari of Redstart Construction, Inc. (top right), and Tech Lighting (bottom right); p. 18: Kohler Co. (top) and Tech Lighting (bottom); p. 19: Just Basements, www.justbasementsottawa.ca (top left), Krause Construction, LLC, Denver, Colo. (top right), and design: Suzanne Martin, LLS, build: Michael Martin, Luxury Renovations (bottom); p. 20: courtesy of IKEA (top and bottom right) and Dreamstime (bottom left); p. 21: design: Suzanne Martin, LLS, build: Michael Martin, Luxury Renovations (top) and Dreamstime (bottom); p. 34: Perma-Seal Basement Systems; p. 35: Perma-Seal Basement Systems (bottom); p. 38: Perma-Seal Basement Systems; p. 39: courtesy of Wellcraft Egress Systems (bottom right); p. 40: Perma-Seal Basement Systems; p. 41: Perma-Seal Basement Systems (bottom); p. 42: Perma-Seal Basement Systems (bottom right); p. 44: Perma-Seal Basement Systems; p. 46: Perma-Seal Basement Systems; p. 47: Perma-Seal Basement Systems; p. 53: Shawn Greene, Green Projects, Chicago (top center and top right); p. 56: Mike Fish, Vogon Construction, Chicago; p. 57: Shawn Greene, Green Projects, Chicago (bottom left and bottom center); p. 58: Tech Lighting (right); p. 59: Tech Lighting; p. 60: Just Basements, www.justbasementsottawa.ca; p. 61: Just Basements, www.justbasementsottawa.ca (bottom); p. 70: Shawn Greene, Green Projects, Chicago; p. 72: Tech Lighting; p. 73: Tech Lighting; p. 75: Just Basements, www.justbasementsottawa.ca; p. 113: Shawn Greene, Green Projects, Chicago; p. 119: SFA Saniflo, Inc., manufacturer of macerating and grinding toilet system (center right); p. 158: Dancer Concrete Design Team (left) and DRIcore Products (right); p. 159: Just Basements, www.justbasements ottawa.ca; p. 160: Just Basements, www.justbasementsottawa.ca (top) and design by Ryan Duebber, architect (bottom); p. 161: Just Basements, www. justbasementsottawa.ca (top left) and Dancer Concrete Design Team (top right and bottom); p. 162: DRIcore Products; p. 163: DRIcore Products; p. 182: courtesy of Armstrong Flooring, Inc. (left); p. 183: Dreamstime; p. 184: courtesy of Armstrong Flooring, Inc.; p. 185: courtesy of Armstrong Flooring, Inc. (top left and top right) and Just Basements, www.justbase-mentsottawa.ca (bottom); p. 195: design: Suzanne Martin, LLS, build: Michael Martin, Luxury Renovations (top); p. 197: courtesy of Daltile; p. 212: Dancer Concrete Design Team; p. 215: Dreamstime; p. 217: courtesy of Wellcraft Egress Systems; p. 218: courtesy of Wellcraft Egress Systems; p. 219: courtesy of Wellcraft Egress Systems; p. 235: Shutterstock

The following manufacturers/names appearing in *Basements Complete* are trademarks: American Standard®, CleanSpace®, DRIcore®, DryTrak®, EverLast™, Kevlar®, Kohler®, National Electrical Code®, Oneida Dust Deputy®, Ping-Pong®, SaniDry™, Saniflo®, SharkBite®, Sheetrock®, Shop-Vac®, SMARTWALL®, Strait-Flex®, Teflon®, WaterGuard®.

Library of Congress Cataloging-in-Publication Data

Names: Cory, Steve, author.
Title: Basements complete : expert advice from start to finish / Steve Cory.
Description: Newtown, CT : Taunton Press, Inc., [2018] | Includes index.
Identifiers: LCCN 2017047734 | ISBN 9781631868467
Subjects: LCSH: Basements--Remodeling.
Classification: LCC TH4816.3.B35 C69 2018 | DDC 643/.5--dc23
LC record available at https://lccn.loc.gov/2017047734

Printed in the United States of America
10 9 8 7 6 5 4 3 2 1

About Your Safety: Construction is inherently dangerous. Using hand or power tools improperly orignoring safety practices can lead to permanent injury or even death. Don't try to perform operations you learn about here (or elsewhere) unless you're certain they are safe for you. If something about an operation doesn't feel right, don't do it. Look for another way. We want you to enjoy working on your home, so please keep safety foremost in your mind.

ACKNOWLEDGMENTS

Many thanks to Mike Fish of Vogon Construction, whose excellent advice, ocean-deep knowledge, and willingness to slow down and pose for photographs were indispensable. Mike's basement provided the setting for many of the photos in this book, and he can be seen as a model throughout. Expert carpenter Gus Luna was invaluable. Also heartfelt thanks to Joe Hansa and Danny Campana for their expertise and information. William Shuman was a model deluxe. The artful and imaginative Chicago remodeler Shawn Greene provided very helpful photographs.

Many thanks to Perma-Seal Basement Systems (www.permaseal.net; 800-421-SEAL). Perma-Seal serves Chicagoland and northwestern Indiana homeowners with their basement waterproofing, crawl space, air quality, sewer back-up, and concrete-raising solutions. Roy Spencer, President and Founder of Perma-Seal, provided many photos showing the company's proven techniques as well as his expertise on the subject of making basements ready for any remodeling project.

DRIcore® Products supplied photos showing SMARTWALL®, an easy-to-install wall system that stays dry and mold-free in damp conditions. Wellcraft Egress Systems provided photos showing their excellent egress windows, which make a basement both safer and more appealing.

Jim Reddington of Safeway Plumbing knows all things plumbing, and his guys—the brothers Eddie and Joe Slazyk—posed and showed the way to install reliable plumbing.

A special thank you to the companies that generously provided high-quality products that appear in the book: The Kohler® Company (kohler.com) and American Standard® (www.americanstandard-us.com) supplied plumbing fixtures. Cork flooring was supplied by WE Cork (www.wecork.com; 800-666-CORK). And the up-flush toilet system was provided by SFA Saniflo® Inc., manufacturer of macerating and grinding toilet systems (www.saniflo.com; 800-571-8191).

The entire staff at The Taunton Press were most helpful at all points, and a joy to work with. As always, my wife Diane Slavik artfully punched my text into readable shape, and stern but always pleasant textmistress Carolyn Mandarano of The Taunton Press made the book truly reader-friendly.

—Steve Cory

contents

FRAMING WALLS AND CEILINGS

74

ROUGH PLUMBING

106

>> >> >> >>

WINDOWS, DOORS, AND TRIM
214

FINISH PLUMBING AND WIRING
234

INTRODUCTION

Many basements are largely forgotten and underutilized spaces, places you visit only if a major appliance like a furnace, boiler, or water heater needs repair. It may be where you store boxes and bins of stuff you rarely need to access.

But a basement can be much more. Even if today your basement looks like a dark cavern with ugly walls, a plain concrete floor, and a ceiling that features all sorts of complicated-looking pipes and cables, it can most likely be turned into livable space. With some imagination and elbow grease, a basement can offer more functionality to your home without having to change the footprint—think space to entertain, relax, work, exercise, sleep, and more.

The first chapter of this book will help inspire you, with ideas for a range of basement rooms that are both practical and fun. Set up with attractive wall surfaces, practical yet good-looking flooring, and ample lighting, basement rooms can look and feel much like upstairs rooms. The next chapter, starting on p. 22, gets down to the gritty reality: Before you start even planning a basement remodel, it's essential that a basement be strong

and stable, and that it be protected against moisture. Here you'll learn how to fix things the right way (and learn when to call in a pro) to ensure good conditions in the future.

The chapter on plan layouts and installations (pp. 58-73) will guide you through the planning process, including developing floor plan options, determining ceiling heights, making electrical and plumbing choices, and deciding on the best ways to create walls, floors, and ceilings for your situation. The rest of the book gives detailed instructions for the most common basement installations: framing walls and ceilings (pp. 74-105); running plumbing lines (pp. 106-135); running electrical lines (pp. 136-157); finishing walls and ceilings (pp. 158-181); laying flooring (pp. 182-213); installing windows, doors, and trim (pp. 214-233); and installing finish plumbing and wiring (pp. 234-249).

I encourage you to read this book before jumping right in so that you understand the scope of what's involved in creating your new living space and learn how to complete the process in an organized, efficient manner.

REMODELING OPTIONS

A FIRST LOOK AT YOUR BASEMENT may present a depressing prospect: dingy walls, cracked flooring, hanging pipes, and ugly utility appliances that seem to be in the way of achieving a decent floor plan. But as future chapters of this book will show, these problems can usually be overcome. So go ahead and start your planning with a little wistful dreaming: It costs nothing to imagine possibilities.

Think about the future as well as the present. If you have small children, they will become teenagers, then leave the house—and it all happens faster than we expect. Of course, many distinct spaces, like a bedroom or a family/entertainment room, can become popular destinations for folks of most any age. A bathroom with a spa may be popular with young people but is also a feature adults might like to soothe older joints and muscles.

This chapter is arranged according to room types. If you want to plan for discrete rooms that serve the needs of different people, or a suite of rooms that might form a sort of apartment, be sure to consider traffic patterns. If people will spend a fair amount of time in these rooms, you will probably want a bathroom, or at least a powder room.

Of course, you'll also need to plan around the utilities—the water heater and perhaps softener, the electrical service panel, and the furnace or boiler. If possible, put them in a separate utility room, where they can be accessed easily but also be safely away from children.

FAMILY ROOMS

The idea of a family room is to create a space that all members of the family will want to use for relaxation and fun. It is a largish room that can combine many of the functions described for the other types of rooms in this chapter: a play area with storage bins for toys, a TV area with seating, a table where groups can play board games, a computer station, and perhaps a pool or Ping-Pong® table.

Creating a family room is pretty straightforward. It's an open, usable space; the simpler the better, so you can rearrange furniture as your family changes over the years. There is no plumbing to run or fixtures to install, other than providing receptacles and lighting, as well as computer and TV hookups. Make it a cheery, well-lit space.

A large cabinet has doors that can hide the television, instantly transforming a video room into a center for interacting with friends and family.

The owners call this their basement loft. The ceiling is the original structural beams and joists system painted white to add the feeling of higher ceilings and to lighten the space. With young children in the family, boxed-in lally columns and walls help to break the large space into age-appropriate areas.

Built-out walls allow for extra wall insulation, as well as an attractive nook for shelving and a television.

Don't be afraid to add splashy colors and age-appropriate art to liven up a living space. Here, sci-fi memorabilia make a fun personalized teen statement.

If one or more basement walls are at least partly above ground, consider installing spacious windows.

ENTERTAINMENT SPACES

A video area **with extra space feels like a real theater. The house lights—a grid of overhead recessed canisters and sconces on the walls near the ceiling—are all on dimmers, to complete the movie-going experience.**

A basement is often more casual than the rest of the house, making it a place where people can let their hair down and have some fun. Of course, "fun" varies from family to family, so plan according to your habits. And you may want to expand your gaming repertoire by installing a pool or Ping-Pong table, or adding a large table and lots of storage for jigsaw puzzles or creative projects. Every home benefits from having a giant table surface somewhere in the house. A pleasantly refurbished basement can become a place where the family draws closer together with new activities.

For many of us, television is king. You may want to celebrate this universal addiction by creating a full-blown viewing center, complete with a giant screen and cushy reclining theater seating that incorporates lighted drink holders, fold-out trays, ambient lighting, and more to enhance your couch-potato time. Or, just position chairs where people can use them either for watching TV, gaming, or reading and relaxing.

If you have children, it's not difficult to adapt a space for them. Be sure to lay flooring that is easy to clean, or replace, and include storage space in your design to make cleanup easy.

Your own personal sound stage is feasible in the basement, which makes it possible to jam into the night, acoustically speaking, without bothering the rest of the family.

This inviting space offers a wet bar with lots of storage and floating shelves on a stone wall, together with a pool table—the perfect setup to unwind.

A couple of arcade games and an old-time popcorn maker are just off the TV viewing area.

Comfortable space for the whole gang makes movie night. Recliners with cup holders and trays make it easy to feast on gourmet snacks. When planning, just be sure there is access to bring in big equipment and oversize chairs.

KIDS' STUFF

A basement can be an ideal place for young children or teenagers: They can have their own space, they can make noise without bothering people upstairs too much, and parents know they are safe. A kids' area can be a simple open space for play, with some creative touches and storage shelves (below). Or, it can be a small space under the stairs, just right for pint-sized imaginations (bottom).

BEDROOMS

Unless you cherish plenty of bright sunlight, a basement can be a fine place for a bedroom–or a great place for a guest bedroom. It's secluded and usually quiet–and nice and dark at night.

Often, teenagers and young adults like to move into the basement, where they can have more privacy and fewer comments from their parents about their cleaning habits. We'll leave it up to you to decide on standards for the teen cave.

Closet units like these assemble in a snap. They are perfect options for a casual bedroom.

This spacious, open bedroom decorated in earth tones is stylishly lit by pendant and floor lamps. It is a sophisticated and comfortable space suitable for guests or family members.

WORKOUT ROOMS

A basement is a great place for exercise equipment: Noisy machines or loud workout music is less likely to bother others; you can get all sweaty and pant without worrying about people watching you; and having a dedicated workout room can make it easier to develop good habits.

Most people find that it helps to have a screen or two, either with good speakers or headphones. You may choose to fully equip a room with nothing but machines, mats, and weights, ensuring that once you enter, you have nothing else to do but work out. Or, include some simple equipment in an all-purpose family room.

You don't need a lot of equipment to stay fit. For many, a simple mat, which can roll up and be stored under the sofa, plus a few small weights, are all that's needed.

This large room has ample space for a Ping-Pong table and several pieces of exercise equipment. Cork tiles on the wall make a forgiving surface in case of mishaps or rambunctiousness.

This workout room located just behind the media area makes it convenient to watch the big-screen TV with surround sound while working out. The bright ceiling color adds upbeat energy to the room.

OFFICES AND CRAFT CENTERS

Many people think of an ideal home office as a sunny place with stunning views out the window. However, those who actually want to get work done often prefer a place with fewer distractions—and a basement may be a better choice.

Unless you're writing Gothic fiction or vampire novels, you probably don't want the office to be positively gloomy, and the projects and tips in this book are full of ideas for making rooms bright and cheerful even where there is little or no natural light.

Install plenty of electrical receptacles. To be safe, the office should be on its own electrical circuit to ensure you will not trip a breaker and lose data. Plan for Internet connectivity, which can sometimes be a problem in a basement, using either a wireless or a cable connection, or both.

If you like to craft but want to keep crafty clutter and perhaps fumes out of the upstairs living areas, make room for a below-stairs arts and crafts area. Keep things as large as possible: a large table or two, and plenty of capacious shelving and bins for storing materials. Make surfaces easy to wipe clean. And be sure you can open a window or turn on an exhaust fan, when ventilation is needed.

Black-and-white is a time-honored color scheme that feels contemporary. Glass cabinet doors make it easy to find stored documents yet keep them from getting dusty. A unit with lots of large drawers is always welcome.

A workspace for a young adult or professional, this small and simple space must be kept tidy to be usable—a great strategy against clutter! Playful wall-mounted strings allow for hanging artwork—or any work in progress.

A spacious room with lots of storage is a crafter's dream. This cheerful space doubles as a sewing and art room, and even includes a sink. Basement rooms can be a good place to recycle old kitchen cabinets.

Straightforward, inexpensive materials combine to keep things well organized without fuss. A strip of wood on the wall holds bars and hooks for all sorts of small items. The desk is a simple slab with wood supports. Wall- and desk-mounted swing-arm lamps can be quickly adjusted to perfectly suit your needs. Traditional file cabinets add to the feel of an office that means business.

A small space tucked in near the stairs combines a library, a sewing table, a chalkboard for children's art, and a desk.

BATHROOMS

A bathroom in the basement is a welcome addition whether people spend the night in a bedroom or just hang out for periods of time. Often a small powder room with just a toilet and sink will suffice, but a shower or tub—or even a spa tub—can be a luxurious place to relax and get clean.

A bathroom in a basement is sometimes inexpensive to install because supply and drainpipes are nearby and easy to run. However, in some situations, the drain may pose difficulties because the only drain lines lower than the bathroom are under the concrete floor. This situation isn't insurmountable, though: You could break into the concrete or install an up-flush system, as shown on pp. 117–119.

Plan for adequate ventilation, especially if your basement does not have many operable windows. A bathroom should have a powerful vent fan that efficiently shunts moist air to the outside.

A powder room tucks under the basement stairway. Behind the toilet is an up-flush unit that pumps waste up to a drainpipe, so you don't have to cut into the floor.

A clean and modern powder room in light, bright hues is a welcome addition to any family basement remodel.

With plenty of lighting, you can forget that the bathroom is in the basement.

Equipping a basement bath with a spa tub—even a small one like this—makes it a soothing refuge from your worries and cares.

CONSIDER A MUDROOM

If your basement has a doorway to the outside, people and pets may feel free to drag in mud and muck. Install a dedicated mudroom area, with flooring that is easily cleaned, such as ceramic or vinyl tiles. Position a bench and a place—perhaps just an empty space below the bench—that is clearly designed for stowing soiled boots and shoes.

A space-saving vanity sink hugs the wall, and a slender storage unit has both open and doored shelving.

Even if only the upper foot or so of your walls are above grade, you can take advantage and install slit windows that let in welcome sunlight.

KITCHENS

A marble countertop surrounds a farmhouse sink; a faucet with an old-fashioned look and painted cabinets contribute to the charming cottage style.

An island that doubles as an eating table with stools is an efficient use of space and brings the cook and noshers close together. Light-colored granite countertops wipe clean in a flash and nicely reflect the pleasant lighting.

Unless you are making a full-fledged apartment in your basement, the kitchen area is likely to be modest, perhaps more of a "kitchenette." You'll want the basics—sink, base and wall cabinets or open shelves, countertop, refrigerator, garbage and recycling bins, and microwave—and possibly a stovetop, or a range and range hood with vent fan. There should be plenty of lighting as well as electrical receptacles that are ground fault circuit interrupter (GFCI) protected. But things can be smaller; for instance, 8 ft. of countertop space may be enough, and even a little bar sink may be all you really need. If you go with a dishwasher, a narrow 24-in.-wide model could be a good choice; a smaller 28-in.-wide refrigerator may also provide entirely enough space.

An advantage of going small is that you may be able to afford more luxurious surfaces, like granite countertops, hardwood cabinetry, and nice tile flooring. Choose surfaces that are easy to keep clean.

BARS AND WINE CELLARS

Basements can be great entertaining spaces, so whether you lean toward fine wines or mixed drinks, you can create a place where it's easy and fun to make your favorite libations.

You'll want the area to be virtually dust free, so your bottles and glasses can stay sparkling with only occasional cleaning. Lighting should be on dimmer switches, so you can adjust the mood to suit the occasion.

This wine "cellar" keeps reds at a perfect 63°F and places them on well-lit display as well.

This elegant basement bar is sure to be a popular gathering spot. The open layout encourages mingling both at and around the bar seating area.

A bar-level countertop with bar stools faces a small kitchen and drink-mixing area. Chairs with high backs encourage guests to linger.

LAUNDRIES

Your typical basement laundry room is a pretty desultory affair, with plain concrete or dingy tiled floors, a washer and dryer, a plastic or old concrete utility sink, and perhaps a table or small countertop. Upgrading the laundry room can really change your attitude toward this inescapable chore. Provide a large easy-to-clean folding countertop or table, so you can easily organize and neatly stack clothing after folding. If you have space, install a nice long hanging rod or two, and drawers or shelves to store cleaning supplies.

You will still need the basics, though: The dryer needs to vent to the outside. The washer should have easy-to-reach supply valves, and its drain hose should be firmly attached to a sink or a drain line. Both should be easy to pull out for servicing, and both need to plug into the correct receptacles.

Provide a sink that is easy and even pleasant to use, for hand washing and general cleanup. The floor should be impervious to water, and there should be a nearby floor drain, in case of overflows. And as is so often the case in a laundry space, the more storage drawers and shelves, the better.

Common in basements is a combination bathroom and laundry. Not only does this speak to the more casual nature of a basement, but all plumbing supplies run to the same area. You can forego a utility sink if this is the case.

Space and storage options are welcome in a laundry room.

A largish powder room can also house laundry facilities.

Crisp tones of black and tan lend a formal feel. Lots of storage, including a built-in area for hanging clothes straight out of the dryer, keeps clutter to a minimum.

Because space is limited, there is no place to add counters for folding clothes. However, the washer and dryer tuck neatly behind doors.

THE GRITTY REALITY

YOU MAY BE TEMPTED TO SKIP RIGHT to planning your new basement, but many homeowners have suffered greatly for neglecting the nonglamorous issues. Whether you are doing work yourself or hiring a pro, you or your contractor must make sure your basement is really ready for a remodel.

There are reasons most basements were originally built with exposed masonry walls, floors, pipes, ducts, and large appliances. Basements can develop a number of problems, and covering things up with a remodel can hide these problems—and then create worse problems as hidden issues quietly grow into a serious situation. So carefully inspect and solve any gritty problems first. It's only prudent.

ANATOMY OF A BASEMENT

To ensure that your basement will be secure and dry, start by gaining an understanding of how it was constructed.

The drawing below shows a fairly typical construction for a basement, plus framing for the floor above. Poured concrete walls (or walls made of block or stone), which are often 8 in. or 10 in. thick, rest on concrete footings that are often 10 in. thick and reinforced with steel. A poured concrete floor is often 3 in. or 4 in. thick and reinforced with metal. If the concrete walls, footings, or floor are not strong enough, or if they rest on soil that is not firm, then walls and floors can sag.

Here drainpipe (often referred to as "drain tile") runs around the exterior of the house at the bottom of the wall. The pipe is encased in gravel, so seeping water can easily enter the drainpipe and flow away from the basement. If a basement does

not have this drainpipe, it should have tile running under the basement floor on the inside. The tile should run into a sump pump, as shown on pp. 31–32.

In this example, there is a massive beam running through the center of the basement ceiling, to support the joists (which are ceiling joists for the basement and floor joists for the first floor). The beam is supported with large posts, which rest on deep concrete footings. This beam is often needed if the width of the basement is too long for joists to span and remain strong. However, if the basement is not very wide, or if engineered joists are used, then the beam may not be needed. During a remodel, the posts are often removed. In order to do this, the wooden beam is replaced with a very strong steel I-beam, which can span very long distances. A "bearing" wall can take the place of a massive beam but will

limit floor-plan options. A "curtain" wall is not needed for support and can be removed.

The joists (which again serve as floor joists for the first floor and ceiling joists for the basement) rest on a sill, which rests on top of the basement wall. This sill should be made of pressure-treated or other rot-resistant lumber. The rim joist, which rests on the sill and runs around the room, should be carefully protected from moisture with building paper and siding.

In this example, one side of the basement has outside soil grade near the height of the basement wall. The other side is a walk-out basement, with the outside grade at floor level. Many basements have walls that rise above grade by a couple of feet or more. In that case, windows can allow light in, and the basement is said to be at "garden" level.

BASEMENT ANATOMY

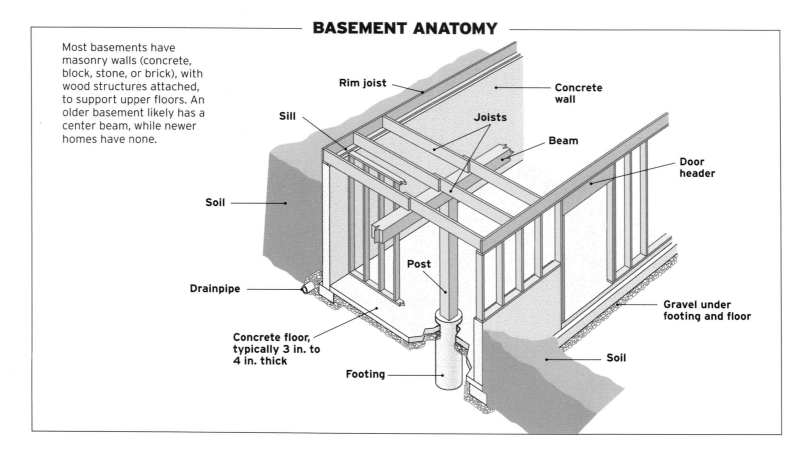

Most basements have masonry walls (concrete, block, stone, or brick), with wood structures attached, to support upper floors. An older basement likely has a center beam, while newer homes have none.

Rim joist

Sill

Soil

Drainpipe

Concrete floor, typically 3 in. to 4 in. thick

Post

Footing

Concrete wall

Joists

Beam

Door header

Gravel under footing and floor

Soil

WALL AND FOOTING MATERIALS

Most basements built after World War II have walls made of poured concrete or concrete block. Basement walls in older homes may be stone, at least at their bottom 4 ft. or so, and perhaps brick or block atop the stone.

Poured concrete

Poured concrete walls usually present a fairly monolithic surface. At their bottoms they rest on a poured concrete footing, which is typically 4 in. or so thicker than the walls. If they were poured correctly, with metal reinforcing bar (called rebar in the trades), concrete walls will be very strong. And if a solid waterproof coating was applied to the outside of the walls before they

were backfilled with soil, the walls should successfully resist water infiltration, unless hydrostatic pressure is very strong (see p. 28). However, some concrete walls were poured or reinforced incorrectly, and this can lead to moisture and structural problems, as the following pages show.

➔ **See Structural Problems and Solutions, pp. 41-55.**

Concrete block

Often referred to as "cinder blocks," structural blocks are actually made of concrete poured into molds. They are typically 8 in. wide by 16 in. long, with open spaces called "cells" inside. The blocks are

stacked on top of each other in a running bond pattern (which means each block rests on two blocks below, rather than just being stacked in vertical rows). Block basement walls usually rest on a poured concrete footing. For strength, the walls should be reinforced in three ways, as shown in the drawing: with horizontal ladder-type reinforcing mesh every two or three courses; by filling at least some of the cells with grout (which is actually a type of concrete); and with vertical rebar embedded in the grout fill every other block or so. Unfortunately, not all block walls are created equal, and some lack sufficient reinforcement—making them susceptible to cracks that need to be sealed and perhaps repaired as well. >> >> >>

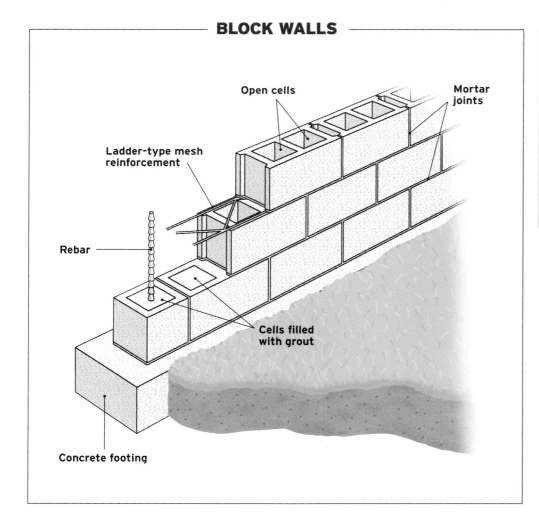

BLOCK WALLS

Open cells

Mortar joints

Ladder-type mesh reinforcement

Rebar

Cells filled with grout

Concrete footing

COLD SEALS

If concrete walls were only partially poured on one day and finished the next, there will be a "cold seal" where the second pour rests on top of the first pour; this is typically a horizontal line running all along the wall. Because new concrete does not bond well with hardened concrete, this line can be a source of leaks, unless it is well sealed from the outside.

WALL AND FOOTING MATERIALS (CONTINUED)

Stone walls

Many older homes have a foundation and a lower wall made of natural stone assembled with mortar joints. Many of these walls remain strong and level for centuries because of their massive size (often 2 ft. thick), the durability of boulders, and the old-world skills used in their construction. Often, a brick wall is installed on top of the stone wall.

These walls were likely installed in the days when people didn't think of living in their basements, and so they may not be very waterproof. Some can stay surprisingly dry, but inspect yours carefully after a heavy rainfall for any signs of moisture. If moisture is a problem, consider having the outside of the wall waterproofed.

In this older home, mortared stones were used to make a footing and about 3 vertical feet of wall. If your house has a wall like this and the mortar between the stones is eroding, the wall has likely been exposed to moisture.

BRICKS IN INTERLOCKING PATTERN

Most brick homes built before World War II were constructed so that the bricks actually form the structure of the house. (Most brick homes built more recently use brick only as a veneer; the foundation and basement walls are most likely poured concrete, and the house's structure is made of wood.)

Usually, the basement wall is three wythes, or thicknesses, of brick. There is typically little if any metal reinforcement. Instead, the bricks are laid in an interlocking pattern. The brick wall shown here, which rests on a stone foundation, was built in 1882. Its walls are almost perfectly plumb, and it is, overall, no more than 1/4 in. out of level.

This common-brick wall has joints with extra mortar for added protection.

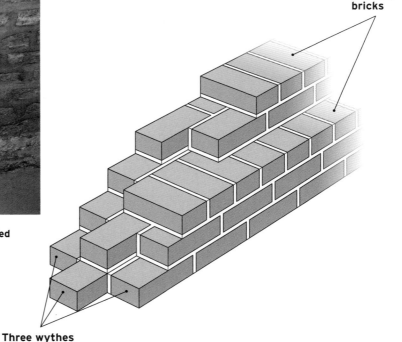

Bonding bricks

Three wythes

MAKE IT DRY

It's a common story: Homeowners want to increase their living space, and so install finished walls, ceilings, and flooring in their basement. A few years down the line, they find that moisture has infiltrated their newly installed framing and surfaces, and they have to tear it all up and fix the problems in order to abate smelly and unhealthy mold and mildew. The moisture may come in the form of a flooded floor during a "hundred-year" storm. Or it may slowly accumulate due to slight but ever-present condensation that you may not even notice.

How dry is dry enough?

Ideally, basement walls and floors should be bone dry, even during rainstorms. However, it is possible—and certainly advisable, even if you think your basement is very dry—to build walls and floors in such a way that small amounts of moisture can seep away so that basement walls can dry out. Pages 34-35 show some methods.

If your block, stone, or brick walls are leaking severely, however, chances are good that interior repairs will not solve the problem. Though it's a drastic fix, you're probably better off sealing from the outside, as shown on p. 38.

>> >> >>

Basement Repair Companies In many areas there are companies that specialize in repairing and sealing basements. Check out these companies carefully, and choose one that has a proven track record of satisfying customers and keeping basements dry. They will likely have solutions that work well in your climate and with your soil conditions. (In Chicago, where I live, I rely on the Perma-Seal company for advice and information.)

WHERE WATER CAN ENTER

Water can seep into a basement via a number of pathways, as shown here. Window wells need to be well sealed and also have a clear drain at their bottoms. Cracks in a concrete wall or masonry joints will of course allow water in. Wherever pipes poke through from the outside, the area around the pipes must be well sealed. A malfunctioning sump pump will fail to eject the water that collects in its well, and during a heavy rain, a flooded floor may result.

Floor drains may need to be rodded, so that water cannot back up through them into the basement. And the cove joint, where the wall meets the floor, is sometimes a trouble spot. All these potential problems are addressed in the following pages.

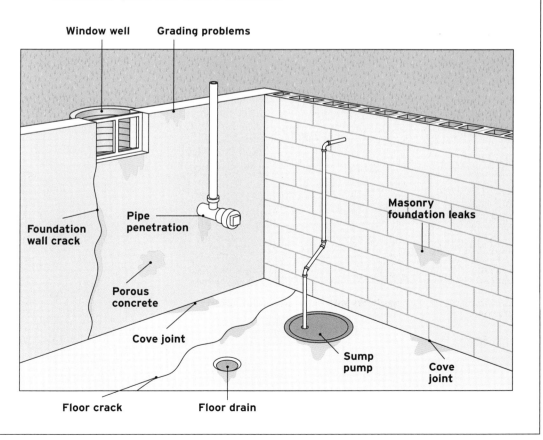

Window well · Grading problems · Pipe penetration · Masonry foundation leaks · Foundation wall crack · Porous concrete · Cove joint · Sump pump · Cove joint · Floor crack · Floor drain

MAKE IT DRY (CONTINUED)

Hydrostatic pressure: a powerful enemy

Water in the soil can become surprisingly powerful. It exerts "hydrostatic pressure" that forces water through cracks, small openings, and even porous materials. This not only makes a basement moist or wet, but it also can cause structural damage, as well as mold and decay. Water often seeps down to the footing and even under the floor, where it can create a good deal of havoc.

In most cases, you can relieve the pressure by directing rainwater away from the house.

Cove seepage

One of the most common leak spots is at the cove—the joint where the wall rests on top of the footing. Because the footing is dried when the walls are poured, the seal between them is "cold," and adhesion is not very good. If the joint is not well sealed from the outside, water can seep in when hydraulic pressure builds up.

The cove joint, where the wall meets the floor, is a common trouble spot where water can infiltrate.

TESTING FOR MOISTURE

Masonry walls and floors may be generating moisture in ways you do not see or even feel. The wetness may be so slight that it evaporates before it becomes visible. However, if you cover these slightly moist surfaces with walls or flooring, the moisture will not have a good chance to evaporate, and can build up, leading to mold, rot, and other problems.

You can easily test for moisture: During the wet season, or shortly after a heavy rainfall, tape a small sheet of plastic or aluminum foil to the wall or floor. Attach with duct tape, pressing firmly to be sure it is tightly sealed ❶. Wait four or five days. If the outside of the sheet becomes moist then your basement air is very humid; it's a good idea to install a dehumidifier. But if you see wetness when you pull the sheet off the wall or the floor, then moisture is seeping in from the outside ❷, ❸. In that case, take some of the steps shown on the following pages, then retest.

1 Firmly tape a piece of foil or plastic to the wall you are testing.

2 After four or five days, pull back the foil or plastic to see if the wall is wet.

3 Perform the same test on the floor.

REDIRECTING RAINWATER

In many cases, simple measures taken outside the house will solve basement water problems. The principle is simple: If rainwater runs off your roof onto the ground near your basement, it can seep down and cause problems. So take steps to direct the water well away from the house.

The lawn or masonry surface that abuts your house should slope away, so water cannot easily soak into the soil and filter down next to your basement. If the area is level or sloped toward the house, do some excavating so that the soil slopes down at a rate of at least ¼ in. per running feet.

Also check your home's soil conditions. If the ground is sandy, then water seeps into it easily; if it is clayey, then the seepage is far less. If you have ground cover, such as gravel or mulch, it's a good idea to scrape it away, lay plastic sheeting or landscaping fabric, and then replace the covering. Consider planting bushes, which can drink up plenty of water.

The solution may be as simple as extending your downspouts. Splash blocks, made of concrete or plastic, extend out about 2 ft., which may be enough if the area around the foundation is sloped so that rain runs away from the house. Often a better solution is to attach a downspout extension that directs water away from the house 6 ft. or more. An extension may be a flexible line made for the purpose. Or, you can simply attach a section of solid downspout.

>> >> >>

Here you can see **two problems: First, the soil does not slope away from the house, so rainwater can easily seep down against the basement wall. (Mulch placed over the soil does not solve this problem.) Second, a disintegrating patio captures rainwater, making it even more likely that it will flow down to the basement wall.**

── DIAGNOSING RAINWATER PROBLEMS ──

One of the best ways to diagnose rainwater problems is to go outside during—or immediately after—a heavy rain. Look at the area around the house to see if water puddles or collects anywhere within 5 ft. Check whether all the water is going into the downspouts (and not spilling out of the gutters) and whether the downspouts are intact (and not leaking).

Some Just Have to Live with Water Problems

In some areas, basement flooding may be inevitable, perhaps every 50 years or maybe every few years. This can be the case in areas with heavy rainfalls or high water tables. Or, maybe your municipal sewer system cannot handle large rainfalls. A reliable sump pump may be your only line of defense here, but if flooding is severe, even that may not prevent floors and walls from getting soaked (especially if water occasionally wells up out of floor drains). Check with your building department, as well as with neighbors who have lived in the area for a long time, to learn if you should plan on occasional flooding.

If you cannot guarantee a dry basement for the next quarter century or so, there still are remodeling options, though they are limited. Consider acid staining the floor, or applying a garage-type finish, rubber flooring, ceramic or resilient tiles, or sheet goods. You could simply paint the floor or leave it a "natural" gray and cover most of it with an area rug.

REDIRECTING RAINWATER (CONTINUED)

If you have a grade problem that is not easily solved by excavating the surface, or if you don't like the look of a gutter extension, consider installing a dry well. This carries water away from the house via an underground perforated pipe.

At the bottom of the downspout, install two elbows so the water comes out a foot or so from the house and about 6 in. above grade. Dig a trench about a foot wide and a foot deep leading to a hole where you want the water to percolate. The trench should slope at least 1/4 in. per running foot. At the end of the trench, dig a hole and set in a perforated basin designed for use with a sump pump (see p. 31), or a garbage pan drilled with a series of 1/2-in. holes. The top of the basin should be about 3 in. below grade.

Fill the basin with large stones, and surround it with gravel; this is your dry well. Lay landscaping fabric in the trench, and partially fill with gravel. Set a grated catch basin directly under the downspout. Attach and run perforated drainpipe from the catch basin to the dry well. Add more gravel above the drainpipe, and cover the basin with a lid. Cover the gravel in the trench with landscaping fabric, then add soil and sod or plantings.

LET IT BLEND

Downspout extensions, while necessary, can be unsightly. They are available in many shapes and sizes, and there are also color options. Choose one that will blend with the siding or trim on your house to help the downspout blend in.

WARNING

If you have a sprinkler system, be sure it does not spray excessive water near the house. Adjust the head(s) to spray at least 2 ft. from the foundation.

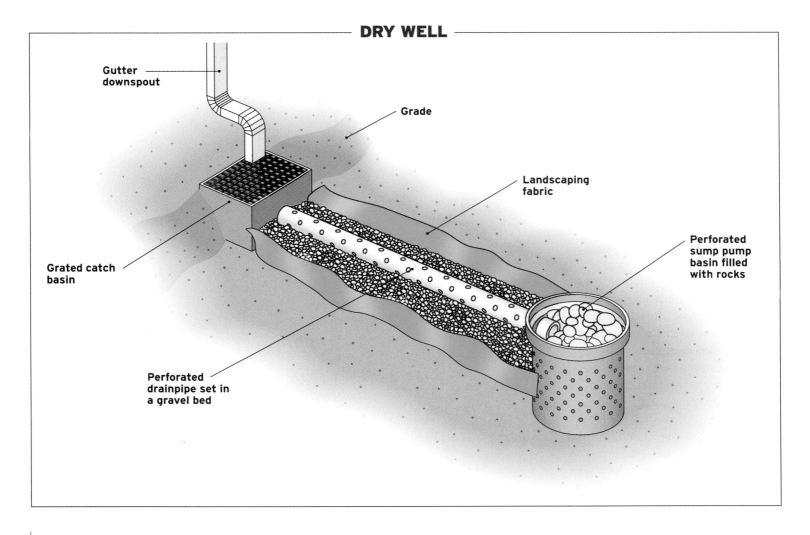

DRY WELL

Gutter downspout

Grade

Landscaping fabric

Grated catch basin

Perforated sump pump basin filled with rocks

Perforated drainpipe set in a gravel bed

INSTALLING A SUMP PUMP AND DRAIN

A sump pump siphons groundwater from beneath a basement floor and expels it, either to the outside or into a drainpipe (also called "drain tile"). A properly installed and maintained sump pump can eliminate hydrostatic pressure and keep a basement surprisingly dry. It may not solve a problem of slight moisture coming through walls, but it will keep a basement from getting positively wet.

Sump pumps reside in special basins (also called liners), which are basically very large plastic buckets. There are two types of sump pump and basin installations. The most effective calls for drain tile (which in an old home may actually be made of clay, but is more often a perforated drainpipe) that runs all around the basement's perimeter. (The drain tile must be embedded in gravel, so its perforations do not get clogged with mud. This arrangement is often called a "French drain.") Groundwater enters the tile at any point around the basement, and the tile carries it to the sump pump basin, where the pump expels it.

In a second type of installation, there is no drain tile. Instead, the basin has a series of holes or perforations. Groundwater slowly makes its way into the basin, and when the water reaches a certain level it raises a float, which turns on a switch so the pump expels it. It should be emphasized that this arrangement works only for a small area of the basement; to expel water from the entire basement with this kind of installation would require a number of basins and sump pumps.

The pumps shown are submersible, but "pedestal" pumps are installed onto the pipe above the floor.

Where does the water go? It may be simply shot out of a pipe that exits the house. Or it may run into a dry well in the yard. Or, it could go to the house's main drain or to the municipal sewer system.

>> >> >>

A basin is buried in the basement floor, with its top just above the floor level. Here, drain tile runs into the basin.

Here the check valve is installed in the discharge pipe. In a "pedestal" arrangement, the pump is also on the pipe.

The sump pump's drainpipe runs outdoors.

This submersible pump is attached to a check valve (just below the rubber fitting), which keeps water from backing up into your home. A discharge pipe rises out of the pump. The pump gets plugged into a standard 120-volt electrical receptacle.

In this installation, the sump pump's drainpipe runs into the house's drainpipe.

INSTALLING A SUMP PUMP AND DRAIN (CONTINUED)

Sump pump tips

Installing a new sump pump where there was none before is a major undertaking that is probably best left to pros, especially if you want to run new drain tile around your basement floor. But maintenance is necessary and well within your reach.

- If you have an existing basin, replacing a pump is a straightforward task. If the pump is not doing its job, or if it runs constantly, try installing a more powerful one. A half-horsepower model will handle most any situation.

- If the pump shunts water out onto your yard only a short distance from your house, it can easily seep back toward your basement. Extend the pipe farther away from the house to better keep your basement dry.

- If your sump pump's pit is uncovered, it is both an eyesore and a danger to children and pets. If possible, buy a cover. Or, you may need to install a new basin that comes with a cover.

- Many inexpensive sump pumps have a "tethered" float switch that sometimes sticks, so the pump does not come on when needed. For peace of mind, spend more for a high-quality pump with a multiyear guarantee.

- It's not uncommon for nasty weather to be accompanied by power outages. Install a reliable battery backup for your sump pump, so it can operate at any time.

TWO SUMP PUMP SETUPS

If drain tile runs under the basement floor around its perimeter, it should empty into a solid basin, where a sump pump can force it out. If there is no drain tile, groundwater can slowly seep into a perforated basin, where the sump pump does the same thing.

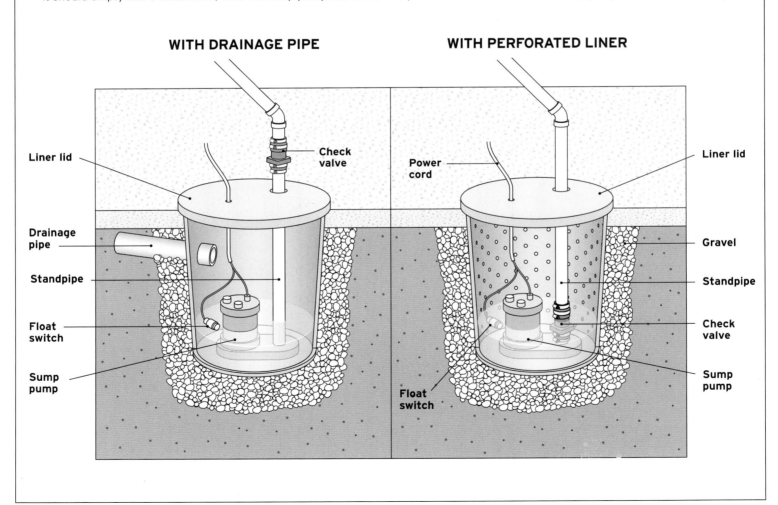

WITH DRAINAGE PIPE

Liner lid
Drainage pipe
Standpipe
Float switch
Sump pump
Check valve

WITH PERFORATED LINER

Power cord
Liner lid
Gravel
Standpipe
Check valve
Sump pump
Float switch

Be Sure the Drains Will Drain

Here's a real heart-breaker: Despite all your efforts to keep a basement dry, during a storm your sewers back up, sending water (and sometimes worse) up through your floor drains. In some cases, it's your municipal water supplier's fault, but sometimes the problem is on your end.

In most homes, all the drain lines in the house lead to the main drain, which likely runs under your basement floor, and from there to the municipal sewer system. (In some locales, sewage water and storm water are on separate systems; in other places, the two are tied together in various ways.) If your municipal system is insufficient—if there is a history of backups in your area that affect multiple homes—then there's not a lot you can do about it; remodel with the expectation that occasional basement flooding will occur.

But also make sure that your drainpipes are clear. To do this, you could rent a large auger and rod it yourself, but it's safer to call in a plumber or a rodding service. Nowadays, these companies not only have powerful augurs to remove obstacles, but they also have cameras that allow them to actually see the insides of the drainpipes. And they can certify that your drains are clear, so you may be able to be compensated by your municipality if backups occur. If backups are a problem in your area, have your pipes inspected every three years or so.

An older home may have pipes actually made of clay, which tree roots can poke into and even crack. If at all possible, have clay pipe replaced with PVC. Of course, this involves a lot of expensive digging and excavating. Depending on local conditions, your municipality may or may not pay for this.

Also consider having a backflow preventer installed onto your drain system. This makes it impossible for water to back up into the house. However, these devices are not allowed in some locales.

Keep floor drains uncovered, and sweep the area regularly, so they can efficiently get rid of water in case of a flood.

OTHER INTERIOR DRAIN SOLUTIONS

There may be other drain solutions short of installing a new sump pump. These may be supplied by local companies familiar with your conditions.

Large interior drain line

If you have a nearby large drain line that leads to your municipality's sewage or storm drain system (in some cases, they are the same system, or are tied together), drain tile can simply lead to this drain instead of to a sump pump. This is a simpler arrangement. It's important to install cleanouts so you can easily clear these lines if they get clogged. It's also important that the drain tile be sloped toward the main drain.

DryTrak®

A system like the DryTrak water drainage system works well when the main problem is leakage from the cove joint—where the concrete wall meets the footing. It is installed on top of the floor, so there is no need to break out concrete and dig a trench. Leaking water is collected and directed to an existing sump pump or to a floor drain.

➡ See "Two Sump Pump Setups," p. 32.

WaterGuard®

A plastic drain strip like this runs around the perimeter of the basement and sends water to a sump pump like standard drain tile. But there is no need to dig a deep trench in the soil to install a WaterGuard drainage channel. It sits on top of the footing, where it can gather water coming from cove seepage, as well as from any moisture dripping down the wall. Because there is no dirt around it, there is no chance that it will clog.

TRADE SECRET

If water is seeping up through the floor, the solution is either to install drain tile and a sump pump on the inside of the basement (pp. 31–32) or on the outside, as shown on p. 38.

The DryTrak system **needs to be installed by a certified installer, but requires no jack hammering of concrete.**

Tying drain tile **to the drainpipe that flows to your municipality's sewage system is a simple arrangement.**

The WaterGuard drainage channel **has a wall flange with spacers for collecting wall seepage, channel holes that allow ground water to enter the drain line, and a large-diameter channel that won't crush.**

Interior wall solutions

The best solutions for sealing basement walls against leakage are done on the outside of the house, or by installing a sump pump. As can be seen on pp. 31–32 and p. 38, these methods involve serious excavating and can be quite expensive. Fortunately, if your problems are not severe, you may be able to solve them from the inside, without lots of digging.

Let's be clear: A repair made on the inside of the basement wall cannot resist built-up hydrostatic pressure; other steps must be taken for that. And if moisture is constantly seeping into your masonry walls, sealing from the inside alone will mean that your walls stay wet on the inside for long periods, which will damage them in time. So the repairs shown here are suitable where only moderate wetness problems occur from time to time.

EverLast™ Wall System

Often only the bottom third or so of walls is subject to moisture damage. With the EverLast Wall Panels, the lower wood studs have been removed and replaced with metal studs, and the drywall has been replaced with waterproof vinyl panels. Behind the vinyl panels, water is directed down into drain tile in the floor, which carries it to a sump pump.

CleanSpace®

CleanSpace liners can be installed with screw fasteners. They direct water into a drainage system in the floor rather than simply sealing the wall (so that the masonry walls do not stay wet for long periods, which can damage them). The liners are completely waterproof and do not have any organic matter, so mold cannot grow. >> >> >>

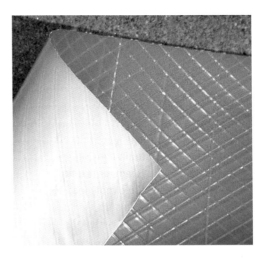

The CleanSpace liner is installed over the walls and floor to create a continuous moisture barrier.

KEEPING THE AIR DRY

If your basement tends to be humid, a plug-in dehumidifier can help. A serious unit like this not only effectively keeps humidity below 50%, but it also has a two-stage air filter to keep the air clean and healthy to breathe.

The SaniDry™ basement air system is humidifier and air filter in one.

AVOID PAINT-ON PRODUCTS

Many stores sell products that are advertised to keep basement walls dry after you simply paint them on. I do not recommend these, especially if you will cover up the walls with framing and drywall. They often do not keep out the moisture, at least not everywhere. And even if they do work, they can cause the walls to stay wet, which can damage them.

OTHER INTERIOR DRAIN SOLUTIONS (CONTINUED)

Sealing cracks with epoxy injection

If walls leak only in certain discrete places and only during or soon after a rain, a leak may need to be repaired. Again, this is best done from the outside, but that is a major project (see p. 38). Cracks can be sealed from the inside with good success. An effective repair can strengthen the wall and ensure that the crack does not grow wider. Epoxy repair materials are available with kits that include the injector ports, two-part epoxy paste, and the two-part epoxy liquid in a caulk tube. Different manufacturers have slightly different methods, but in general you will first clean the crack and "cap" it with epoxy paste, and then inject liquid epoxy to fill the crack.

There is no need to chisel out the crack. Clean the crack and the surrounding area with a wire brush or a wire-brush drill attachment. Pry out any loose debris and remove any concrete crumbs ❶. Every 8 in. to 10 in. along the crack, drill a hole of the size recommended by the patch manufacturer. Insert an injector to be sure it will seat all the way against the wall ❷.

Mix the two-part epoxy paste until it achieves a uniform gray color ❸. When removing each part from the containers, take care to use one of the mixing sticks for each of the parts: If you get a small amount of one part in the container with the other part, you could ruin it for future use. Carefully twirl an injector port's flange in the epoxy, taking care not to get any into the hole, and press an injector into each of the holes you drilled in step 2 ❹. Slather the epoxy all along the crack, pressing it gently into the crack. Avoid getting epoxy in the port holes ❺.

Allow the sealer to cure; curing time varies depending on humidity, but 12 to 24 hours is common. Remove a cap and insert a plunger into the caulk tube that contains two-part liquid epoxy. Move the plunger up and down 20 times or so to

1 Clean the crack thoroughly with a wire brush. Pry out any loose material.

2 Drill holes every 8 in. to 10 in., and test that the injector will seat against the wall.

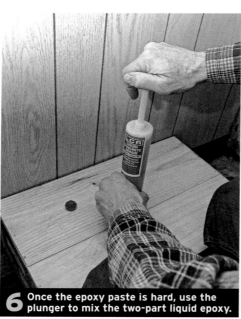

6 Once the epoxy paste is hard, use the plunger to mix the two-part liquid epoxy.

7 Squirt liquid epoxy into the bottom port.

completely mix the two parts ❻. Remove the plunger and screw on a nozzle; now you can put the container into a caulk gun. Insert the tip of the nozzle into the lowest port hole, and start squirting the liquid ❼. Keep squirting until liquid starts to seep out the port above. Then insert the cap into the hole of the bottom port and start squirting

into the next-highest one ❽. Repeat until you get to the top. When liquid starts to seep out the top of the crack, you are done ❾. You can now snip off the port caps and smooth over the entire crack with additional paste ❿.

3 Mix a batch of two-part epoxy.

4 Apply a small amount of epoxy to an injector port's flange, and press into place.

5 Apply epoxy all along the crack.

8 Once liquid starts to flow out the next-highest port, cap the bottom port and squirt into the next-highest one.

9 Repeat until liquid seeps out the top of the crack.

10 Snip off the port caps and smooth over the entire crack with additional paste.

Don't Use Hydraulic Cement In the past, hydraulic cement has often been used to repair basement wall cracks. However, this repair often lasts only a few years and then starts leaking again, because it cannot stop the wall from moving. The epoxy injection method shown above is far superior and is definitely recommended, especially if you will cover up the concrete wall.

SEALING FROM THE OUTSIDE

Where walls leak profusely, fixing from the inside may not do the job. In that case, the solution is to dig a trench around the basement to expose the outside walls and the footing. A trench is filled with perforated drainpipe and gravel, to get rid of water. Then the walls are coated with a watertight sealer. In days gone by, a single viscous sealer was applied with a roller or a spray gun. For a more sure solution, sealer is applied, then a membrane is applied over the sealer. Unless you have excavating equipment and some experience, this is not a do-it-yourself project; you should hire professionals. Do your homework and hire a company with plenty of satisfied customers.

First, the footing and walls are cleaned with a pressure washer. Any cracks are repaired with epoxy. Then a special heavy-duty waterproofing membrane is installed, such as rigid insulation board; often a tarlike waterproofing is applied first. Rigid insulation may be applied over the membrane. Gravel is laid, and a drainpipe is set in the gravel, sloped toward a dry well, a municipal drainpipe, or a sump pump. More gravel is poured and landscaping fabric is placed on top, so the drainpipe will not get clogged. Then the trench can be backfilled with soil. The grade is sloped away from the house.

Rigid insulation is fairly expensive, but will ensure against condensation inside the basement and will cut down on heating costs as well.

If you are going to the trouble of digging a trench down below the top of the footing, the fix should be done right.

WINDOWS

Basement windows often get and stay moist for long periods, and so rot faster than upstairs windows, especially if they are at or below ground level. Also, they are prime entryways for intruders, so they often need to be made secure.

If your basement has simple sash, slider, or casement windows, checking for rot and replacing them may be no different from what you would do for upstairs windows. On both the outside and inside, poke wood parts with a slot screwdriver; if it feels soft and spongy, you've got some rot. Rot that is only 1/2 in. deep or so can usually be repaired with epoxy wood filler and repainted. If the rot goes deeper, consider replacing the window and its frame. Consider rot-resistant vinyl windows, or glass block.

Basement windows are often low quality and not well insulated. Since you will be living in your future remodeled basement, you may want to add a storm window to existing windows, or replace them altogether with ones that have thermal glass. Also be sure to caulk around the window frame, and check that the seals are tight when you close the window; you may be able to fix a leaky window with weatherstripping.

You may want to replace a standard sash, slider, or casement window with another type that is suited to your needs. Some local codes demand that if you are using your basement as a living space, you must have an "egress" window, also called an escape window. These are designed to be easily opened, are large enough for a person to fit through, and may have a built-in set of steps. If your basement walls are only partially below grade, you may be able to simply install a window above grade. Otherwise, you will need to excavate and install a large window, as shown on p. 40.

>> >> >>

A window like this **shows signs of rot and needs to be sealed with caulking; it also has only single-pane glass and so will let in the cold in winter and heat in summer. Replacement is the best option.**

Glass block is an old-style solution that still makes sense in some situations. Glass block is a good deal more difficult to break into than a standard glass window pane. (It's actually not as solid as it looks, but the looks alone can deter intruders.) And the block lets in light, but outsiders cannot actually see inside.

An egress window is installed in any sleeping room so that occupants can exit in case of an emergency. Check your local building codes for specifications.

WINDOWS (CONTINUED)

The drainpipe's grate is placed at a low spot at the bottom of the window well. The grate, and the surrounding gravel, should be a couple of inches below the masonry window opening. It's important to keep the grate clear of leaves and other debris that could clog it.

This window has a rusty metal frame, which can be repaired by painting with rusty metal primer, then a finish coat. The area around the frame has been filled with caulk and covered with waterproofing fabric. A gap at the bottom has been filled with mortar.

WINDOW WELLS

An effective window well directs water away from the window to a drain system that directs it away from the house. Things to check for:

- The window well itself—typically a large, metal half-cylinder that is wider than the window—should be in sound condition and should be well sealed against the house.

- The well should retain its part-circular shape. If soil has pressed against it and deformed its shape, the area should be excavated and a new well installed.

- Water should flow easily through the well. The best method is to have both a gravel bed and a drainpipe embedded in it. The drainpipe's top should have a grate that is free from obstructions like leaves.

- Children and animals should be kept away from a well. It may help to install a cover.

WINDOW WELL WITH DRAINAGE

To ensure that water does not puddle in a window well, a drain is positioned in a gravel bed at the bottom. Water drains down through the pipe, which may lead to a dry well away from the house (see p. 30), or to a gravel-filled trench with a drainpipe, as shown here.

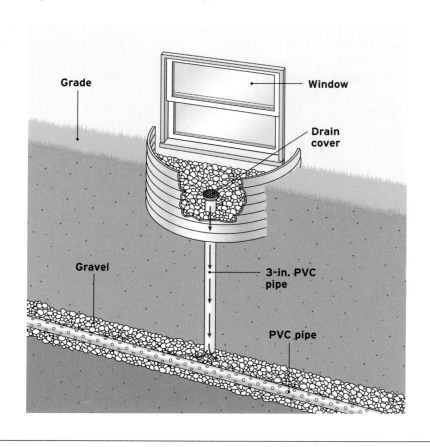

Grade

Window

Drain cover

Gravel

3-in. PVC pipe

PVC pipe

SPOTTING PROBLEMS

A newer basement may have walls and ceilings that are solid and secure. Older basements often have problems that must be attended to. In some cases, the fixes are fairly quick and easy; in other cases, serious surgery is called for, which can be performed only by professionals.

Problems with basement walls and floors—often called a house's foundation—are visible not only in the basement itself but also on upper floors, as shown in the drawing on p. 43. When these problems manifest themselves, you should take steps to fix them in a timely manner, or they can get worse and damage the rest of your home. They certainly should be repaired and shored up before attempting any basement remodeling—which can often cover up the problem, so it grows worse when out of sight.

In general, look for cracks that are wider than 1/4 in. or that are offset. Also see if your walls or floors are uneven. The drawing shows other signs of structural problems.

If a chimney leans so it pulls away from the house at the top, the problem may simply be with the chimney. Or, it could be that the foundation it rests on is sinking or leaning. This can lead to damage to your house's siding, and even its structure.

>> >> >>

If brick, stone, or block **shows signs of surface deterioration, the problem is very possibly only skin deep. As long as the wall as a whole is plumb and free of bulges or indentations and the floor above is not sinking, damage like this can be fixed by filling in with mortar.**

If cracks in a basement wall **are uneven or offset, like those shown here, there could well be a problem with the underlying concrete or stone footing. This problem will not fix itself and is likely to get worse. Have it looked at by a professional.**

⚠ WHAT CAN GO WRONG

If a floor has a crack wider than 1/4 in., or if it is uneven so that one area is more than 1/2 in. higher or lower than an area less than 8 ft. away, the basement floor is likely in trouble. However, unless the floor is separating from the wall, the problem can often be solved by reinforcing the floor, perhaps by adding another layer of concrete. Or, you may need to break out the old concrete and pour a new floor.

SPOTTING PROBLEMS (CONTINUED)

Crumbling and falling ceilings

Older basements with lath-and-plaster ceilings often end up looking something like the photo at right. If the damage is not severe, you may be able to "skin over" the ceiling by attaching sheets of drywall that hold the old material in place. However, if it looks like this or worse, you should remove the plaster and the lath—an extremely messy process, so wear a respirator and ventilate the basement with outward-pointed fans as you work.

Old plaster often fails in a basement. Depending on the amount of damage, you may repair, replace, or cover over it.

Bowed walls are a sure sign of trouble. Hold a 6-ft. or 8-ft. level against the walls at a number of places. The walls should be reasonably plumb (though they do not have to be perfect), and they should be straight. If you see a bulge, or if a wall is out of plumb by more than half the level's bubble, call in a basement expert for assessment.

If you see gaps under baseboards—either in the basement or on the first floor—that means the floors are sinking, which most likely means that the house's footing is sinking. If the gap is more than an inch, the problem could be serious, and you should have the house's footings inspected.

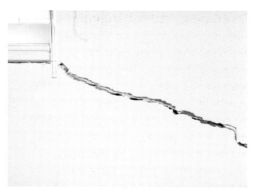

If cracks like this near a window develop on the first or second floor of the house, have the foundation inspected. This is often a sign of a sinking footing.

If windows or doors in the basement or on the floor above are noticeably out of square, they will not close properly. The problem could be that the house's foundation is sinking in some places. You could reinstall the windows or doors, using shims to keep them square, but the underlying problem may remain and get worse. The foundation likely needs to be fixed.

BASEMENT STRUCTURAL PROBLEMS

Many times cracks occur for superficial reasons, but if walls or floors are bowed or uneven, or if cracks are wide or offset, you should have a basement professional check them out.

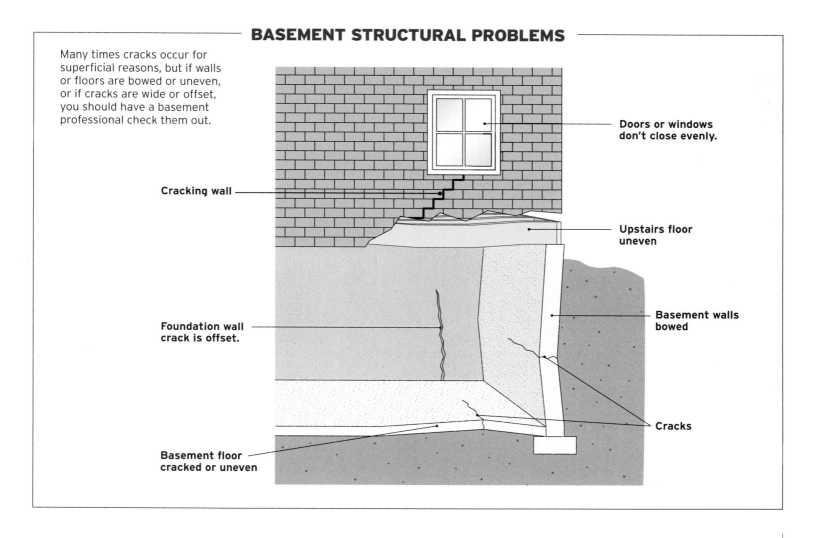

Doors or windows don't close evenly.

Cracking wall

Upstairs floor uneven

Basement walls bowed

Foundation wall crack is offset.

Cracks

Basement floor cracked or uneven

SOLVING PROBLEMS

Unfortunately, foundation repairs are not do-it-yourself projects. Find a company with a long history of foundation repair in your area. The company should have plenty of references you can call, and the salesperson should explain clearly the type of work they will do. Two common repairs are adding carbon armor straps and neckties.

If a wall is bowing in the middle due to soil pressure, the bowing can often be stopped with the installation of special foundation straps that are typically made of super-strong carbon fiber. These can be installed quickly and on the inside of the basement, so no excavation is required. They can be painted over or hidden behind walls that you frame out.

If an entire wall is leaning at its top, the process can be stopped by use of a foundation strap with the addition of a necktie. Made of exceptionally strong Kevlar® or fiberglass, a necktie is bolted with special hardware to the outside or rim joist, to hold the wall in place.

If the floor is sinking, the foundation likely needs to be raised and reinforced. A basement repair company can insert foundation piers, as shown on p. 46.

>> >> >>

Neckties will combat **top wall movement** of load-bearing and non-load-bearing walls.

A carbon strap won't fix a bowed wall, but it will stop the wall from continuing to bow. The strap—and bowed wall—can be hidden behind drywall.

A floor that is 1½ in. below the bottom of the wall (left) has sunk and needs to be raised and reinforced. After raising the foundation with a foundation pier and supporting it by pumping in concrete, as shown on p. 46, the floor is brought up to meet the wall and will not sink any farther (right).

WALL ANCHOR SYSTEM

Straps and neckties stabilize walls that lean slightly. But if a wall is leaning or bowed seriously, and you need not just to keep it from getting worse but to actually move it into better position, then solutions from the outside are called for. A wall anchor system can be installed with surprisingly little disruption to your yard.

With almost surgical precision, heavy-duty wall anchors are inserted into the soil and secured with threaded steel rods that poke into the basement. Inside, you see a series of wall plates. Bolt heads on the plates can be turned to adjust the wall's position.

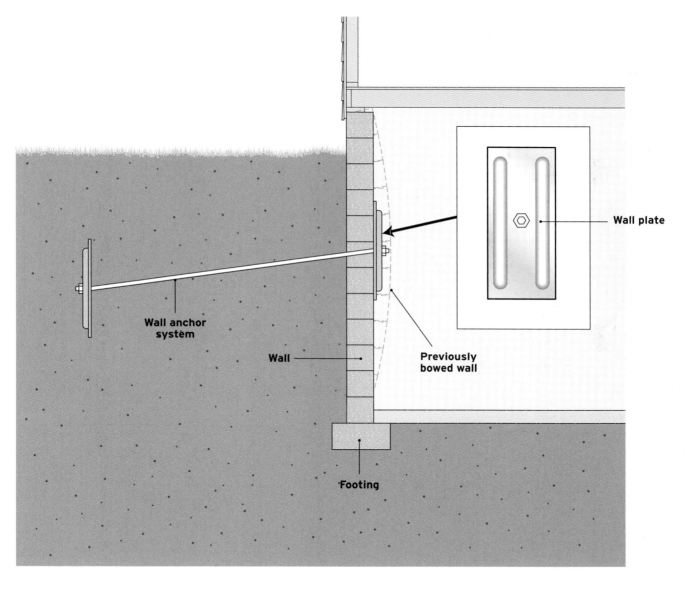

Wall plate

Wall anchor system

Previously bowed wall

Wall

Footing

SOLVING PROBLEMS (CONTINUED)

Raising a sunken foundation calls for digging a big hole and firing up heavy-duty equipment in order to add a bracket for support.

Installing wall anchors

Companies that specialize in repairing bowed and damaged basement walls have developed methods to limit the damage to interior walls and the lawn outside. Here are some techniques used by the Perma-Seal company in the Midwest. There are likely companies in other areas that follow this or a similar technique.

Using heavy-duty drills and massively long masonry drill bits, holes driven through the interior wall are generally only 2 in. or so in diameter ❶. Through experience and some calculating, the workers know pretty much where the drill bits will end up on the outside. Holes are dug from those locations. ❷. Here, the sod is neatly cut out so it can be replaced later.

Large threaded rods are pushed through the hole in the interior wall to the outside holes, where they are attached to wide plates ❸. From the inside, the threaded rod's hole is filled with a very strong epoxy that keeps out any possibility of moisture infiltration ❹. A large plate is attached temporarily while the wall is ratcheted back into straight vertical ❺. The plate is left in place ❻. It may need adjusting in the future. You may leave it exposed, or cover with framing and drywall.

FOUNDATION PIERS

If your walls and floors are sinking, the concrete footing they rest on is likely sinking. Believe it or not, footings can be raised. However, this is the most extreme repair, involving digging a wide trench around the house, inserting a steel push pier deep into the ground next to it, and raising the footing up with steel brackets attached to the pier. The process can take some days, as the footing is raised slowly with hydraulic pressure. Once raised, concrete is pumped into the space under the footing, and the house will remain stable for a century or more to come.

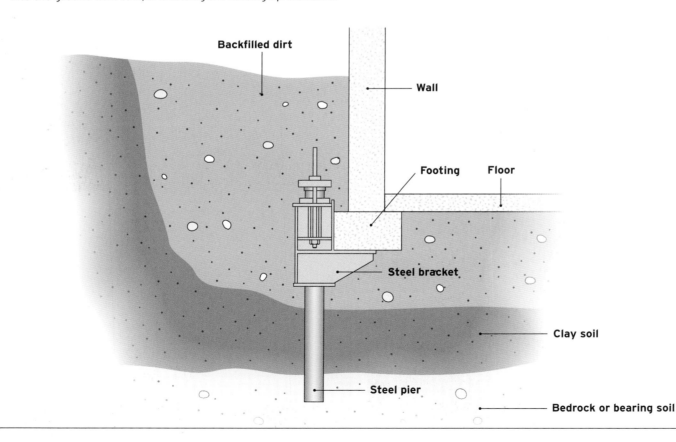

- Backfilled dirt
- Wall
- Footing
- Floor
- Steel bracket
- Clay soil
- Steel pier
- Bedrock or bearing soil

1 A large bit drills holes through the basement wall.

2 Holes dug from the outside will be neatly filled later.

3 These plates are wide enough to stay still while the wall is pulled back into position.

4 The hole is sealed against moisture.

5 From the inside, the wall is pulled until straight.

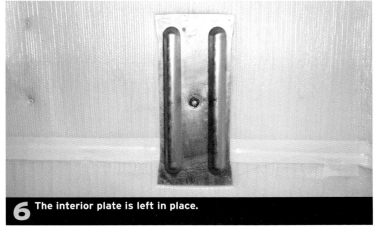

6 The interior plate is left in place.

POSTS AND BEAMS

The first floor's floor joists—which are also the basement's ceiling joists—are often made of 2-by material, but in newer homes, the joists may be made of "engineered" materials laminated together for greater strength. If they are very strong, these joists can span across the entire width of a basement; in that case they need not be supported in the middle. But in older homes, or if the basement is very wide, a beam (or two) must support the joists in the middle, to keep the floor above from sagging. This is done with a beam that is supported with posts.

You may decide to leave the posts in place, and do your remodeling around them: you can incorporate them into walls, or wrap them with trim. This limits layout possibilities, but eliminating posts is difficult.

If you have posts and a beam, inspect for damage and straightness before you proceed. Posts should be close to plumb in both directions. If you see substantial cracks, or if poking with a screwdriver reveals substantial rot, then the post or a part of the beam should be replaced. The beam—and the floor above—should also be reasonably level. If not, you may be able to shim it up, as long as the condition is not severe. Adjustable posts, also called floor jacks, can be used to support and also raise a beam ❶. Rest the post on a piece of lumber at the bottom, to spread out the load on a concrete floor. Turn

2 Find a level spot under the beam for the post anchor, then secure it to the concrete floor with a masonry screw.

1 Use adjustable posts to raise the beam, then insert pieces of wood between the top of the post and the underside of the beam.

3 With the post set firmly and level in the anchor, secure the two together with screws or nails.

the handle at the top to raise the beam. If you need to raise more than an inch, raise it a bit, wait a few days, then raise again, to avoid cracking the beam and joists.

Posts—which are often 6x6s—should rest not just on the concrete floor, which is typically only 3 in. to 4 in. thick. Instead, they should be supported by concrete footings that are at least 2 ft. deep, and deeper if possible. You probably cannot see how deep your footings are, but if a beam sinks more than ½ in. at the post, or if the concrete footing appears cracked or loose, it's a good idea to repour a footing: Support the beam temporarily on each side, remove the post, break up the footing and pry it out, dig a deeper hole, and pour concrete.

Attach a wood post at the bottom with a post anchor made for a 6x6 or 8x8 post ❷. Use a level to mark a spot directly below the beam. Drill a hole with a hammer drill and masonry bit, and attach the anchor with a masonry screw or with injected epoxy. Set the post in the anchor, check it for plumb, and attach with nails or screws driven through the holes in the anchor ❸.

Replacing a section of wood beam

If a portion of a beam is damaged by cracks or rot, you can replace it. Be sure to temporarily support all the joists that will be left unsupported when you remove the section ❶. Cut the beam at the center of a post on each side. You may need to modify the beam piece to get it to fit. In this case, a long notch was cut ❷. Raise the beam piece in position and attach it with screws to the posts, the beam on each side, and the joists ❸.

>> >> >>

1 Temporarily support the joists before removing the damaged beam section.

2 Often a beam needs to be notched in order to fit.

3 After setting in the beam, attach securely with angle-driven screws.

POSTS AND BEAMS (CONTINUED)

INSTALLING A STEEL I-BEAM

A steel I-beam is stronger than a typical wood beam, so by installing one you can eliminate some posts and make the basement space more wide open. Check with a building inspector or an engineer to be sure the beam will be strong enough for your situation.

As you may expect, a steel beam is very heavy. Because a crane cannot fit into a basement, manpower is the way to move one. Start by temporarily supporting the joists on each side. Cut channels in the masonry walls where you will insert the beam or supply a code-approved way to support the beam at each end.

In this example, a beam was threaded through a small basement window ❶ ❷. Plenty of manpower was needed to carry

it, raise one end into the channel cut into the brick wall, and then raise the other end so temporary adjustable posts could be placed below ❸. The beam was then slowly raised nearly into final position by turning the handles on the adjustable posts ❹. After raising some joists by almost an inch, it was decided to wait a few days before raising the beam all the way.

SEALING DUCTS AND PIPES

Basements have lots of pipes and ducts that poke outside, as well as plenty of places where the outside can infiltrate. Take the time to seal these nice and tight before remodeling. On a cold and windy day, you can often feel some of the places where extra sealing is needed. Materials of choice for sealing include foil-type duct tape, high-quality caulk, and spray-foam insulation.

This gas pipe is pretty well sealed with mortar, but mortar cracks. A good bead of flexible caulk on the inside and outside will take only a few minutes to apply, and will keep the outside air outside.

This old duct arrangement is in need of repair. Ducts should not exit through a window but rather through a rim joist or the masonry wall. In addition, duct fittings should be substantial enough to withstand years of use. The fittings shown are too thin and are duct-taped. Foil tape is better.

Examine all your ductwork, and seal it nice and tight. Here, a flexible pipe is tightly sealed where it enters a furnace, first with the proper fitting, then with foil tape.

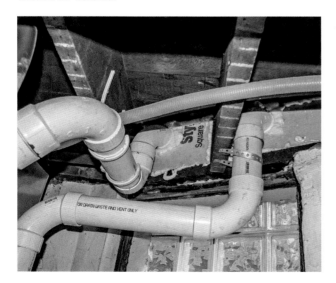

Spray-foam insulation, available in canned form, makes an excellent sealer where looks are not important.

UPGRADING MAJOR APPLIANCES

Most of the engines that make our lives comfortable live in the basement, where they are for the most part out of sight and out of mind. Part of your goal in remodeling will be to hide them from sight as much as possible. That may mean moving some of them, so they can reside behind walls in a utility room that takes up as little space as possible. Now is also the time to assess your appliances and decide if you need to make some changes.

Laundry

Fortunately, laundry facilities can be moved without much trouble; see p. 131 for setting up a shiny new launderette. If your machines are old, consider buying a more energy-efficient and high-load washer and dryer. The extra-large laundry tub shown below left has antique charm, and you may want to refurbish one like this. But for most of us, a simple single-basin tub will do the job.

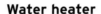
➡ See "DWV Plans," p. 111, and "Rough Plumbing Configurations," pp. 128-131.

Water heater

Standard water heaters usually need to be replaced every 10 years or so; yours may be due. Consider a larger-capacity unit if you sometimes run out of water, especially if you will install a new basement bathroom. Or, you may be better off with a tankless water heater.

Boiler and furnace

Have your heating plant—boiler for hot-water, radiant, or steam heat or furnace for forced-air heat—inspected by a heating company to see if you might be able to save money in the long run with a newer, more energy-efficient unit. An older boiler like the one, below left, can be fairly efficient if well maintained, but new high-efficiency models like the furnace, below right, have a pair of PVC pipes rather than a single metal duct arranged so far less heat is lost to the outside. They also have improved gas burners or electric heating elements, to sip rather than gulp expensive energy.

A standard tank-type water heater like this is still the most common choice. If your family sometimes runs out of hot water, consider buying a new unit with a larger capacity.

An older "slop sink" gets the job done, but a remodeled laundry area will make your weekly laundry chores much more pleasant.

Although some older boilers (left) are fairly efficient, a high-efficiency furnace (right) can save plenty on energy costs over the years.

Service panel

Your electrical service panel should be neatly arranged with wires running to plenty of breakers. (If you have a fuse box that actually uses fuses, it is certainly time to upgrade.) There should be plenty of service capacity—at least 100 amps for a smaller home and 200 amps for a larger home. And you will need open slots for future breakers that you will use when installing new services in your basement. It's a good idea to have an electrician assess your wiring for safety.

A well-organized service panel has wires that are neatly routed to their breakers.

OLD BASEMENT PIPES

A basement usually houses the main plumbing drain, as well as a bunch of branch drains. If you have a newer home with plastic PVC drainpipes and have no problems with major clogs, you are probably in fine shape. In an older home, opening a drain may reveal a nightmare like the one shown below left. Make sure cleanouts—places where you can remove a plug and insert an auger to rod the line—are in good working order; the one below right needs replacement. Any old galvanized pipes will corrode and clog soon, and should be replaced with extruded or cross-linked polyethylene tubing (PEX) or copper. Even copper pipes can also corrode and need to be replaced.

This main drain is almost completely clogged, which is not that unusual in an older home.

An old cast-iron drain stack with a cleanout at the floor will likely be rusted; it is usually a good idea to replace the cleanout and some of the pipe.

This tangle of tubes includes electrical conduit and cable as well as a black gas pipe and water supply pipes in copper and galvanized steel. Galvanized pipes almost always should be replaced. In this case, the copper pipe shows signs of decay as well.

LOWERING A BASEMENT FLOOR

In an older home, the basement ceiling may be uncomfortably low, and covering pipes and ducts may make it lower still. The solution is rather drastic: Chop out and haul away the existing concrete floor, then dig out the new floor to a depth of about 5 in. lower than the future depth of the new concrete floor. Add and tamp a layer of gravel and pour a new concrete floor.

This all sounds nearly impossible, but it is actually done pretty often. The difficulty of the job depends largely on how hard it is to get the concrete and soil out, as well as how hard the soil is to dig. There may be construction companies in your area that are experienced in this work; get prices from two or three of them.

The floor is usually lowered below the level of the concrete footing, which poses a problem: If you dig under the footing, you will compromise the structure of your basement—and house. Some contractors dig a small section, fill with concrete under the footing, and move on to the next section.

A more common—and safer—method is to use a "bench footing," as shown in the drawing below. This can be done without undermining the existing footing. However, it will lessen your usable floor space. The bench footing must be sloped no steeper than 3 and 2 (see the drawing). So if, for example, you lower the floor by 12 in., you will lose about 18 in. of floor space at each wall.

LOWERING A BASEMENT FLOOR WITH A BENCH FOOTING

Using a bench footing is the safe way to proceed because you do not undermine the basement's footing. However, it does cause a loss of floor space.

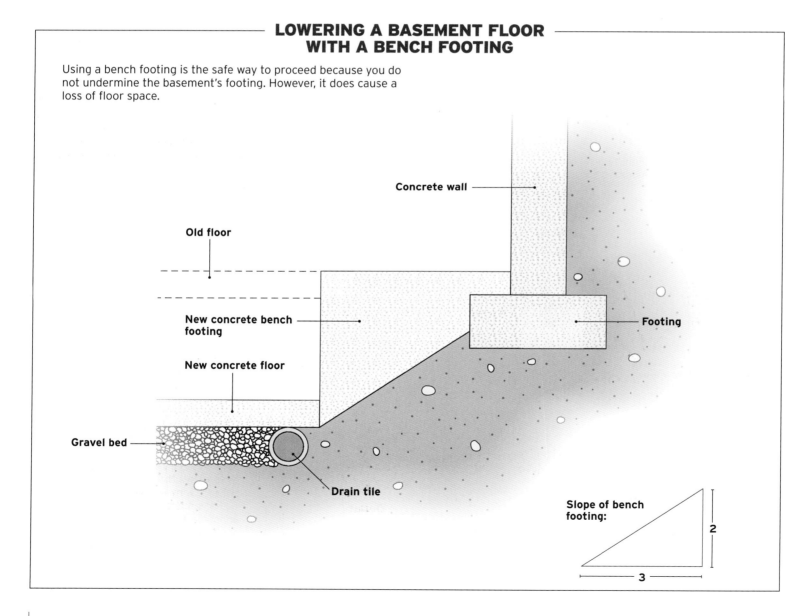

Concrete wall

Old floor

New concrete bench footing

New concrete floor

Gravel bed

Footing

Drain tile

Slope of bench footing:

2

3

PESTS

A basement is a moist place that is warmer in the winter and cooler in the summer than the out of doors, and so is a magnet for insects and other pests—including mice and rats, and even snakes in some areas. But the most common and troublesome pest is the termite. These critters take a variety of forms, depending on their role in the social structure and the phase of life, as shown below.

Of course, the most telling sign of their presence is wood that has been eaten away. However, the channels they dig while devouring are most often inside the wood, where you cannot see them. Poke your sill plate, posts, beams, and joists with a screwdriver at many points. If you feel sponginess or a hollow space, dig it away. If you see channels that are eaten away, call in a pest control company for evaluation.

These wood eaters need not only food but water, and so they have two main forms of habitation: A *primary infestation* will be outdoors, in an underground nest. The termites live there, and make daily trips to your house to gather food in the form of your lumber. In a *secondary infestation*, they live inside your home in a space with a reliable source of moisture.

If you see an actual colony of termites inside your home, then you have a secondary infestation that can most likely be taken care of by killing the queen and eliminating the moisture permanently. A primary infestation is more difficult to deal with.

This is serious stuff. Termites can cause very expensive damage, and in some cases can even destroy a home. Don't try to abate termites yourself; a pest control company will have a much greater chance of success. They may use a trap system, or they may work on the outside to destroy the colonies there.

You can test for the presence of wood-eating bugs or rot by simply poking with a screwdriver.

TERMITES AT VARIOUS STAGES

It can be difficult to identify termites because they take on a good number of forms. Here are some of the most common.

- Supplementary reproductives
- Reproductive nymph
- Alate
- Worker
- Older nymph
- Young nymph
- Soldier
- Eggs
- King termite
- Queen termite
- Dealate

COMBATTING MINOR PESTS

The best way to eliminate cockroaches is not with the spray stuff that kills them instantly; you won't get them all, and they will return. Instead, carefully spread poufs of boric acid around the perimeter of the inside of your basement and wherever else they travel. Keep pets and small children away from the powder. It will take a week or two, but pests will carry the powder back to their lairs, where the queen and the entire colony will be killed.

For spiders, ants, and other annoyances, a "bug bomb" usually does a very good job. Seal the area, open the bomb, and leave for a day or so.

RADIANT FLOOR HEAT

Nothing makes a basement more comfortable than radiant heat, which transforms a cold and clammy concrete floor into a delicious place of even, gentle warmth. The warmth rises up to heat the basement and can even help heat the floor above as well.

Electric radiant heat is suitable in areas with cheap electricity, or for small spaces like a powder room. Tubing can be laid on top of the concrete floor, just before setting tiles. For a large area, hot-water radiant is usually a better choice. Hot-water radiant pipes are embedded in the concrete, so you'll need to plan early, before you start framing out the basement floors and walls; see the photos here for installation.

Running tubing in concrete

In the most common installation, PEX tubing is embedded in concrete. Use aluminum-reinforced PEX, which will hold its position once bent. Two layers of plastic sheeting are laid on the floor to protect the PEX from condensation. Then wire reinforcing mesh is cut to fit and placed over the plastic. Once this is done, run PEX tubing in loops, so it is fairly evenly spaced throughout the floor. Take your time creating a pattern that covers most of the floor area ❶. Where you will install the boiler that heats the water, run the PEX up and out of the floor ❷. Once all the tubing is laid, be sure that it all lies flat on the floor. Pour and finish the concrete ❸. Unless you have experience installing heating systems, hire a plumber or a heating company to hook the tubing to a heat source.

1 Run aluminum-reinforced PEX in a pattern throughout the floor.

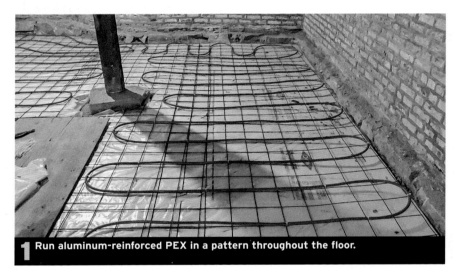

2 The tubing should run up the wall near where the heating unit will be.

3 Pour and finish the concrete floor.

Installing the heating unit

This is a job for pros, and I won't even try to give instructions. Here we see a tankless water heater with dual use—it supplies hot water to the floor and to the plumbing in the rest of the house as well. You also could have a separate boiler for the radiant heat. Much of the plumbing to hook up the heating unit is done on the floor, where shutoff valves and initial fittings are sweated in place **❶**. Then the unit is mounted onto a heatproof surface, and the rest of the connections are made **❷**.

1 Assembling lines with shutoff valves for two or more services is a complicated process and best done on the floor, where everything can be spread out and sweated in place.

2 The final connections are made after the heating unit is mounted onto a heat-proof surface, here a piece of plywood covered with metal sheeting.

RUNNING PEX IN FRAMING

If the floor needs to be raised, spread reflective insulating sheets on top of the concrete floor. Build floor framing as needed. In this example, the framing is raised a couple of inches, and the PEX tubing is run under the framing. Another option is to lay the framing on the sheets and thread the PEX through holes drilled in the framing. Arrange the PEX in loops so there are no gaps greater than 16 in. or so. Once the PEX is run, attach plywood or oriented strand board (OSB) subflooring to the framing.

PLAN AHEAD TO AVOID PUNCTURING PIPES

When you install framing, you will drive masonry screws or powder-actuated nails into the concrete to attach bottom plates. If you hit a pipe in the concrete, the results can be quite devastating: a slow leak that will not quit, requiring you to tear up the concrete to make a repair. So take photos of the installation, and note the distances away from landmarks, so you can be sure to avoid the pipes.

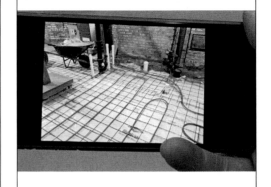

PLAN LAYOUTS AND INSTALLATIONS

BEFORE YOU START DEMOLISHING or building, it's important to take time to plan exactly how you will make the installations.

Some of your plans—such as how you frame your walls and provide a subfloor for your finish flooring—will depend on local conditions. Be sure to check with local codes, and get a permit for all electrical and plumbing work. Look through the rest of the book to make decisions on things like how to insulate the walls, what sort of windows to install, lighting and electrical receptacles, and plumbing fixtures. Even think through the furniture you want, and make sure there is ample room for it.

Detailed drawings, planning exactly where everything will go, will be necessary not only so you can decide which tasks you want to tackle yourself and those that you'll hire out, but also for required permits. And although basement work does not usually affect the family's life in the rest of the house, it's important to set a timetable for the work to be done so your basement remodel doesn't become long and protracted.

SIMPLE SOLUTIONS

Minimalist Approaches, p. 60

LAYOUT CONSIDERATIONS

MINIMALIST APPROACHES

The most common approach to basement remodeling includes installing flooring, wall, and ceiling surfaces that look very much like those in upstairs rooms. We are creatures of habit, comfortable when surrounded with smooth walls covered with paint, paneling, or tile, as well as floors that are tile, hardwood, or carpet.

But there's another way of thinking about a basement: It need not be like all the other rooms in the house, and may actually have a sort of rustic (or industrial or Bohemian) charm if treated more lightly. The idea is to "let a basement be a basement." Once

you achieve this attitude, all sorts of funky elements—pipes, ducts, exposed joists and beams, rough masonry walls and floors, and even some appliances—no longer appear as eyesores. Instead, they achieve (in one's mind, anyway) the status of "utilitarian beauty."

Perhaps the greatest virtue of the minimalist approach is that it can save tons of money. Moving pipes and ducts, framing walls and floors, and installing drywall surfaces, as well as finished-looking lights and plumbing services, consumes lots and lots of time and materials. And, in many

cases, such hardcore remodeling is strictly cosmetic and does not actually make a basement more comfortable or usable. Plus, strategies like leaving walls and floors unfinished or merely painted ensure against expensive damage in case of a flood.

All that money you save can go toward things that make a basement memorable, such as artwork for walls, fancy rugs, and fun stuff like a pool table or wine cellar.

However, do not neglect safety and comfort concerns. If you have nonmetallic cable for wiring, it should not be in easy reach. Perhaps replace it with solid conduit

A bare concrete floor makes an ideal surface for skateboarding ramps. Plywood walls make an ideal canvas for painted murals.

In this basement, a hardwood floor was laid, but the walls were simply spray painted; ceiling joists are left exposed, and electrical supplies are on display. Rather than hiding large ducts, they are celebrated for their shininess. Overhead canister lights are also left exposed, as is the wiring leading to them. A wall of glass block adds to a Euro style.

(pp. 151–153), or cover it up with a simple frame and drywall or paneling. And if your walls and floors get very cold, you may choose to insulate and seal them up (pp. 164–166). Window and exterior door replacement may also be a good idea (pp. 216–222).

Often the minimalist approach involves spray-painting walls and ceilings (including pipes). If a concrete floor is relatively uniform in appearance, acid staining may look great. If it varies in texture and has other imperfections, consider simply painting it.

➤ See "Acid Staining the Floor,"
   pp. 212–213.

Even exposed black steel gas pipe can be appealing, especially if it is neatly installed and clean. Here, the excess pipe dope or Teflon® tape has been carefully removed.

GETTING READY TO GET READY

Before you start planning room types and sizes, open up your space by clearing out all unnecessary stuff—including all those storage items that you can put elsewhere. Take steps to ensure that the space is dry and will stay dry, as discussed previously. If your basement is riddled with posts, or your large appliances are sitting in the middle of the basement, planning around these obstructions can be complicated and frustrating. You may want to install new beams and remove posts to give you a clean slate on which you can make your plans.

Keeping clean

Doing construction work in a basement can be dirty and dusty, so one of the first orders of business is to figure how to handle the mess. It has been said that the first tool a remodeler should buy is a high-quality Shop-Vac® with a really good collection system. You may not opt for the high-end setup shown below, but at least get a large-capacity vacuum with a HEPA filter and plenty of dust collection bags. Plan to clean often—at the least, at the end of every workday.

As much as weather permits, open windows and put outward-facing fans in them. Simple inexpensive box fans can do a remarkably good job of lessening or eliminating airborne particles.

Construction dust—and especially drywall dust—has an amazing ability to seep through even tiny cracks and infiltrate other rooms. How it travels upwards we may never know, but it does. Whenever possible, use plastic sheeting and tape to seal off areas of the house not being worked on.

SAFETY ALERT

Before removing a basement wall, be sure it is not load bearing. A bearing wall runs perpendicular to the joists in the basement ceiling and supports them where needed. If you want to remove a bearing wall, you will need to replace it with a beam that is approved by your building department as strong enough.

A great dust collection system often starts with a high-quality shop vacuum. But even if you have a standard Shop-Vac, the addition of a secondary unit, like Oneida's Dust Deputy® will greatly increase its efficiency. This unit spins dust cyclonically and removes most of the dust even before it reaches the vacuum.

You can prevent marital and familial hard feelings by carefully taping off "innocent" rooms that are not involved in the construction. It can be an annoyance to keep these areas sealed every day, but it's well worth the effort: Cleaning infiltrated dust can be a major job in itself.

Working with Your Building Department

Local building codes cover many operations you may perform while remodeling a basement, from structural support to insulation of outside walls, electrical and plumbing installations, and more. Though your basement may seem out of sight, it is recommended that you consult with your local building department before starting work. Building codes may seem strict, but they are designed to keep your basement safe and secure. You will probably need to schedule inspections of various types at various stages of work, for instance:

framing, rough electrical, rough plumbing, finish electrical, and finish plumbing. The building department may require that some of the work be performed by a licensed electrician or plumber.

If you're tempted to skip the building department, keep in mind that when you go to sell your home you could get into trouble. And if you are caught working without permits, the inspector may make you tear up walls or the floor to uncover the work they need to inspect—a very expensive and difficult proposition.

PLANNING AND DRAWING

Use a computer program or just a pencil, graph paper, and straightedge to plan your room(s). Start by carefully measuring your available space. Make a scaled drawing of the empty space—including all the little obstructions and bump-outs—and make a number of copies, so you can sketch onto them.

Overall plan

Make an overall plan view (top view) drawing, showing where all the important things go. A family room may have wide open spaces, so you can later put in a pool table or exercise equipment. A bathroom and utility room, on the other hand, have elements that need to be precisely planned. >> >> >>

OVERALL PLAN

An overall plan shows where all the stuff goes. Be sure to take into account the full thickness of walls—which may be as thick as 8 in. around the perimeter, depending on how you construct them. Also include doors (and the way they swing), windows, major appliances, shelving units, and bathroom fixtures.

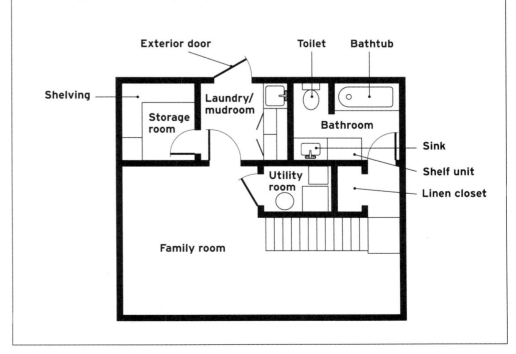

PLANNING AND DRAWING (CONTINUED)

Individual plans

Also make detailed drawings of the bathroom, utility room, laundry room, and any other room where precise placing of appliances and fixtures is important. In addition to a plan view drawing, side views (elevations) help you visualize the final look.

>> >> >>

WHAT COMPUTER PROGRAMS CAN DO

Computer drawing programs generate 3D images that make things more real. Once you've made the drawing, you can rotate it to look from above or from any side.

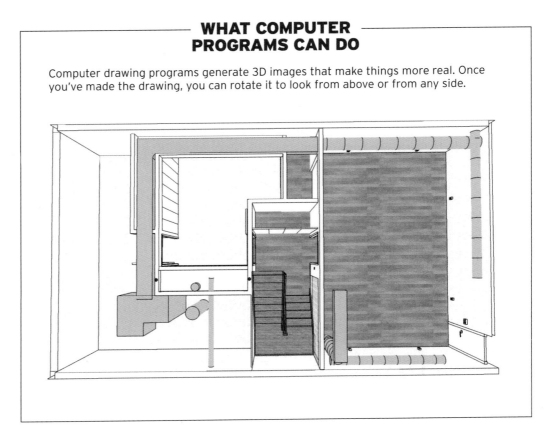

LAUNDRY ROOM DRAWING

A side-view drawing—either computer generated like this one or drawn by hand—helps you gain a greater feel for how spacious or cramped the folding table, shelving, and other elements will be.

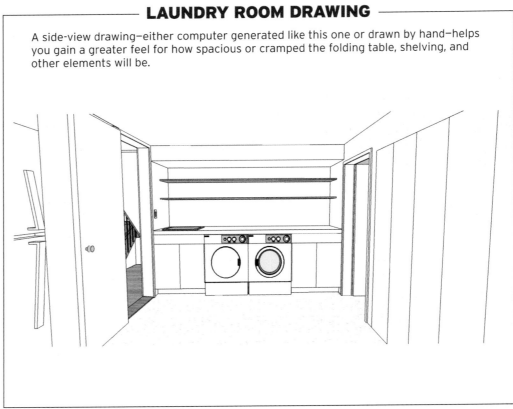

BATHROOM PLAN

This bathroom plan-view drawing includes not only the toilet, sink, and shower unit but also a towel bar, a niche in a shower wall, and recessed medicine cabinets. Precise dimensions help to place elements where they will be comfortable to use without wasting space.

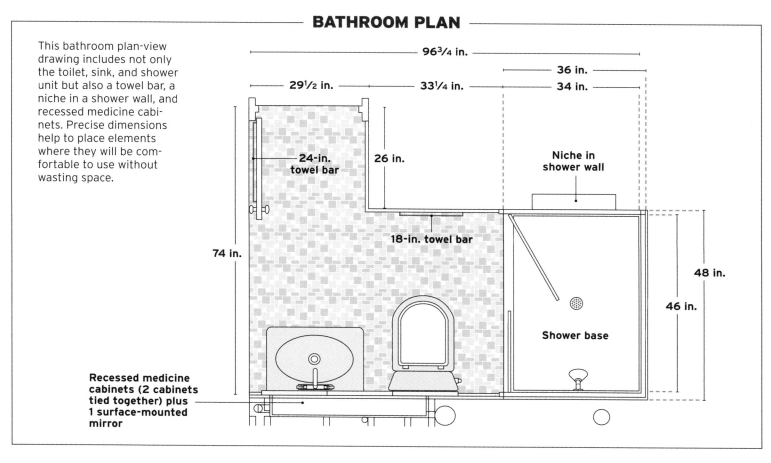

96³/₄ in.

29¹/₂ in.　　33¹/₄ in.　　36 in.

34 in.

24-in. towel bar

26 in.

Niche in shower wall

18-in. towel bar

74 in.

48 in.

46 in.

Shower base

Recessed medicine cabinets (2 cabinets tied together) plus 1 surface-mounted mirror

BATH ELEVATION

This elevation-view bathroom drawing is so detailed that it shows the shower tiles to scale, to get a complete feel of the room.

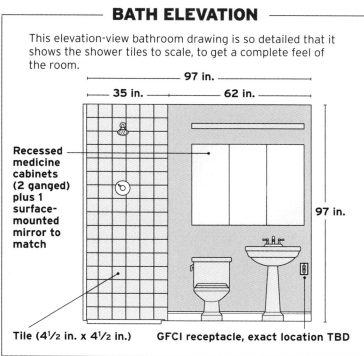

97 in.

35 in.　　62 in.

Recessed medicine cabinets (2 ganged) plus 1 surface-mounted mirror to match

97 in.

Tile (4¹/₂ in. x 4¹/₂ in.)

GFCI receptacle, exact location TBD

ELECTRICAL PLAN

Also make an electrical plan showing the locations of light fixtures, switches, and receptacles.

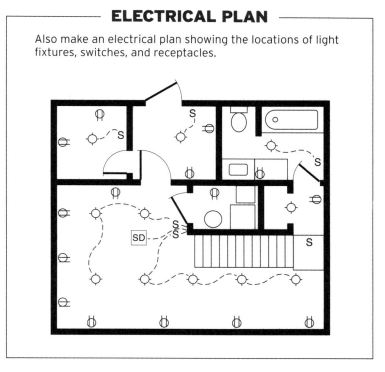

PLANNING AND DRAWING (CONTINUED)

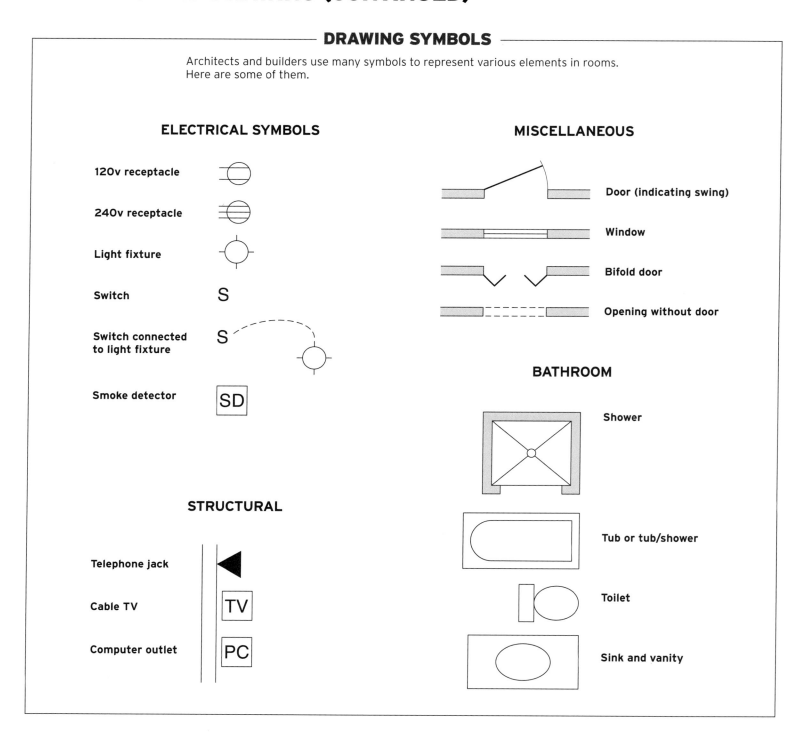

— DRAWING SYMBOLS —

Architects and builders use many symbols to represent various elements in rooms. Here are some of them.

ELECTRICAL SYMBOLS

120v receptacle

240v receptacle

Light fixture

Switch

Switch connected to light fixture

Smoke detector

STRUCTURAL

Telephone jack

Cable TV

Computer outlet

MISCELLANEOUS

Door (indicating swing)

Window

Bifold door

Opening without door

BATHROOM

Shower

Tub or tub/shower

Toilet

Sink and vanity

WORKING WITH SUBCONTRACTORS

Plumbers, electricians, drywallers, framers, and other tradesmen all can do their work faster than you can—unless you are one of them. You no doubt want to save money by doing much of your own work. But even professional contractors often hire "subs" because it just makes things go more smoothly.

Permits

You can be the general contractor on the job, or you can hire someone else to do that. If you hire, say, a plumber to run the rough plumbing or drywallers to hang and finish the drywall, they are your subcontractors. Be clear on which permits you need to pull and which they need to. Plumbers and electricians usually pull their own permits and are present for the inspections.

Bids and the contract

You may have heard that you should get three bids on a job and go for the one in the middle. That's not always true, but it often is. Don't just shop around for the cheapest price, or you may get shoddy work. Vet the subcontractors: Take the time to ask around and find out if a sub is reliable, if his work stands the test of time, and if he will do the job when you want it done. Many subs do good work but take on so much work that they may be weeks late in getting to your job.

The contract does not need to be elaborate, but it should specify:

- The exact materials to be used, including brand names.
- A payment schedule that holds back a significant sum until you are completely satisfied with the work and it has been inspected and approved.
- Which materials they will supply and which you will. For example, you may provide the sink, toilet, tub, and light fixtures, and subs may provide pipes, cables, and all the behind-the-walls stuff.
- A schedule of when things should be finished, and penalties if work is not done in a timely manner. This does not have to be punitive and unfriendly, but if the sub is weeks late, he should feel a wallet pinch.
- A statement of who will actually do the work. You don't want the sub to sub-sub it out to someone you don't know.

THE ORDER OF WORK

To keep the job going at a reasonable pace, start out with a loose schedule of when things will happen. In general, a basement job follows this path:

1. Making repairs to the concrete surfaces, and taking steps to ensure dryness
2. Moving large appliances and heating units, if needed
3. Lowering the floor and/or moving up pipes and ductwork, if needed
4. Getting permits
5. Making structural repairs and installations, such as to beams and posts
6. Insulating the exterior walls
7. Framing exterior and interior walls
8. HVAC installations
9. Rough plumbing
10. Rough electrical
11. Insulating between studs, if any
12. Installing windows
13. Hanging and finishing drywall
14. Installing doors
15. Finish carpentry—trimming doors, windows, and base
16. Painting and staining
17. Installing subflooring and flooring
18. Finish plumbing
19. Finish electrical
20. Installing bathroom accessories
21. Installing door handles, thresholds, and transition strips; paint touchup

ELECTRICAL AND PLUMBING INSTALLATIONS

As part of your own basement inspection, you'll want to catalog the mechanical systems—particularly the current electrical and plumbing. Your home's electrical system will definitely play a part in your basement remodel, as will the plumbing system if you intend to add or update a bathroom or laundry room.

Unless your house was built fairly recently, your basement may have a number of sketchy or confusing electrical and plumbing installations that need to be dealt with before you can proceed with a remodel.

If you see something that you do not fully understand, call in a professional, at least for a consult.

Electrical

There's a lot of wiring even a novice can do in a basement, but installing a service panel isn't on the list. Your home's service panel houses incoming cables from the meter outside your house as well as breakers (or fuses, sometimes found in older homes and service panels) and wires that distribute electricity to individual circuits. Each breaker or fuse is rated to trip when a circuit is overloaded, cutting voltage to those wires delivering electricity.

When remodeling a basement, you—or more likely a licensed electrician—will need to determine if the service panel is large enough to provide enough amperage for your home. If not, an additional or larger panel can be installed.

➡ See "The Service Panel," p. 138.

>> >> >>

The electrical circuits in this service panel are neatly labeled, so if one overloads, you can easily find the breaker to flip. Also, there are many available slots for installing new circuits, which you will likely need when remodeling a basement.

If your service panel is an old fuse box like this, it almost certainly needs to be replaced with a new circuit breaker panel. You'll probably also need to upgrade service to 200 amps. Consult with a professional electrician.

Nonmetallic cables can be safe, as long as they are correctly connected inside boxes at each end, are firmly stapled, and are kept protected from drywall screws, if the area will be finished. Here, the cables are installed loosely and are not well attached.

The wires in this panel are run haphazardly, which is not good practice though it can still be safe. This panel carries only 100 amps, which may not be large enough for your house, and there are only two slots available for new circuits.

SAFETY ALERT

To work safely on existing circuits, always turn off power at the service panel and use a voltage tester at the outlet to verify the power is off.

ELECTRICAL AND PLUMBING INSTALLATIONS (CONTINUED)

Plumbing

For many, a large part of a basement remodel might be to section off a dedicated laundry room, even if the laundry is located in the basement already, and to add a powder room. Perhaps your dream has been to turn your basement space into an adult hangout, complete with mini-kitchen, or maybe you're remodeling to create an apartment-like space for an adult child or aging parent. Some newer homes might even be plumbed to allow easy installation of a basement bathroom.

Adding or changing plumbing requires you to locate the main drain, or stack, the sewage line that runs to either your septic system or city sewage system, any gas or HVAC lines, and any other drain lines. Local building codes as well as practical considerations will dictate your layout and plumbing plan, so be sure to consult a professional as well as your local building official.

As with electrical services, those who live in an older home might encounter some outdated plumbing situations, such as cast-iron pipe or runs that might not be up to code. Don't panic—a pro can help you update and remodel your plumbing system.

Cast iron can last a long time, but in the case of the installation at far left, the lower pipe section is rusting badly and the cleanout is all but useless. The lower section of the plumbing was replaced with PVC pipe, with a cleanout located a foot or so up from the floor (see the photo at near left). The neoprene repair fitting that joins the PVC to the cast iron is easy to install and is approved in most areas as a permanent fitting.

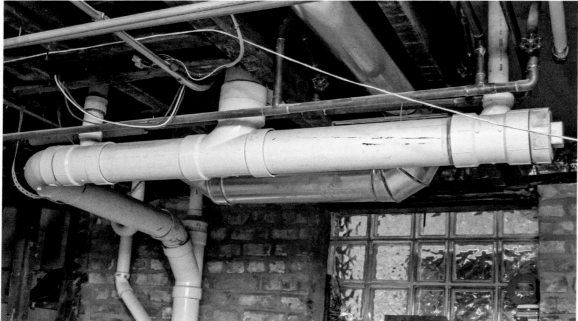

Here, a large horizontal PVC pipe has three vertical pipes attached to it, which lead to a sink, toilet, and shower in the bathroom above, on the first floor. The pipe slopes downward at a rate of 1/4 in. per ft. or more and leads to a PVC vertical stack, which runs to the main drain line under the concrete floor. Copper pipes supply water to the upstairs bathroom fixtures. Each has a shutoff valve, which must be kept accessible for future repairs.

The green bubbles and stains on this copper gas pipe mean that moisture has been allowed to collect. This type of gas pipe installation is no longer up to code and needs to be replaced with approved gas pipe.

When running new drain lines into an existing old main drain, it's a good idea to chip away the concrete and find out the condition of the pipe. You can see plenty of rust, which is partially encased in concrete and will some day cause the pipe to fail. This should be replaced with PVC piping.

If you see a cylindrical fitting under the floor, like this brass cleanout, you have an old-fashioned drum trap. It will likely last, but it would be better to tear up the floor and replace the fitting with a P trap. In any event, if you install flooring here, be sure to provide access to this fitting in case you need to rod the drain line in the future.

This gas line looks unusual but is actually just fine, though it may not be up to local code. Although the gas pipe is a bit rusty, it is not in danger of failing. Blue Teflon tape at the fittings is approved for use on gas lines.

CHOOSING LIGHTING

Basements usually get little in the way of natural light, so planning the lighting is an important consideration early in the remodeling process. In general, more is better, as long as you have dimmer switches that can adjust the levels of all the lights.

Your electrical plan will need to take into account your basement design and how "finished" your new space will be. Your plan should identify your lighting needs before rough in and inspection.

Plug-in lights like these do not need their own electrical boxes, and can be easily moved around and adjusted.

A modest yet classy flush light like this makes a simple but elegant statement.

These are flush-mounted lights, but their trim and shape give them the sleek feel of recessed canisters.

Three mini recessed canisters directly over the bed provide general illumination when wanted; individual hanging pendant lights make for good reading while the partner is asleep.

If a fixture box is mounted on a wall, you can install an individual wall sconce, or a system like this, for highlighting favorite artwork.

Pendant lights, which can be easily adjusted for height, come in a dizzying array of colors and styles; all attach to the ceiling box in the same way.

If you opt for a minimalist approach, a pointable floodlight ties in handsomely with the exposed conduit.

FRAMING WALLS AND CEILINGS

Framing a basement usually proceeds in this order: (1) the exterior walls, (2) the interior walls, (3) the ceiling where necessary, and (4) soffits and box-ins to cover up pipes, ductwork, and other obstructions. With this order of work, after framing walls you can attach horizontal nailers to begin framing the ceiling. (And often there is no need to actually frame the ceiling; you can use the existing joists.)

Framing in a basement can get pretty complicated, so plan carefully by making drawings that show where all the framing members go, as well as the paths for plumbing and wiring lines. Even with good planning, you will likely need to do some improvising, especially where you need to frame around obstructions. Building in this way can be slow, so allow plenty of time.

PREPPING OUTSIDE WALLS FOR FRAMING

Keeping the Framing and Insulation Dry, p. 76

FRAMING

A Basic Framed Wall, p. 80

Planning and Buying Materials, p. 81

FRAMING BASIC WALLS

Laying Out on the Plates, p. 82

Building a Wood Wall Frame on the Floor, p. 83

Piecing in Wood Framing, p. 86

Framing with Metal Studs, p. 88

Framing Windows and Doors, p. 90

SPECIAL FRAMING SITUATIONS

Lowering a Ceiling, p. 94

Building an Interior Wall, p. 96

Framing a Plumbing Wall, p. 98

Framing and Finishing a Curved Wall, p. 100

Framing around Obstructions, p. 101

KEEPING THE FRAMING AND INSULATION DRY

Moisture issues are addressed in detail on pp. 22–57. To quickly summarize, take these steps:

1. Seal the outside of the basement wall and the joint between the wall and the footing.

2. Direct rainwater away from the house.

3. Provide effective drainage inside the basement, most often with a sump pump and a perimeter drain of some sort.

However, most of us cannot take all these steps to keep the water out, and even if we do, a heavy flood may send moisture into the walls. Plus, a small amount of moisture can develop due to condensation, when there is a difference in temperature between two sides of a wall.

If you build framed walls adjacent to the outside walls and then hang drywall, you will create a pretty tight space inside the wall; if even a small amount of moisture builds up inside this space, it may not dry out for a very long time. This can lead to mold, wet rot, and other horrors. So even after you've taken the steps described previously to ensure your walls and floor will stay as dry as possible, you'll want to install an effective vapor barrier to keep moisture from becoming trapped in the framing cavity, where it can grow on studs, the back of drywall, and perhaps fiberglass insulation, if you install it.

Prior to framing, consult with your building department and local builders to find the most common and approved ways of preparing basement walls. Your building department will probably also have insulation requirements (often, R-19 or greater). Here are some of the more common approaches to keeping framing dry.

WHAT CAN GO WRONG

No matter which method of insulation you choose, be sure to avoid providing "food" for mold. If you apply anything remotely organic—including ingredients in most construction adhesives—you will be installing a mold banquet. The methods on the next few pages use only inedible materials, so even if there is a bit of moisture, there will be no mold.

BEWARE OF THIS INSULATING METHOD

For many years, installing wood framing and hanging fiberglass insulation between the studs and a plastic sheet stapled to the face of the studs to act as a "vapor barrier" or "moisture barrier" was the most common way to frame and insulate outside basement walls.

In theory, this arrangement works well to keep moisture from inside the room from reaching the studs. But the extremely large problem with this method is that moisture almost always comes from the concrete or masonry wall, not from inside the room. So not only is there nothing to prevent moisture from reaching the studs and the fiberglass insulation, but also the plastic "vapor barrier" actually helps hold the moisture in, allowing it to collect on the wood and fiberglass, where it can be harmful. Sometimes walls built this way manage to stay reasonably dry, especially if there is a gap at the bottom where moisture can escape. But there are many stories of people smelling something funny, removing a section of drywall, and discovering heavy mold accumulation and rotted boards.

A possible exception: If you live in an extremely arid climate and are sure your masonry basement walls will stay dry, then the source of moisture may actually come from inside the room, and this arrangement may make sense. Check with your building department and local contractors.

Plastic wall liner

Probably the gold standard solution is a special plastic wall liner coupled with the floor drain, shown on p. 34. A system like this is typically installed by specialist contractors and is not usually a do-it-yourself project. Once the liner is installed, you can install wood or metal framing next to it. The framing can touch the liner, but should not press the liner against the concrete wall. Make sure the bottom plate of the framing does not interfere with the floor drain. Be sure to position the framing so you can add fiberglass insulation between the studs thick enough to satisfy local codes.

A thick plastic liner with a running drain below ensures against moisture buildup in the framing cavity.

Spray-foam insulation

You can hire an insulation company or rent equipment yourself to spray foam insulation on the masonry surface. This is a very effective barrier. However, it is also quite expensive, so you may want to apply it only in certain areas that are difficult to cover in other ways.

Spray-on foam insulation is worth its price tag when used in hard-to-cover areas like these.

Rigid foam sheets

Another method is to attach rigid foam insulation sheets directly onto the concrete or masonry wall, and then tightly seal all the joints. The sheets should be at least 1½ in. thick; thinner sheets may not form an effective vapor barrier.   >> >> >>

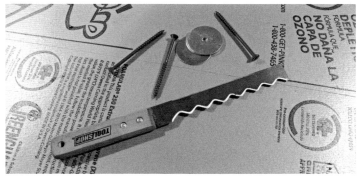

Cut 1½-in.-thick rigid foam insulation with a special knife and attach with masonry screws and fender washers that are at least 1½ in. in diameter. Do not use adhesives.

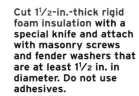

Foam insulation can be sprayed directly from the can, but a gun-type tool makes application easier.

KEEPING THE FRAMING AND INSULATION DRY (CONTINUED)

1 Cut foam insulation using a serrated knife.

2 Drill pilot holes with a masonry bit.

Measure and cut the sheets carefully, so you don't end up with large gaps to fill **❶**. Most saws will make crumbly edges, so use a long knife. A serrated bread knife works OK, but a tool made especially for the purpose is well worth its low cost. Butt sheets tightly together so they are also snug against other surfaces. Drill pilot holes with a masonry bit of the right size for the masonry screws you will install **❷**. Slip a fender washer onto a masonry screw and drive it into the concrete or block **❸**. Drive enough screws so that the sheet is firmly attached and not loose or floppy at any point.

Cover or fill all gaps with foam insulation or tape, or with both. Apply ample amounts of foam insulation, which expands as it dries **❹**. You can leave the squeezed-out foam in place, or trim it with a sharp putty knife if it may get in the way of framing. Tight seams can be covered with building-paper tape **❺**. Press firmly and work carefully, so there are not even small gaps in coverage. If there are chunks of concrete or other obstructions that may get in the way of the framing, cut or chip them away **❻**.

TEST FOR GAPS

Rigid insulation doesn't just help keep the cavity dry—it insulates as well. Here, an inexpensive heat-sensing device that attaches to a cell phone indicates warm and cold spots on the wall. The area with insulation is a nice warm red; uninsulated areas are various shades of less-warm color. A tool like this does not give precise insulation data but does helpfully alert you to any spots that need coverage.

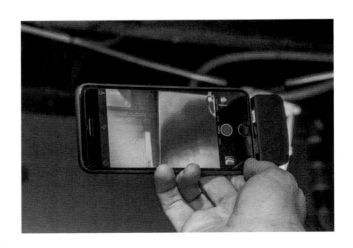

3 Secure the sheets with masonry screws and fender washers.

4 Seal all gaps with spray-foam insulation.

5 Building-paper tape can be used to seal joints between sheets.

6 Chip away any obstructions that may get in the way of framing.

A BASIC FRAMED WALL

Most commonly, walls are framed with wood or metal 2x4s, though smaller- or larger-dimensioned studs and plates can be used. Studs are most commonly spaced 16 in. "on center," meaning that the center of one stud is 16 in. away from the center of the next stud. The resulting space between studs is 14½ in. If planned correctly, this spacing ensures that the end of a full sheet of drywall—which is most often 96 in. long—will fall in the center of a stud, so no extra framing is required. When you reach the end of a wall, the last stud is almost always spaced less than 16 in. on center.

Sometimes studs are spaced 24 in. on center, to save on material costs. However, this is not recommended: It creates a wall that is less sturdy, and it really saves very little money.

Often builders use a combination of wood and metal studs. When building with wood, it's common to use pressure-treated lumber for the bottom plate and standard non-treated boards for the studs and the top plate. When building with wood, it's best to build with 2x4s, but if space is tight you may choose to go with 2x3s. Metal framing comes in various widths, with 2½-in. and 3½-in. widths being the most common.

FRAMING A BASIC WALL

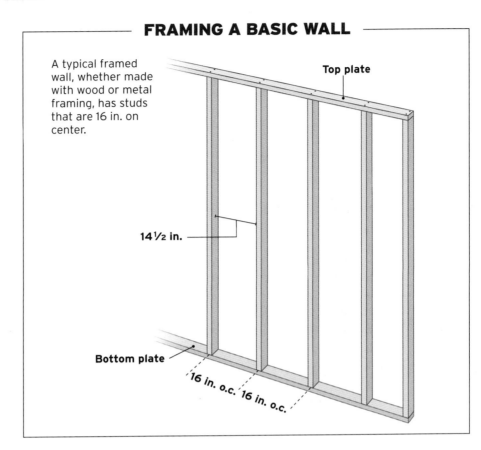

A typical framed wall, whether made with wood or metal framing, has studs that are 16 in. on center.

Top plate

14½ in.

Bottom plate

16 in. o.c. 16 in. o.c.

HOW FAR AWAY FROM THE WALL?

Building wall framing an inch or so away from the wall surface will leave ample room for adding R-13 insulation between the studs. However, if you need to add more insulation, consider moving the framing farther away. If, for instance, you place the framing 2½ in. away from the wall, you will have enough space for R-19 insulation. Your building official can provide details on which insulation is required.

➤ See "Installing Insulation between Studs," pp. 164-166.

CORNER FRAMING

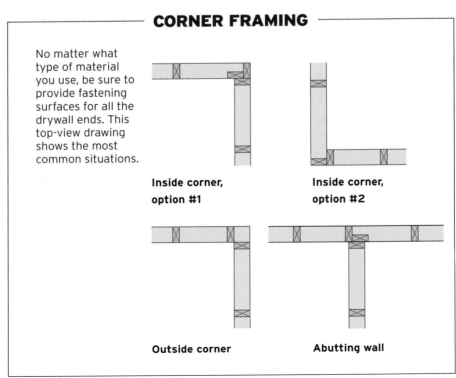

No matter what type of material you use, be sure to provide fastening surfaces for all the drywall ends. This top-view drawing shows the most common situations.

Inside corner, option #1

Inside corner, option #2

Outside corner

Abutting wall

PLANNING AND BUYING MATERIALS

It's usually easiest to first frame the outside walls, then the interior walls, and then around obstacles. However, you may want to snap chalklines for all your planned walls first, following the guidelines in chapter 3, to gain a good feel for the overall plan. With the lines chalked, you can walk around the layout and perhaps spot areas where a wall or two should be moved for more comfortable foot traffic.

➔ See "Getting Straight Lumber," p. 103, for selecting wood framing and "Framing with Metal Studs," pp. 88-89, for selecting metal framing.

Calculate framing materials

- Start by figuring your top and bottom plates. Looking at your plan, list the distances for all of your walls. (Don't deduct for doorways.) For wood framing, buy two boards for each wall—one top and one bottom plate. Boards come in 2-ft.-long increments, so, for example, if a wall is 10 ft. 4 in. long you will need two 12-footers. (The waste will probably get used elsewhere.) Metal top and bottom plates are called channels and generally come only in 10-ft. lengths.

- Then estimate the studs you will need. If you are using wood, 8-footers will be long enough, unless your ceiling is higher than 8 ft. 3 in. above the floor. Studs are placed every 16 in., but you'll need lots of extra pieces for corners and at windows and doors. Rather than trying to add up all the extra pieces, you can't go too

far wrong by figuring on one stud per every foot of wall length, and then adding 10%. So for instance, if your walls all add up to 100 ft. in length, buy 110 studs.

- Buy a dozen or so more 2x4s than you think you need. You almost always end up needing them, and you may need to return boards that are twisted or damaged.

- If you need to box in pipes, ductwork, or other obstructions with a soffit, first determine if you will use 2x4s or 2x2s. Then figure on 3 ft. of framing material for every foot of soffit or chase. Also throw in a sheet or two of ½-in. OSB.

➔ See "Framing around Obstructions," pp. 101-105.

- For plumbing walls you will need extrawide studs. Often 2x6s are wide enough, but you may need 2x8s. Buy plates and studs of the same width.

➔ See "Framing a Plumbing Wall," pp. 98-99.

- For fasteners, buy one masonry screw or powder-actuated nail for every 16 in. of all the walls' lengths. There's no sense trying to calculate other nails and/or screws. For a typical basement, two 5-lb. boxes of nails or one large box of power nails plus one 5-lb. box of 3-in. screws will meet at least most of your needs.

- You'll also need two or three large bundles of shims.

GET A COMPRESSOR AND NAILER

You can build these walls by pounding nails by hand or by driving screws, but nowadays you can buy an air compressor with a framing nailer for a fraction of the materials cost of your basement. An air gun not only shoots nails much faster than hand nailing but also reduces mistakes and enables you to hold a board with one hand while you drive with the other. This can save you plenty of time and aggravation. Once you adjust the compressor to the right pressure, it will drive nails at just the right depth almost every time. The setup here includes a compressor, a framing nailer, and a finish nailer.

LAYING OUT ON THE PLATES

Whether you build a frame on the floor or piece in the studs one at a time, start by laying out the positions of the studs on the bottom and top plates. Position the plates according to your plan for framing a corner as shown in the drawing on p. 80. Draw V-shaped marks with their points indicating every 16 in., minus 3/4 in. (15¼ in., 31¼ in., and so on) **❶**. Then use a square to draw a line through the V points and across both plates, and draw an X next to the lines indicating which side of the line the studs will fall on **❷**.

1 Draw V marks every 16 in., minus 3/4 in.

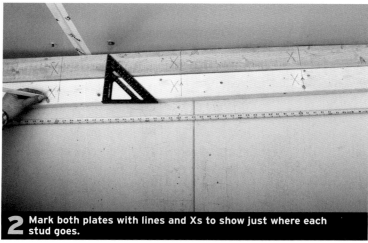

2 Mark both plates with lines and Xs to show just where each stud goes.

BLOCKING WHERE NEEDED

Where joists run parallel to the wall you will not be able to attach to joists at the top of the wall. So cut pieces of blocking—any 2-by lumber will do—and install them every 16 in. or so.

TRADE SECRET

For an extra measure of protection against water damage to your framing, put a layer of composite or vinyl decking material under the bottom plate. Be sure to use better-quality decking; cheap composite decking can swell with moisture. Rip-cut the decking to a width of 3½ in. and fasten it to the bottom of the bottom plate. Of course, be sure to take the decking's 1-in. thickness into account when you cut studs.

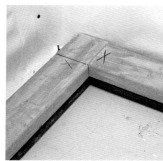

BUILDING A WOOD WALL FRAME ON THE FLOOR

If you have plenty of floor space and your joists are at a fairly consistent height, building a wall on the floor and raising it into position can be the fastest and most efficient way to build.

Determine the length of the studs. Stack two 2x4 scraps on top of each other, to represent the bottom and top plates, and measure from the top of the stack to the underside of the joists that the wall will attach to at the top ❶. Measure at every joist, because the distance can vary. Take the shortest of the heights and subtract ¼ in. or ³⁄₈ in. Cut the studs to this dimension. (If the height gradually lengthens or shortens as you move along the length of the wall, you can cut the studs to gradually longer or shorter lengths; just be sure to number the studs and install them in order as you build the wall.)

Cut the studs to length. You can use a circular saw, perhaps with a speed square as a guide. If you have a power miter saw (also called a chopsaw), that is better. Set up a work surface on a table, on horses, or on the floor so you can easily position boards for cutting. Measure and mark with a square line and an X indicating the waste side, and make the cut ❷.

Often, studs are not straight; they usually have a "crown"—a slight curve along their length. For a straight-looking wall, all the studs' crowns should face the same way. Sight down along each stud, and draw an arrow indicating the direction of the crown ❸.

>> >> >>

TRADE SECRET

Power saws are often set up a little imperfectly, resulting in imprecise cuts. Before you start cutting boards, make a test cut on a 2x4 and check that the cut is square through its thickness. If not, adjust your saw until you get perfectly straight cuts. This will take only a few minutes and will make the job go more smoothly.

1 Measure for the stud lengths, using two blocks to indicate the plates.

2 Cut studs to length.

3 Find the crown on the studs and install them all facing the same way.

BUILDING A WOOD WALL FRAME ON THE FLOOR (CONTINUED)

Arrange the plates and studs on the floor; the studs should have their crowns facing up. To fasten each stud, place its end to cover the X mark and align its side with the square line. Hold the stud so its edge is flush with the edge of the plate and drive two fasteners through the plate and into the stud ❹. Raise the stud wall into position ❺. Place 1-in. spacers between the bottom plate and the wall and check every few studs for plumb ❻. If the wall is loose, tap in shims at the bottom or top to snug it up ❼. The wall should be at least 1 in. away from the insulation at all points. If needed, you may have to move the bottom plate out a bit farther.

Once the wall is snug and plumb, attach the bottom plate to the concrete floor. You can drill holes and drive masonry screws, but a faster way is to use an inexpensive powder-actuated nailer. Buy 2-in. or 2¼-in. nails and powder charges of two or more power levels. To use the model shown, load a nail, insert a powder charge (which has actual gunpowder), press the tip against the wood, and tap with the butt of your hand on top of the tool ❽. Drive screws or nails every 16 in. or so. If the nail does not sink all the way in, or if it goes in too far, use a charge of a different power. Fasten the top plate to joists with nails or screws ❾.

4 Fasten the studs to the plates, keeping them carefully aligned.

6 Use spacers to hold the wall away from the insulation, and adjust for plumb.

8 Shoot nails or drive screws every 16 in. or so with a powder-actuated nailer.

9 Attach the top plate to framing with nails or screws.

5 Raise the stud wall into position.

7 Where needed, tap in shims to make the wall fit snugly.

⚠ WHAT CAN GO WRONG

Few of life's tragedies match the heartbreak of building and raising a just-too-tall wall, trying to knock it into position, then having to give up and take the thing apart so you can cut the studs a wee bit shorter.

Don't try to be precise or tight fitting. Build a wall that is ¼ in. or ³/₈ in. shorter than you think is needed.

CORNER TREATMENTS

Consult the drawings on p. 80 to plan and install corner framing. Here are two examples. In the situation at left, scraps of 2x4 are attached with screws to provide a nailing surface. Below, stud positions are carefully planned so they fall 16 in. on center, taking into account the installation of drywall on the other wall first.

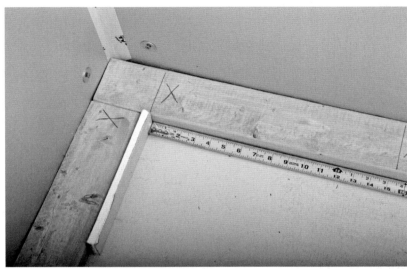

BEWARE OF FRAMING WITH 2X2S

Many basements have been framed with 2x2s (or flat-laid 2x4s) nailed directly to the concrete wall. Sometimes the 2x2s are attached with powder-actuated nails, but that is a poor approach, since those nails are really designed just to keep boards from moving from side to side, not to attach boards structurally. Framing attached with powder nails is notorious for coming loose. Attaching with masonry screws is a far more secure approach.

But even if you use masonry screws, there is no guarantee that the boards will not become water damaged; mold is not uncommon inside walls built this way. Also, the mere 1½-in. thickness of the framing means there is precious little room for insulation. And framing this way can be more difficult than you expect, since concrete walls are often uneven; a lot of shimming and testing for straightness is needed if you want to end up with walls that are fairly straight.

For those reasons, this type of basement framing is less common today than it used to be. Still, if you are quite certain that your walls will stay dry, don't need insulation, and are not bothered by walls that wave a bit, this can be an economical approach.

PIECING IN WOOD FRAMING

Because basement floors and the framing above can be uneven, many builders prefer to install the bottom and top plates, and then piece in the studs one at a time. On a long wall this is more time-consuming than building on a floor (especially if you are hand nailing), but it makes large mistakes less likely. On smaller walls, or where there are obstructions, piecing in is the only reasonable approach, as seen on pp. 101–105.

Start by attaching the top and bottom plates, which must be away from the wall the desired distance and plumb with each other. To mark for the positions of the plates, it helps to make this odd layout tool: Cut spacers to the desired distance that you want the framing to be away from the wall,

and attach them to one edge of a 2x4 that is a bit longer than the wall height. Then tape a level to the other edge of the 2x4. Hold this tool against the wall, and adjust its position until the level reads plumb; you may need to pull it away from the wall a bit. Draw a pencil mark where the front edge of the 2x4 rests on the floor ❶. Holding the 2x4 in position against the floor mark, also draw a mark on the framing above ❷. Test for plumb and mark the top and bottom in the same way every 3 ft. or 4 ft. along the length of the wall. Choose marks that are the closest to the wall near each end, and snap chalklines between them, to mark the positions of the top and bottom plate ❸.

Cut and mark top and bottom plates as shown on p. 82 ❹. Attach the plates to the floor and to the framing above ❺. At each stud location, measure between the plates for each board ❻ and cut. Ideally, each stud should fit fairly snugly, such that you need to tap it into place ❼ but don't have to pound; that would lead to a curved stud. Attach the studs with four angle-driven fasteners, also called toenails. They are usually driven two on each side, but you can also drive one in the front edge. Toenailing is easily done with a power nailer ❽. If you are hand nailing, use 8-penny nails (often labeled "8d"). Or drive 2-in. or 2½-in. screws; two screws per board should be strong enough.

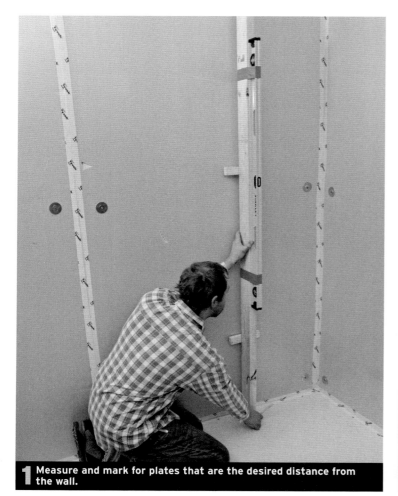

1 Measure and mark for plates that are the desired distance from the wall.

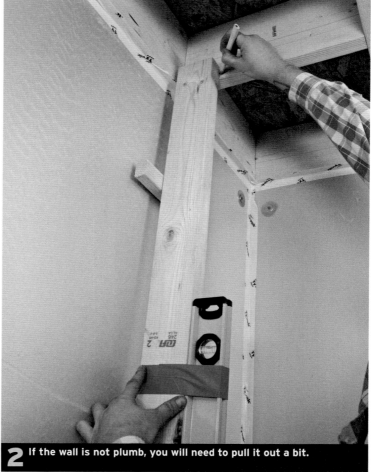

2 If the wall is not plumb, you will need to pull it out a bit.

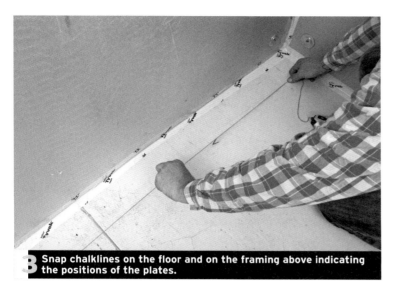

3 Snap chalklines on the floor and on the framing above indicating the positions of the plates.

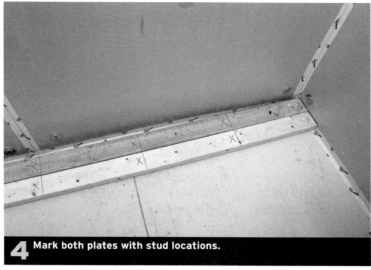

4 Mark both plates with stud locations.

5 After attaching the bottom plate with powder-actuated nails or masonry screws, screw the top plate to the framing.

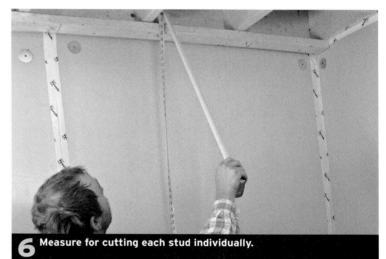

6 Measure for cutting each stud individually.

7 Tap studs into position; aim for a snug but not tight fit.

8 Drive nails or screws at angles to attach the studs to the plates.

FRAMING WITH METAL STUDS

Metal framing is close to being as economical and easy to install as wood framing, but it is not as popular among do-it-yourselfers. Once assembled, metal framing seems flimsy. But after the drywall is attached, the wall is plenty strong. You can buy metal framing that mimics the dimensions of 2x4s, or in smaller sizes. Wear gloves when installing, because the edges are quite sharp.

There are two parts: channels are simple U shapes and are used for the top and bottom plates. Studs slip into the channels. Mark for cutting with a felt-tipped pen ❶. You can cut metal framing with a chopsaw equipped with a metal-cutting blade, but it's also easy to cut with tin snips. Cut both of the sides with the snips ❷. Then bend the cutoff up a bit and cut the width of the channel or stud ❸. Or, simply bend back and forth a few times until the stud or channel breaks.

Attach the bottom channel to the concrete floor using powder-actuated nails ❹, or drill pilot holes and drive masonry screws. Attach the top plate with drywall or all-purpose screws driven into wood framing members. At a corner, mark for cutting a flange to the width of the other channel, cut, and fold down ❺. Mark the channels for studs 16 in. o.c. and cut to span between the channels. Position a stud and drive self-tapping screws made for metal studs ❻.

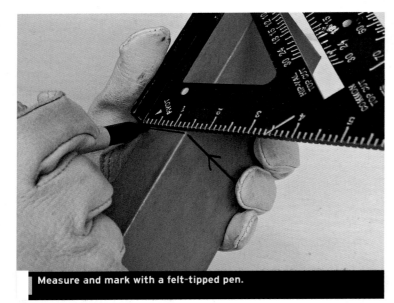

1 Measure and mark with a felt-tipped pen.

2 Cut the sides.

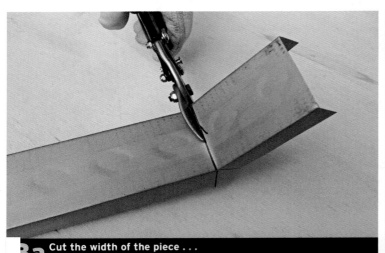

3a Cut the width of the piece . . .

3b . . . or bend back and forth until it breaks.

4 Anchor the bottom channels with powder-actuated nails.

Protect Your Hands Wearing gloves is often dangerous when working with power tools. But metal framing has some surprisingly sharp edges that can easily cut bare skin. So as long as you are using hand tools only, I recommend that you wear gloves when installing metal framing.

5a At a corner, cut and bend a flange . . .

5b . . . for the other channel to fit over.

6 Attach studs with self-tapping screws.

IMPROVISATION

When framing around windows or other features, you will need to cut channels to create flaps that can be attached. This is usually not difficult, but may sometimes take a bit of trial and error. In the example shown, a channel is cut with a flap so it can be secured to the stud on the side of the window. Below, a short section of channel is cut and bent so it can be attached to both the stud and the concrete wall, using masonry screws, to add rigidity to the wall.

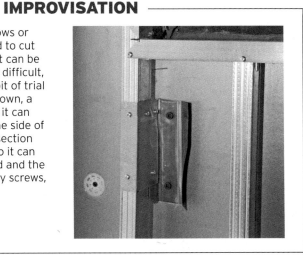

FRAMING WINDOWS AND DOORS

Walls are often interrupted by windows and doors, which need to be framed in specific ways. Basic framing should still be maintained, with vertical pieces spaced 16 in. o.c., but the window and door must be surrounded with additional framing pieces. As the drawing below shows, king studs and trimmers frame the rough openings (so called because they will be trimmed out later) vertically. A header runs horizontally at the top, and a sill completes the frame at the opening. To maintain the 16-in. spacing of studs, short studs called cripples are installed above doors and above and below windows.

Framing a window

Many experienced carpenters measure and then lay out on the plates for all the king studs and trimmers, but the following method is more mistakeproof. Start by drawing layout lines on the plates with studs 16 in. o.c., as if there were no window. Then measure to determine which of the studs will be interrupted by a window, and draw a C (for "cripple") for those ❶; draw simple large Xs for all the full-length studs.

➡ **See "Laying Out on the Plates," p. 82.**

Build a wall that includes all the full studs but none of the cripples. You can build it on the floor, or by piecing in ❷. To determine the locations of the king studs on either side of the window, measure over from the nearest stud to the window ❸, and subtract ¼ in. to allow for an opening that is slightly larger than needed. Check the stud for plumb as you measure. Transfer the measurements to the plates and install the king studs ❹.

>> >> >>

FRAMING WINDOWS AND DOORS

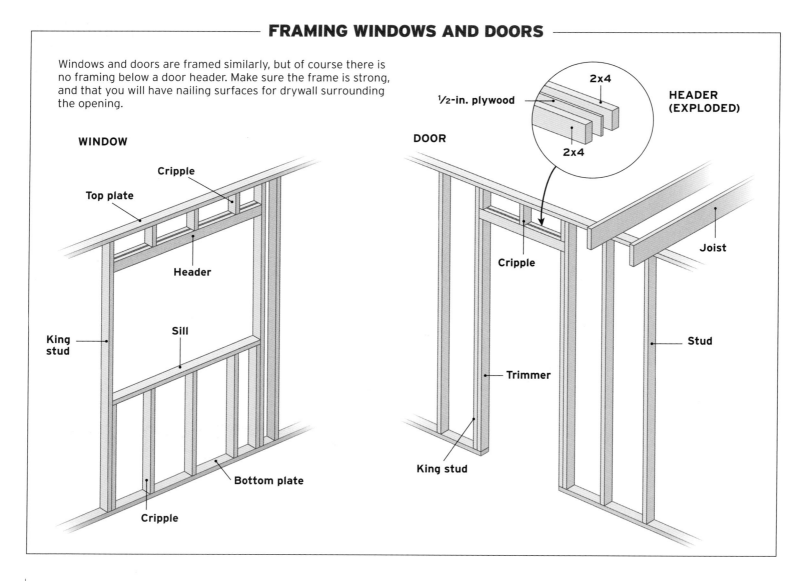

Windows and doors are framed similarly, but of course there is no framing below a door header. Make sure the frame is strong, and that you will have nailing surfaces for drywall surrounding the opening.

WINDOW

Cripple
Top plate
Header
King stud
Sill
Bottom plate
Cripple

DOOR

½-in. plywood
2x4
2x4
HEADER (EXPLODED)
Joist
Cripple
Stud
Trimmer
King stud

1 Lay out for full studs and cripple studs (not the king studs) on both plates.

2 Install a wall with the full studs only.

3 Measure over for the locations of the king studs.

4 Install the king studs.

FRAMING WINDOWS AND DOORS (CONTINUED)

Measure for the horizontal pieces at the top and bottom, then measure up and mark for their positions on king studs **5**. Again, place the boards ¼ in. lower or higher than the needed opening; you will install with shims later. Install the horizontals, then measure and cut cripples at the top and bottom **6**. Check the opening as you work to be sure it will be plenty wide and tall.

5 Measure for the bottom and top horizontals.

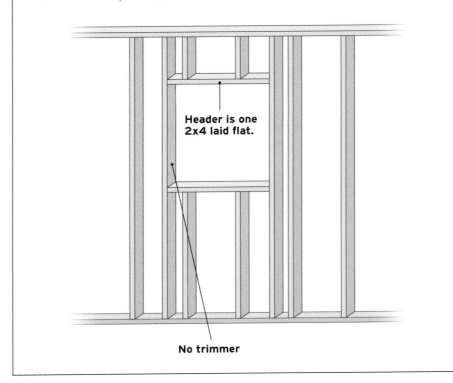

A LIGHTER APPROACH TO FRAMING A WINDOW

The drawings on p. 90 show a rather hefty approach, with a strong laminated header and sides made of king studs and trimmers fastened together. However, if a window is narrow, or if the wall is not load bearing, you may opt for the lighter approach shown here. The header is simply a flat-laid 2x4, and the sides are framed with only king studs and no trimmers. Some carpenters build this way even if the window is wide, because it saves on materials costs. Be sure to check with local codes before choosing this approach.

Header is one 2x4 laid flat.

No trimmer

6a Install the horizontals . . .

6b . . . and the cripples.

POSITIONING THE ROUGH FRAME

Each piece of the rough frame that you are building around the window should be 1/8 in. to 1/4 in. wider than needed. When you later install the window's jamb and stool (after the drywall is installed), you will use shims to ensure that the trim pieces perfectly align with the window. In the example shown here, the jamb will be 3/4 in. thick, the same as the window frame.

➤ See "Trimming a Window on the Inside," p. 226.

Framing a door

A door is framed in much the same way as a window, but the door itself is not in place, so you have to rely on measurements. If possible, have the door on site so you can measure its jamb to be sure of the opening dimensions. Make the opening about 1/2 in. wider and taller than the jamb; you will use shims to install the door jamb later. To build a header, cut two 2x4s to the rough opening dimension, and also cut a strip of 1/2-in. plywood to 3 1/2 in. wide and the same length. Fasten the pieces together. (The plywood is added to make the header 3 1/2 in. thick, the same as the width of the 2x4s.) In the example shown below (bottom), extra strength was needed, so the header was reinforced with flat-laid 2x4s on the top and bottom of the header.

If you are framing around a 6-ft.-wide sliding door or another type of wide door, make the header out of 2x6 or 2x8, for the strength needed for the span.

➤ See "Installing an Interior Prehung Door," p. 220.

Build a header with two 2x4s and a strip of 1/2-in. plywood.

This header is reinforced with two flat-laid 2x4s for extra strength.

LOWERING A CEILING

It's common for a basement to have pipes, ducts, and other obstructions in the ceiling, and attractively boxing them in can be a major challenge. (You may want to go "minimalist" and leave them on display, if that suits your aesthetic; see pp. 60-61.) The easiest way to lower a ceiling is with a hung ceiling, but most people are dissatisfied with this arrangement after a few years. Here, we'll show some methods for lowering framing so you can install drywall, which has a more substantial look and also makes a finished basement look like a contemporary living space.

If you need to lower a ceiling by mere inches or less, you could simply nail 2x2s or other boards to the bottom of the joists. However, if you also want to straighten the ceiling, use string lines, a laser level or some string levels, and "sister" boards. A laser level, which you can buy or rent, emits a ray of light that is perfectly level.

Attach it at the desired height of the ceiling and turn it on. Now you can stretch mason's lines (don't use regular string, which can sag) across the ceiling; make sure the light shines on the lines at every point.

With the lines strung and level, attach sister boards, which are simply 2x4s or 2x6s, to the sides of joists. Their bottoms should be just a hair above the lines, so you don't move the lines out of position. Instead of a laser level you could use an inexpensive line level for each of the lines, but that is more time-consuming and not quite as accurate.

You can also use a laser level in more complicated situations. Because its light shines over a wide area, you can use it as a guide for installing a top plate in a plumbing wall or other difficult spot.

A laser level **makes it easy to keep track of a ceiling's level over even a large area.**

Here, the laser level **shines on string lines and bottoms of sister boards to keep the new ceiling perfectly level.**

A line level **lets you know when an individual mason's line is level.**

The laser line **can be seen on the wall, the side stud, and pipes.**

IMPROVISATIONAL CEILING FRAMING

Even the best-laid plans will require some on-the-job improv, as shown in these two examples.

Ducts are usually difficult or expensive to move upward, and often they are at close to the minimum comfortable height, so you may end up framing just barely below the bottom of ducts. In the situation below, the metal framing is placed as close to the ducts as possible; still, the ceiling drywall will have to span about 18 in. between metal joists—OK but not ideal. It may be a good idea to apply construction adhesive to the underside of the duct when installing the drywall, for a bit of extra strength.

At this steel beam (right), first a series of blocks is cut to fit snugly, construction adhesive is applied to their backs, and then they are tapped into place. Next, a 2x4 is attached horizontally to the blocks. Drywall will be attached to the 2x4 on the side and glued to the underside of the steel beam.

Moving Pipes Up In some cases, you may be able to move a pipe or two up and out of the way so it's hidden in the ceiling, but that is usually difficult to do. You'll need to shut off the water or gas, cut and/or disassemble the pipe, and reconfigure with elbows that move the pipe up and over. If the pipe will travel through joists, you'll need to cut holes for them to travel through.

If you go this route, consider upgrading your pipes.

➤ See "Rough Plumbing" on pp. 106-135 for information on working with various types of pipe.

BUILDING AN INTERIOR WALL

Start by marking the outline of the interior walls on the floor using a chalkline. Cut treated boards or metal channels to fit and lay several of them in place. Position them on the floor and check for square and correct alignment ❶. You could attach these plates with powder-actuated nails, but interior walls are more likely to be bumped, so masonry screws are a more secure choice. Every 16 in. or so (closer for a short wall), drill pilot holes with a masonry bit of the correct thickness

of the masonry screws you will drive ❷. Turn the boards over and run a bead of construction adhesive on their bottoms ❸. Reposition the boards and drive 2½-in. masonry screws to fasten a 2-by board, and 1½-in. screws to fasten a metal track. Where two wood plates abut, drill steeply angled pilot holes and drive wood screws to attach the pieces together ❹.

If the concrete floor has imperfections or changes in height, you can either chip away

the concrete or improvise with framing ❺. Where possible, attach the stud to a side wall with masonry screws or to an already-framed outside wall ❻. Then proceed as you would for piecing in framing: Attach the top plate, cut studs to fit, and toenail the studs into position ❼.

➡ See "Piecing in Wood Framing," pp. 86-87.

1 Carefully lay out bottom plates for interior walls.

2 Drill pilot holes with a masonry bit.

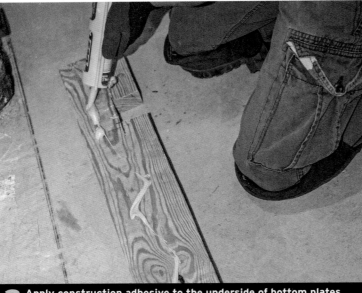

3 Apply construction adhesive to the underside of bottom plates. Reposition the board and drive masonry screws through the pilot holes from step 2.

4 Drill pilot holes and drive screws at a steep angle to attach two boards together.

5 Basement framing often calls for improvisation. Here, a change in the concrete floor's elevation is accommodated by simply attaching a short board.

6 Where possible attach studs to a concrete wall or to framing. Be sure to use a stud finder if the wall is already framed.

7 Attach studs with toenails or angle-driven screws.

Blocking and Fireblocks

Plan ahead for where you will install heavy items or bars and racks. The top photo below shows framing for a television: Wide wood pieces are secured to the metal studs, and short lengths of metal framing are anchored to the wall, then to the studs, for added stiffness. The bottom photo shows two types of blocking: the 2x4s on edge (with the wide part facing inward) are positioned where towel racks will be installed. The flat-laid 2x4s are "fire blocking," which is required in some areas and is always a good idea because it stiffens the framing.

FRAMING A PLUMBING WALL

A plumbing wall encases large pipes, and so must be built with 2x6s or even 2x8s. Because the framing must be cut out substantially to accommodate pipes, work carefully to make the wall as strong as possible. Make your plate cutouts to fit snugly around pipes ❶. Attach the top plate to ceiling framing wherever possible and drive plenty of masonry screws for the floor plate. You may need to put studs at odd spacings. Mark the bottom plate for the stud locations and set a laser plumb tool on the layout line pointed up ❷. Where the level's dot hits the top plate, draw a layout line ❸. (Be sure to put the X on the same side as on the bottom plate.) Cut studs and attach with toenails ❹.

1a Cut top and bottom plates precisely and attach for maximum strength . . .

1b . . . notching studs so they fit snugly—but not tightly— around pipes.

2 Position a laser plumb tool pointing up from a layout line.

3 Draw a layout line on the top plate that runs through the laser dot.

4 Attach studs with at least three nails driven into each joint.

Provide access where needed

Wherever there is a cleanout, shutoff valve, or other plumbing part that may need to be accessed for servicing, be sure to install a removable panel. The same goes for any electrical box; it should not be permanently covered over.

Always frame out for an access panel for the plumbing behind a shower.

An opening is framed for an access panel to get at a shutoff valve.

AVOID PIPES IN THE FLOOR

If there are pipes or tubing in the floor, and you have taken photos of them as recommended on p. 57, be sure to refer to them to avoid disaster. Let the photos serve as a guide when you drive masonry screws or powder-actuated nails, so you don't poke into the pipes.

➡ **See "Plan Ahead to Avoid Puncturing Pipes," p. 57.**

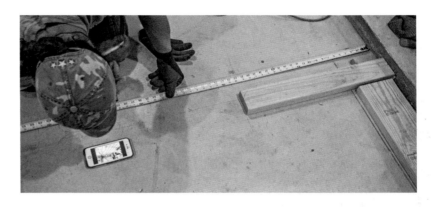

Framing a shower stall

If you will use a formed concrete or plastic shower base, you must frame the shower to the size of the base, following the manufacturer's specifications. (Here we will make a custom tiled base, so the exact size of the opening is not important.) For comfort, most people appreciate a shower that is at least 36 in. square. The sides are framed with blocking pieces to a height of 16 in. or so. At the front, two 2x4s are stacked and attached to the floor to form the step into the shower.

➡ **See "Making a Custom Shower Pan," pp. 132–135.**

A well-framed shower stall includes blocking pieces at the bottom so the wall will stay firm even if kicked.

FRAMING AND FINISHING A CURVED WALL

A curved wall section adds surprising elegance in a basement, and can actually make better use of space so that traffic flows more easily than it would with a squared-off wall. It's a high-end feature, but will likely take less than an extra day to install. Here, we'll jump ahead to drywalling to give an overall impression of the job.

A feature like this can be made with wood framing, but is easier with metal. To make each curved plate, cut one flange off the entire length of a piece that is a foot or so longer than needed. Then make a series of cuts, spaced several inches apart, to allow you to bend the channel. Fasten to the floor with short masonry screws ❶. Use the same technique to make the top channel. Cut a piece of 3/4-in. plywood or OSB to match the curve on the floor, and attach it at the top of the wall. Use a level or a laser plumb tool to position it. Attach the curved metal plate to the underside of the plywood. Install metal studs spaced 6 in. apart to the top and bottom plates ❷.

When it comes time to install the drywall, use two layers of 1/4-in. drywall, which is somewhat flexible. To make it more bendable, soak the backside of each sheet ❸ and wait 15 minutes or so for the water to soak in. Now the drywall can be bent into place and attached to the studs with drywall screws ❹.

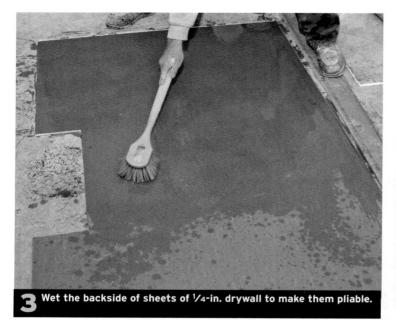

1 Cut off one flange and make a series of cuts to create bendable plates.

2 Attach the top plate to plywood framing, and add closely spaced studs.

3 Wet the backside of sheets of 1/4-in. drywall to make them pliable.

4 Work with helpers to bend and attach two layers of drywall.

FRAMING AROUND OBSTRUCTIONS

If you have ductwork, pipes, or other obstacles that need to be covered but are too difficult or expensive to move, box them in with framing that will get covered with drywall. (Often, a horizontal frame box is called a soffit while a vertical box is called a chase, but the terms are not used consistently.) Building soffits and chases may look complicated, but it is usually pretty straightforward. Envisioning the finished structure can be difficult, but you usually do not need to plan carefully; you can change and add pieces as you build.

Before you build, see if you need to provide access to any part of the stuff being covered. In our example, there is a cleanout plug, which must be reachable in case you need to rod the drains in the future. Some ductwork also needs to be accessed. Build so you can install a removable panel where needed.

Plan so you will provide a nailing surface for the drywall in the corners. If you end up with a place where a drywall end will not be attachable, you can usually install cleats with little trouble.

Measure the length, depth, and height of the obstructions ❶. When you build, give yourself an inch or two of extra room to make sure you don't run into trouble and have to start over again. Measure each pipe or duct at several places, because they may slope or angle; build to accommodate the largest dimension. Attach pieces of blocking wherever needed to support a framing piece. In our example, blocking is added to each vertical piece where a horizontal piece will be attached (see steps 4 and 7) ❷. On the floor, attach nailers that outline the

>> >> >>

1a Measure the obstacles in several places . . .

1b . . . and build to frame around the largest dimension

2a Attach blocking pieces where needed to support chase framing.

2b Also add blocking as needed around a soffit.

FRAMING AROUND OBSTRUCTIONS (CONTINUED)

chase, so the pipe is comfortably encased ❸. The nailers tell you the width and depth of the chase. Build a ladderlike soffit frame. In our case, it has a top "leg" that extends by the same length as the chase frame (see step 3) ❹. Attach the soffit frame so it is plumb with the floor blocking.

Measure and build another ladderlike frame to fit the chase ❺. Tap the chase frame in place and fasten with nails or screws ❻. Attach the chase frame to the blocking from step 2, as well as at

the top and bottom. Then build another chase frame to fit going the other direction, and attach it ❼. Use a level to mark the position of a horizontal nailer ❽. Cut a nailer so it is as long as the soffit frame and attach it to the studs.

Stand back and look to see if you will need any more pieces when it comes time to install drywall. At a place where you need to provide access, build a simple frame ❾.

>> >> >>

3 Install blocking on the floor to outline the chase.

4 Build a soffit frame.

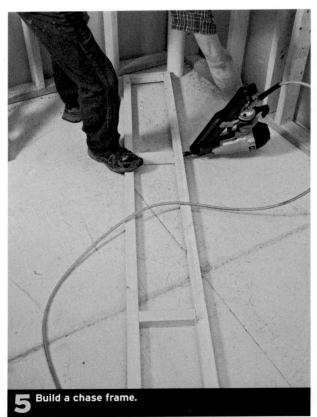

5 Build a chase frame.

6 Tap in and attach one of the chase frames.

7 Attach the first chase frame, then build and attach another chase frame.

8 Mark for the position of a horizontal nailer.

9 Finish the frame around the obstruction, providing access where needed.

Getting Straight Lumber

Most smaller soffits and chases are built with 2x2s. However, many 2x2s sold at lumberyards and home centers are significantly warped, which makes building difficult. That's why many carpenters buy 2x4s and rip them in half, yielding boards just slightly wider than standard 2x2s. Another option: Use 2x3s, which cost less than 2x4s and are usually pretty straight.

CONSIDER SCREWS INSTEAD OF NAILS

The steps on these pages show attaching boards with a power nailer, which is quick and easy. However, if you are not completely certain about your framing plan, it may be safer to build with screws, which take a little longer to drive but can be removed easily if you need to disassemble and rebuild. Remember, though, to drill pilot holes before driving screws near the ends of boards, to avoid cracking the boards.

FRAMING AROUND OBSTRUCTIONS (CONTINUED)

MORE FRAMING EXAMPLES

Here are some ways to deal with framing situations you may encounter. Often, improvisation is called for when working to cover up various types of obstacles. In addition to 2x4s, you will find that 2x2s come in mighty handy for these situations; occasionally you may need to use 1x4s or 1x2s as well. Be sure to have straight pieces on hand, and keep them neatly stacked until use, so they don't start to twist and bend. If you do have distorted lumber, you should probably throw it out and buy straight stuff—it's a small price to pay for getting straight lines and having material you don't need to struggle with.

Carefully cutting around pipes preserves precious inches of ceiling and room space. Install protective nail plates to keep from accidentally driving drywall screws into pipes.

Here, two ducts at different heights are meticulously framed around. Frame so that ceiling drywall does not have to span more than 18 in., or it will sag in time.

An old post could be left in place and celebrated for its rustic charm, or you can frame and drywall around it for a much sleeker look. A narrow column like this will show any imperfections, so make sure all the pieces are plumb and parallel with each other within 1/4 in.

Around a shutoff valve or a cleanout, provide ample room for future maintenance. Here, just 8 in. or so is plenty of width for reaching in to turn off a shutoff valve, but a wider area is needed if you have to open a cleanout with a wrench.

On the outside you may need to frame around a window. Often, however, only the bottom piece needs to be replaced. Use pressure-treated lumber, and apply a generous bead of caulk where the wood meets a masonry surface.

Where ductwork leads into the room and a grill will be installed, firmly attach the duct with straps and extend it 1/2 in. from the framing, so it will be flush with the drywall surface.

This basement has a bump-out where the stone foundation extends inward. A short wall extends to just below the windows. Good use will be made of this situation: A long, wide wood shelf will be installed at window stool (or sill) height.

In some situations—especially around a window— you may need to attach framing directly to masonry. Carefully check that these boards will be on a plane with the other framing, so the resulting walls will be straight. Attach by drilling pilot holes and driving masonry screws.

ROUGH PLUMBING

WITH THE FRAMING IN PLACE, it's time to run plumbing and electrical lines. This chapter covers only the basics. For a deeper understanding of plumbing systems, and for instructions on more challenging installations, consult such books as Taunton's *Plumbing Complete*. Always work according to local codes, and get permits from your building department for new installations. In general, replacing existing fixtures like toilets and light fixtures does not require a permit. But if you need to run new supply or drainpipes or new electrical cable, then you should pull permits.

Much of this work is straightforward. Difficulties arise when installing new drainpipes, which must be vented and sloped properly. Don't rush into this work. Spend time understanding your systems, so your installations will be safe.

UNDERSTANDING DWV PIPES

The term *DWV* commonly refers to drain, waste, and vent lines. Drain and waste pipes (we need not worry here about the difference between the two) are easy to understand: They carry liquid and solid waste out of the house. Vent pipes are not as well known but are just as important. They provide air behind the flow of waste, so the waste can flow smoothly, without gurgling. Vent pipes also keep noxious gases from entering the home.

Stacks

Somewhere in the basement you will see at least one large-diameter (usually 4-in.) vertical drainpipe called the "main stack" or "soil stack." Typically, drainpipes from two or more bathrooms in floors above—and other plumbing fixtures as well—feed into the main stack. The main stack runs down to a horizontal building drainpipe that usually runs under the concrete floor.

Most homes have more than one stack. Often there is a secondary stack, perhaps 2 in. or 3 in. in diameter, usually serving the kitchen. Secondary stacks also run into the building drainpipe under the basement floor.

Drainpipes and vent pipes

A number of "branch" drainpipes run from fixtures, either vertically or horizontally at a downward slope, into a stack. These pipes are often 1½ in. or 2 in. in diameter. (Nowadays plumbers typically use 2-in. pipes.) A horizontal drainpipe must slope at a rate of at least ¼ in. per running foot.

Vent pipes are needed to ensure that there will always be air behind the flowing waste. If there is no air, the waste will not flow smoothly and may get stuck in the pipes. Also, without proper venting, waste can siphon up into sinks and toilets. And vent pipes ensure against the entry of poisonous gases into your house.

Vent pipes must lead all the way up and out the house's roof. In some cases, a single vent pipe runs from a fixture up through the roof, but more often vents from several fixtures tie into a main vent that runs out the roof.

DRAIN-WASTE-VENT SYSTEM

This overview shows common plumbing installations in a house. Here there are no vent pipes in the basement; in some newer homes, a vent pipe is provided.

If you are lucky, there may be an existing vent pipe nearby in the basement. Often the solution is to run a vent pipe up to the first floor and tie into an existing pipe there.

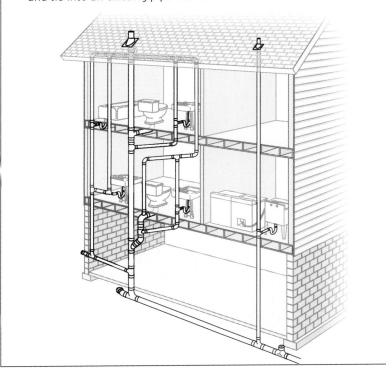

DRAINPIPE SLOPE

A horizontal drainpipe must slope downward at least ¼ in. per running foot. An easy way to test for this is to tape a ½-in.-thick block to one end of a 2-ft. level; when the bubble reads level, the slope is correct. A stronger slope is fine—even preferable—but a flatter slope at any point along the pipe's path will lead to drainage problems.

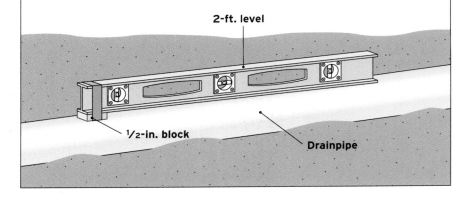

2-ft. level

½-in. block

Drainpipe

THE IMPORTANCE OF VENTING

Unless local codes allow for the use of air admittance values (AAVs) (see p. 110), the first question you must ask when planning new plumbing service is: How will it be vented? Remember that a vent must run all the way up through the roof; starting in a basement, that can be difficult. "Wet venting," using a main stack as a vent pipe even though it also acts as a drainpipe, is often not allowed.

Arcane and complicated rules apply to plumbing vents, and you should consult with a plumber or your building department before running any vent lines. Perhaps the most important code is this: A horizontal revent pipe, which ties into a nearby vertical vent pipe, can, in most cases, be no longer than 5 ft. Therefore, any new services need to be pretty close to the existing vent pipe.

If you are lucky, there may be a vent pipe already installed in your basement. (That is often the case in newer homes.) If not, you may need to run a vent pipe up to the first floor and tie into an existing pipe there. Worst-case scenario: You have to run a new vent pipe all the way up through the ceiling.

CLEANOUTS

Drainpipes do get clogged from time to time, so codes require that there be cleanouts—places where you can unscrew a plug and insert a plumber's rod—at certain points. If you remove a cleanout, be sure to install another one nearby. And if you install new pipes, be sure to include new cleanouts. Cleanout plugs must be accessible, which sometimes means installing a removable panel in a wall.

RUNNING A VENT PIPE UP

Running a vent pipe up through the basement ceiling and tying into a vent on the first floor is not complicated plumbing, but it can be a real pain to get at the pipes; often you must cut walls open, plumb, and then replace, patch, sand, and paint the drywall or plaster. If possible, position your new service so its vent pipe will be directly below the vent pipe above.

Open up the wall on the first floor to expose the vent pipe. Use a level or laser level to locate the spot on the first-floor bottom framing plate that is directly above your basement vent pipe. Drill a locator hole up through the plate (a long drill bit helps), then drill a large hole down from the first floor. Make a connection in the basement ❶ and tie into the first-floor vent pipe with a horizontal revent pipe ❷. In extreme cases you may need to run a vent pipe all the way up and out the roof ❸. In that case, you should probably hire a roofer to patch the hole, install rubber flashing around the vent pipe, and install roofing as needed.

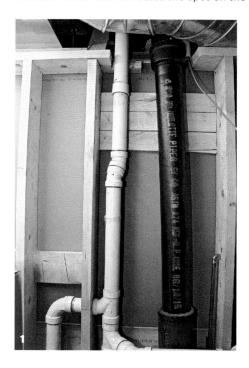

AAVS TO THE RESCUE, MAYBE

All this venting trouble may be avoided if your local codes allow for the use of AAVs. Sometimes called mechanical vents, these handy little devices have internal flaps that open when the pipe is draining and close when the draining is finished. Though they are looked down upon by many plumbers and are not installed in new homes (which are vented entirely with pipes), they do have a proven track record.

In most cases, each AAV serves only one fixture and is installed near it. Because AAVs can fail, they should be accessible so you can change them if need be. Check with local plumbers and your building department to see if you can use AAVs, and, if so, exactly where they should be installed.

Buy AAVs that fit **your pipe size, or attach with reducer fittings.**

AAV PLACEMENT

Air admittance valves may be placed on the trap arm inside the room or on the drainpipe. If they are installed on the drainpipe, there should be an access panel so you can change the AAV if needed.

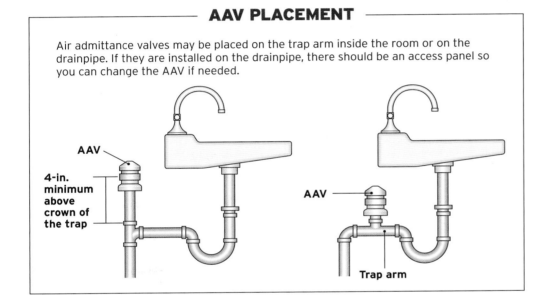

AAV

4-in. minimum above crown of the trap

AAV

Trap arm

PIPE MATERIALS

Newer homes use only PVC (white plastic) pipes and fittings, often referred to as "schedule 40 pipe." It is not only inexpensive but also strong and nearly eternal. In an older home you may find black plastic pipe, acrylonitrile butadiene styrene, called ABS; if so, consult with your building department about tying into it with PVC. You may find galvanized pipe for smaller stacks and drains, and cast-iron pipe for larger stacks and drains. Transition fittings are available for changing from older pipe materials to PVC. As can be seen in many of the photos in this chapter, cast-iron pipe, though strong and solid, can often corrode in time.

When transitioning **from galvanized to PVC drainpipe, you could use flexible fittings like the one shown in photo 4b on p. 115. Here, threaded transition fittings are used.**

DWV PLANS

O f course, there are many possible approaches to planning a plumbing layout, depending on where you want the new fixtures, where your existing pipes are, and the range of your venting possibilities. The drawings here show two approaches to help you plan.

DWV OPTIONS

DWV SETUP #1

In this plan, a single vent pipe serves the toilet, sink, and shower drain. A 3-in. horizontal drainpipe runs through the middle from the toilet, and the sink and shower drains tie into it. The shower has an under-floor P trap; the sink has a P trap inside the room; and the toilet needs no trap.

Drainpipes

Vent pipes

DWV SETUP #2

Here, vent pipes travel up through the wall and over through basement ceiling joists. The drainpipes for the shower, sink, and toilet all tie in and enter the main drain at the same point.

4-in. main stack and drain

Drainpipes

Vent pipes

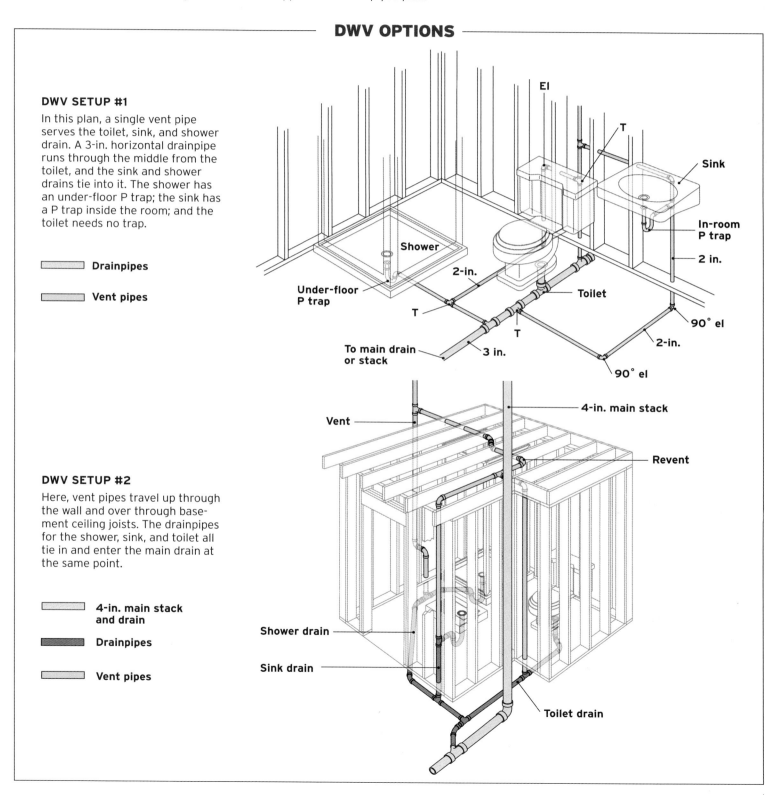

WORKING WITH DWV PIPE

PVC pipe is easy to cut and attach, but don't take the task lightly. In most cases, the pipe must be cut to the exact correct length; all the pieces must be carefully configured so they face in just the right way; and each joint must be properly primed and glued, or it will leak.

In some cases, it is easier to work on a table when cutting the pipe, but often you will need to assemble pipes in place. (For clarity, the following photos show cutting and assembling on a table.) When you measure pipes for cutting, be sure to include the distance the pipe will travel inside the fitting—usually about 3/4 in. Experienced plumbers often simply cut with a handsaw

or a reciprocating saw, but a do-it-yourselfer should use a hand miter saw, as shown, or a power miter saw, to ensure a straight cut. (If the cut is not at a reliable 90° angle, the joint will not be as strong as it should be.)

Mark for cutting with a felt-tipped pen and then make the cut ❶. After cutting, scrape off all the burrs with the side of a knife blade or a screwdriver ❷; crumbs will flow through the pipe and can clog things up. Attach five or six pipes and fittings together in a dry run, test that they are facing in the right direction, and draw reference lines to be sure you will attach them in just the right way ❸. (Once the parts are glued, it is not possible to disassemble them or adjust their positions.)

Wipe the ends of pipes and the insides of fittings with a rag; there should be no debris. Apply PVC primer, which is usually purple, to the pipe ends and the insides of fittings ❹. (Do not skip this essential step.) The primer will dry in a few seconds. For the next two steps you need to work pretty quickly, with no interruptions: Apply a fairly thick coat of PVC glue to the inside of the fitting, and then to the outside of the pipe end ❺. Push the pipe into the fitting; some glue, but not a lot, should squeeze out. Twist the pipe a bit, perhaps to align layout lines, and hold the fitting and pipe firmly together for a count of ten ❻. Do the same for all other joints.

1 Make a straight, clean cut in the PVC pipe.

2 Scrape away any burrs and crumbs.

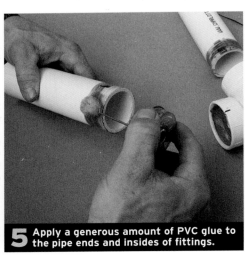
3 Assemble pipes and fittings in a dry run, and draw layout lines where needed.

4 Apply PVC primer to the pipe ends and insides of fittings.

5 Apply a generous amount of PVC glue to the pipe ends and insides of fittings.

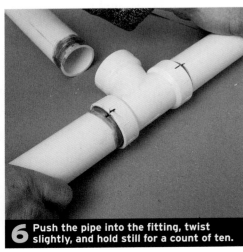
6 Push the pipe into the fitting, twist slightly, and hold still for a count of ten.

RUNNING DRAINPIPES UNDER THE FLOOR

Cutting away a concrete floor in order to run drainpipes through it no doubt sounds like extreme labor. And it is indeed messy work that calls for some elbow grease. But it may not be as difficult as you imagine. Basement floors are usually only about 3 in. or 4 in. thick, so cutting a trench does not call for heavy equipment. Draw lines on the floor showing where the pipe will go, and cut out a space at least three times as wide as the pipes. First cut lines with a rented masonry cutoff saw, or, if you don't have a lot of cutting to do, use a circular saw equipped with a diamond blade. Then use a rented electric jackhammer to finish the cutting, and haul the broken concrete and underlying gravel and soil away with a shovel and wheelbarrow.

The new pipes will need to tie into the house's main drain. If the main drain is PVC, simply make the connection with a PVC fitting. If the main drain is cast iron or another material, use a flexible fitting. Before you make the final connection, make sure the main drain is free from obstructions.

Set up the pipes in a dry run, checking and rechecking to be sure the drainpipes will emerge from the floor in the correct locations. Also check that every pipe slopes downward at a rate of at least 1/4 in. per running foot. Work carefully to get the slopes right. You will likely need to dig away soil or support the pipes with chunks of concrete at various points. As you connect the pipes, take special care to keep the pipe ends and insides of fittings clean; dirt or debris can ruin a joint. Disassemble and apply primer to pipe ends and insides of fittings and glue together.

Recheck that the horizontal pipes slope downward at all points and that the verticals emerge at the correct positions. Shovel in some soil, then gravel, and tamp firm with a hand tamper or a 2x4 or 4x4. Pour concrete and finish the surface.

➡ **See "Patching and Repairing a Concrete Floor," p. 186.**

See "Patching and Repairing a Concrete Floor," p. 186.

TYING INTO A STACK

Sometimes you can run a drain directly into an existing stack. Here, the existing cast-iron stack had a cleanout at the floor. The area around the cleanout was cut away, and a PVC pipe with a cleanout was installed. With some transitional fittings, a sink, toilet, or shower can drain directly into the drainpipe.

Install a main drainpipe as well as branch pipes, check that they are all sloped downward, and make sure they emerge at the right points in the floor.

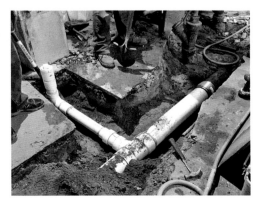

Cut channels in the concrete and connect new pipes to the existing drain line.

RUNNING DRAINPIPES THROUGH A WALL

Often you need to tap into existing plumbing and run drain and vent pipes through framing. Where the pipes will be large, a "plumbing wall" made of 2x6 studs is needed. For smaller pipes, 2x4 framing is just large enough.

Determine the height at which the new pipes will run. A standard height for a sink drain is 16 in. or 17 in. ❶. Hold a T fitting at the desired height and mark the existing pipe for cutting in two places ❷. Cut PVC or steel pipe with a reciprocating saw equipped with a metal-cutting blade ❸. If the existing pipe is somewhat loose, you can simply pull the pieces out and insert the ends into the T fitting ❹. If the pipe is firm, you may need to cut out a larger section; slip a flexible fitting onto the pipe and slide it up; add a short length of pipe to the top of the fitting; prime and glue the fitting to the lower pipe and the short section; and slide the flexible fitting down to complete the joint.

>> >> >>

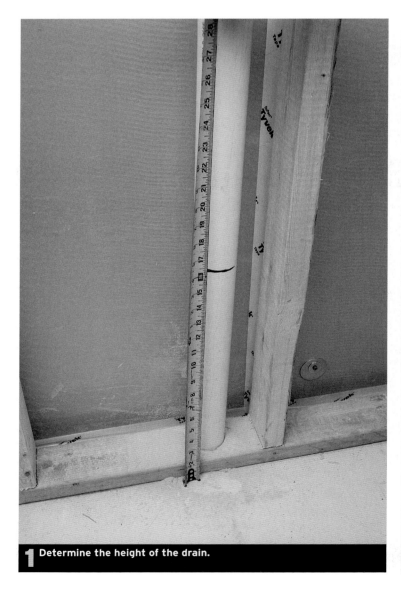

1 Determine the height of the drain.

2 Mark for cutting the existing pipe in two places.

3 Cut with a fine-toothed blade.

4a Move the pipes and slip in the fitting . . .

4b . . . or use a short pipe length and a flexible fitting.

5 Mark stud faces for plumb.

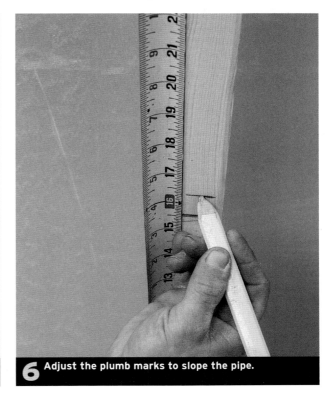

6 Adjust the plumb marks to slope the pipe.

RUNNING DRAINPIPES THROUGH A WALL (CONTINUED)

To run pipe horizontally through framing, hold a level positioned at the center of the fitting's opening and mark the front edges of studs for level **5**. Then mark lines that will lead to a slope of at least 1/4 in. per running foot. **6**. Use a sliding square to mark a square line, then to mark the center of the stud **7**. Drill holes with a right-angle drill. The holes should be slightly larger than the outside diameter of the pipe **8**.

To run pipes through more than two framing holes, you have two options: cut a notch rather than a hole in some of the studs, or use couplings and shorter pieces of pipe, as shown **9**. Double-check that the pipes slope downward **10**. Where a pipe stubs out for a drain trap, install a trap adapter **11**.

7 Mark the centers of the studs.

8 Drill holes through the studs.

9 Slip sections of pipe through the holes.

10 Recheck for slope.

11 Stub out and add fittings as needed.

UP-FLUSH SYSTEMS

If you don't want to cut into your basement floor, consider installing an up-flush system, also called a macerating unit. This has a pump that powerfully ejects waste—both liquid and solid—and sends it as far as 150 ft. to the nearest drainpipe. Various models may serve just a toilet, a toilet and a sink, or a toilet and a shower. The unit can be inside the room, just behind the toilet. Or, if you prefer, you can install it behind the wall, out of sight once the bathroom is finished. If you do that, be sure to install an access panel so you can service the unit in the future. You will need to purchase a special toilet made for use with the up-flush system. It is very similar in appearance to a standard toilet, though its inner passageways differ.

The steps that follow show installing an up-flush unit behind the wall for a toilet. For this type of installation, there must be 12 in. of space behind the wall framing. Additional fixtures can be connected to the unit, as long as they are on the same level as the toilet.

Set the up-flush unit on the floor either behind or in front of the wall framing. If you set it in front, leave room for installing drywall, or install drywall first. Install an elbow onto the unit, then run 3/4-in. PVC discharge pipe from the up-flush unit toward the nearest soil stack. At all points, the discharge pipe should be at least 12 in. above the floor ❶. When running the drainpipe, it's important that you never use 90° elbows or Ts; always use 45° fittings, so waste can flow more smoothly ❷. Run the discharge pipe into a Y fitting at the main stack ❸. Run a cold-water supply line, using copper or PEX pipe, to a place behind the toilet that is 10 in. to 12 in. above the floor and install a shutoff valve either now or after you add drywall ❹. Install a new 15-amp circuit in

>> >> >>

1 Position the unit and run the discharge pipe.

2 Use 45° elbows to run the pipe.

UP-FLUSH SYSTEMS (CONTINUED)

your service panel and run cable to a box near the unit. Install a GFCI receptacle, into which you will plug the up-flush unit ❺.

➤ **See "Working with Copper Pipe," pp. 120–122, and "Working with PEX," pp. 124–127.**

➤ **See "Running a New Circuit," p. 157.**

Run a vent pipe from the vent outlet on the unit to a nearby vent pipe ❻. If you want to connect other fixtures, like a sink or shower drain, the up-flush unit may have a port with a removable plug; remove plugs and run PVC pipe to the ports ❼. (Make sure any sink or shower you connect to the unit does not use water hotter than 104°F.) Hook up the toilet to the up-flush unit. If the unit is behind the wall, use an extender fitting. Be sure to leave 1 in. to 1½ in. of space between the tank and the wall framing to accommodate the tank lid and drywall ❽. Attach the toilet to the floor using plastic anchors, and plug into the receptacle.

The toilet is now hooked up ❾. When you drywall the room, be sure to install an access panel for servicing the unit later.

3 Install a Y fitting onto the house's stack, and run the discharge line into it.

4 Run a cold-water supply pipe to a shutoff valve near the unit. Be sure it's 10 in. to 12 in. off the floor.

5 Install a new 15-amp circuit and hook it to a GFCI receptacle.

6a Connect a vent pipe to the up-flush unit . . .

6b . . . and also to a house vent.

7 Connect other fixtures to the unit if desired.

OTHER UNITS

Companies, such as Saniflo, offer a variety of macerating units. This one can be installed remotely, has extra power for large discharge, and includes a control panel and an alarm console.

8 Connect the toilet to the unit, leaving space for the tank lid and drywall.

9 Screw the toilet to the floor and finish making connections.

SUPPLY PIPES

Supply pipes, which bring pressurized water to your fixtures, are generally installed after the DWV pipes have been installed. Planning and running supply pipes is far less complicated than running DWV pipes. Supply pipes can be sloped in any direction and can run hither and yon, the only caveat being they must be connected correctly so they don't leak.

Older homes often have gray-colored galvanized steel supply pipes. It's a very good idea to replace these with either copper or PEX pipe, because galvanized pipes corrode and clog, often leading to low water pressure and leaks after some decades. Some homes have white plastic PVC supply pipe, which has proved unreliable and may leak in time. Chlorinated polyvinyl chloride (CPVC) pipe, which is a cream-colored plastic, is more trustworthy. In the following pages, I'll show how to install the two most common supply pipes: copper and PEX.

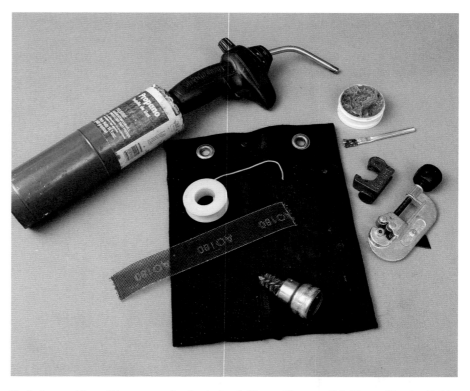

Tools for working with copper: standard-size tubing cutter; small tubing cutter for tight spaces; plumber's tape (sanding mesh); wire brush; flux and a flux brush; propane torch; protective heat shield.

WORKING WITH COPPER PIPE

Though PEX has surpassed it in popularity in some areas, copper is still a very common choice for supply pipe, and is required by codes in many locales. The process of soldering copper pipes to fittings may seem daunting at first glance. But with less than an hour of practice you will likely be able to "sweat" copper with ease. For the sake of clarity, I'll first show sweating on a tabletop, although much sweating is done with pipes assembled in place.

Though none of the steps for cutting and soldering copper are difficult, it is important that you do all of them. Skipping any step will result in faulty joints.

Measure for cutting pipes by holding them in place or using a tape measure. To cut, slip the pipe onto a tubing cutter and gently tighten the tool until the cutting wheel starts to bite into the copper ❶. Turn the tool all the way around the pipe until you stop feeling resistance. Then tighten the knob a bit and turn again until you stop meeting resistance. Repeat until the cut is complete ❷. Insert the reaming blade of the tool, or insert the head of a pair of pliers into the cut end and twist to remove burrs ❸.

Dry-assemble a number of fittings and pipes to be sure they all fit, then dismantle them in order and start sweating. First, use a small piece of sandpaper called "plumber's

WHAT CAN GO WRONG

Deburring the cut end of copper pipes should become a habit, because it's important. Any burrs left in the pipe will slightly impede water flow, and a good number of them will seriously slow the flow.

cloth" or a wire brush to burnish the outside ends of the pipes until they gleam brightly. Then do the same for the insides of the fittings ④. Then apply a generous amount of flux to the burnished pipe ends and fitting insides ⑤.

Reassemble the pipes. (In a normal installation, you might cut, burnish, flux, and assemble 12 or more pieces, but for clarity I'll show sweating just one joint.) Turn on a propane torch and adjust so the flame makes a pointed shape about 4 in. to 6 in. long. Apply its tip to the fitting—not the pipe—until you see the flux begin to bubble ⑥. Once the fitting is very hot, apply the tip of plumbing solder to a joint. It should melt and suck into the joint all around ⑦. If it does not melt and suck in, reheat the fitting and start again. If two or more attempts fail, disassemble the parts and start again with burnishing and fluxing. Once all the ends of a fitting have been soldered, brush them with flux to start smoothing things out, then wipe with a damp rag ⑧.   >> >> >>

1 Tighten the cutting wheel on the cut line.

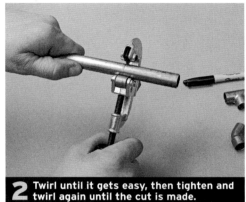

2 Twirl until it gets easy, then tighten and twirl again until the cut is made.

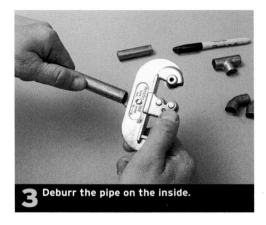

3 Deburr the pipe on the inside.

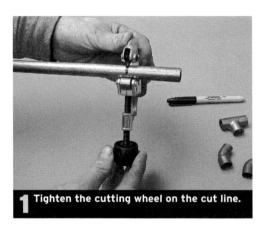

4 Burnish the outsides of the pipe ends and the insides of fittings.

5 Apply flux to the pipe ends and inside the fittings.

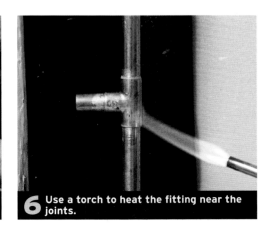

6 Use a torch to heat the fitting near the joints.

WORKING WITH COPPER PIPE (CONTINUED)

7 Apply solder so it sucks into the joint all around.

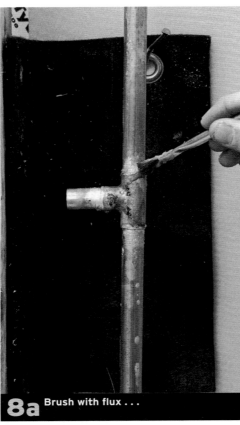

8a Brush with flux . . .

8b . . . then wipe with a damp rag.

RUNNING COPPER PIPE THROUGH WALLS

Although it's extra trouble to keep pipes in the center of studs, it is there where they are safe from the sharp tips of standard-length drywall screws or nails. You may choose to run pipes in simpler ways, but if so, be sure to use protective plates to protect them from drywall fasteners.

To tap into existing supply lines, be sure to shut off the water to those pipes and open faucets downstream to clear out all water. Mark for cutting them in two places so they can be inserted into a T fitting **1**. Make the cuts using a small tubing cutter if space is tight. Tighten, twirl the cutter all the way around, tighten, and repeat until the cut is made **2**. Dry-fit the Ts. If you need to go around a pipe and stay in the center of a stud, use a number of "street elbows," which have one female and one male end **3**. Measure to the centers of the pipes and mark nearby studs for cutting holes **4**. Use a right-angle drill to bore holes for the pipes to travel through **5**. Assemble all or most of an installation in a dry run **6**, then disassemble, burnish, apply flux, reassemble, and solder all the joints.

1 Mark for tapping in with T fittings.

2 Cut the pipes, using a small cutter if needed.

3 Use a number of fittings where needed.

4 Mark for boring holes.

5 Bore holes with a right-angle drill.

6 Assemble in a dry run, then disassemble and solder.

Protective Plates
A screw or nail can easily pierce copper pipe, causing a serious problem. If a pipe is run through the center of a 2x4, a $1^5/_8$-in. drywall screw driven through $^1/_2$-in. drywall will not be able to reach it, so no protective nailing plate is required. (And most drywall screws are only $1^1/_4$ in. long.) If the pipe is nearer to the edge of the framing, be sure to attach a metal protective plate.

STUBBING OUT

A strap like this holds copper pipes firmly in place where they emerge from the wall. Run pipes through the holes and screw the strap to studs. Apply flux and solder the pipes to the strap.

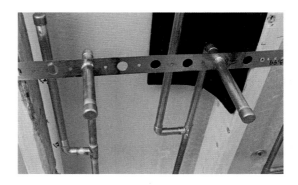

WORKING WITH PEX

Extruded or cross-linked polyethylene tubing, usually referred to as PEX pipe or tubing, is a common material for water supplies in many parts of the country. It is certainly the most economical solution: The material itself is far cheaper than copper, and it is much easier and quicker to install. Whereas sweating copper takes some practice and skill, connecting PEX is quite simple, as long as you make sure to fully tighten all the joints.

There are three different ways to join PEX. Pros may use a very expensive tool to make expansion joints. Another method uses crimp rings; this method is less expensive, but some people find it difficult to fully tighten joints. Here, I'll show the simplest and least expensive method: PEX clamps, which require some muscle but not as much as crimp rings. If you have only a few connections to make, consider using push-on (SharkBite®) fittings, which are expensive but very easy to attach. PEX fittings may be plastic or metal. Both types have proved themselves reliable.

➜ See "Push-on Fittings," p. 127.

Measure for PEX lengths, taking into account any bends you may need to make. Because the tubing is so flexible, you can add an inch or so. Mark for cutting with a felt-tipped pen ❶. PEX is easy to cut. Do not use a saw, which will leave burrs that need to be scraped away. A PEX or tubing cutter like the type shown makes quick work of cutting ❷. Be sure the cut is nice and square; an angled cut may produce a joint that leaks. PEX fittings, which may be Ts, elbows, or other types, slip inside

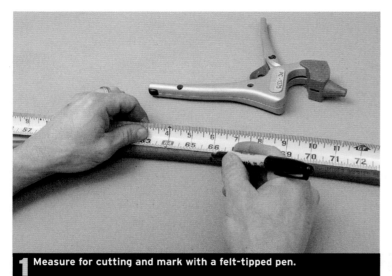

1 Measure for cutting and mark with a felt-tipped pen.

2 Make a clean, straight cut using a PEX or tubing cutter.

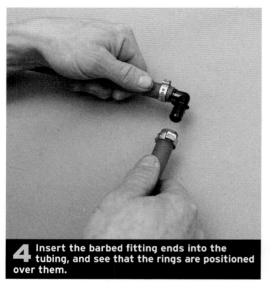

4 Insert the barbed fitting ends into the tubing, and see that the rings are positioned over them.

5 Place the clamp tool's end over the fitting wings and tighten all the way.

the tubing. To make a connection, first slip clamps onto each of the pipe ends ❸. Then slip the tubing onto the fitting at each end ❹. You may need to slide the clamps down a couple of inches, slide the pipes onto the fitting, and then slide the clamps back into position. Check to be sure that each clamp is positioned completely over the barbed end of the fitting, so it will fasten securely to the fitting. Slip the tip of the clamp tool onto the clamp's wings. Use two hands to start tightening, then finish by tightening the

handles all the way together ❺. Check that the clamps are completely over the barbed fitting ends ❻. If you cannot fully tighten the tool, or if the clamp is partway off the fitting's barb or at an angle, cut the tubing and start again.

>> >> >>

WHAT CAN GO WRONG

PEX is even easier to puncture with a screw or nail than copper. Protect tubing with metal plates, as shown on p. 123.

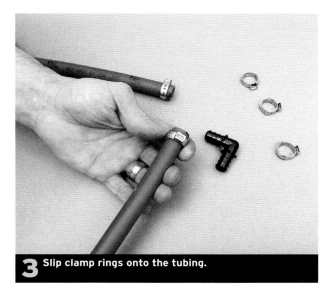

3 Slip clamp rings onto the tubing.

6 Check that the clamps are straight and secure over the fitting's barbs.

PEX TOOLS AND MATERIALS

PEX comes in red and blue colors, for hot and cold supplies. Cut with a tubing cutter made for PEX. Fittings such as elbows and Ts may be plastic or metal. Instead of the clamp tools and rings shown in the steps here, you may choose to use crimp rings and a crimping tool.

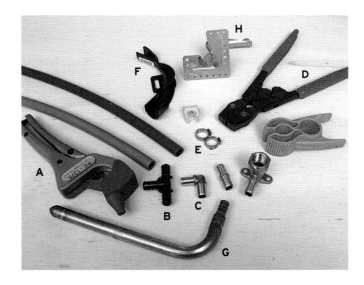

A	Pex cutters	**E**	Clamp rings
B	Plastic fitting	**F**	Right-angle bracket
C	Metal fittings	**G**	Stub-out
D	Clamp tool	**H**	Metal bracket

WORKING WITH PEX (CONTINUED)

Turning a corner and stubbing out

PEX is just flexible enough to turn a right angle by itself, but doing so requires a fairly wide sweep, and you may accidentally crimp the tubing. Instead, use right-angle brackets. These are plastic, with tabs for attaching to a brace. You can also buy metal brackets without tabs, for tighter spots. Attach wood framing braces between studs. Drive screws to attach the brackets, and snap the PEX into the brackets **1**. Cut the tubing to the same height **2**.

PEX is rigid enough that you could actually poke it out of the wall and connect a stop valve directly to it, but for a firmer installation use special copper stub-outs. Screw plastic clamps just above the cut ends of the tubing **3**. Attach stub-outs to the PEX ends, and snap them onto the clamps **4**.

1 Attach right-angle brackets and snap the PEX into them.

2 Cut the PEX ends.

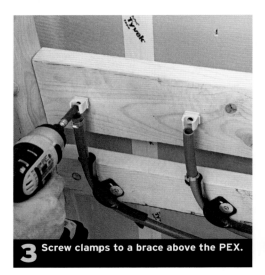

3 Screw clamps to a brace above the PEX.

4 Install copper stub-outs.

TRANSITION FITTINGS

When connecting two different types of pipe—most commonly copper, PEX, or galvanized steel—use a fitting made for the purpose. In this example, a straight coupling is soldered onto a copper pipe and will be joined to PEX pipe with a straight coupling. Transition fittings may also be elbows or Ts and can accommodate any type of supply pipe.

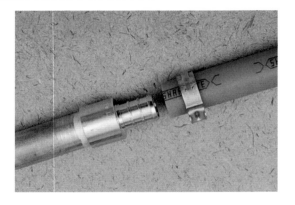

Push-on fittings

Often referred to by the brand name SharkBite, push-on fittings resolve many supply-pipe situations with amazing ease. Once you buy the correct fitting and make clean cuts in pipe ends, you simply push the pipes into the fitting—usually with no tool required—to achieve a reliably watertight connection. Fittings may be elbows, Ts, couplings, or other shapes. And they can connect to copper or PEX. The downside is the price—about $10 per fitting—but if you have only a few connections to make, or if you are in a tight or hard-to-reach spot, push-on fittings are well worth the cost. Here, we show installing a T fitting onto existing copper pipe, and connecting to PEX pipe.

Cut the copper pipe to receive the T, and use plumber's cloth or a wire brush to remove any raised edges or burrs from pipe ends ❶. Push copper pipe into two ends of the fitting and make sure they seat all the way into the fitting ❷. Pull hard on all the pipes to make sure the connection holds.

Push the PEX pipe into the remaining fitting ❸. You can also use this fitting for CPVC pipe, if your home happens to have that.

1 Cut pipe ends nice and straight, and then clean with plumber's cloth.

2 Push pipe ends into the fitting until they seat.

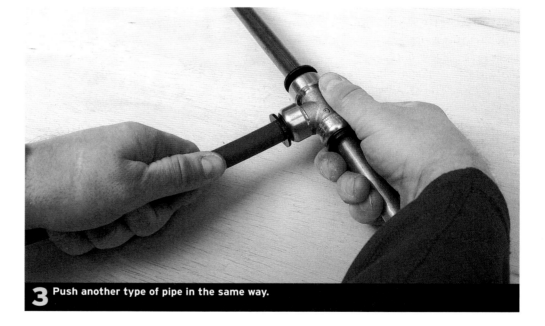

3 Push another type of pipe in the same way.

ROUGH PLUMBING CONFIGURATIONS

he following pages show some common rough plumbing arrangements for various types of rooms and fixtures. Of course, it's impossible to show every permutation; your room designs and fixture choices, as well as local codes, will probably require altered plumbing arrangements. But many of the principles shown in these configurations should apply, and some of the actual configurations should work.

➡ See "Working with Your Building Department," p. 63.

Shower-only plumbing

If you will install a custom shower pan, the drain for a shower-only unit can be anywhere that is vaguely near the center of the shower floor. However, if you will install a precast or plastic shower pan, the drain must be precisely positioned. Install a precast pan onto the drain before you run the supply pipes; you can make a custom shower pan after the supply pipes are run and the backerboard is installed.

➡ See "Making a Custom Shower Pan," pp. 132–135.

If you will be installing a shower stall (not a tub), position the faucet (the valve, where the control handle will go) about 48 in. above the floor. The fitting for the shower arm (where the showerhead will go) is usually positioned 72 in. to 80 in. above the floor; people of various heights may have definite preferences on this. Both the faucet

Remember the Finish Wall Materials When
determining the position of the drainpipe, factor in the thickness of the finish wall materials—usually ½-in. concrete backerboard plus ³/₈ in. or so for tiles or other finish materials.

Shower-only supply plumbing includes two supply pipes that fasten to Ts for vertical hammer arresters, and then into the sides of the faucet. A single vertical pipe rises from the faucet up to a drop-ear elbow, which has threads that will accept a showerhead's arm.

Position the temporary plastic cylinder so it protrudes the correct amount from the studs. Leave the cylinder in place and don't remove it until you have finished tiling or installing another finish surface.

and the head should be centered side to side in the interior of the shower.

You may need to reposition a stud in order to accommodate the three vertical supply pipes. Provide blocking pieces (braces) for securely fastening the faucet and the showerhead fitting. In the arrangement shown here, the supply pipes come from above; yours may come from below or from one side. Most shower faucets come with round removable plastic guides. Follow the manufacturer's instructions to position the guide at the correct depth in relation to the framing; in most cases, the face of the guide should be out from the studs by 1/2 in. (for the backerboard) plus the thickness of your tiles or other finish material.

Run all the pipes in a dry run. Install two vertical hammer arresters that are at least 12 in. tall, one for the hot water and one for the cold. Also run the center vertical pipe up to a drop-ear elbow, where you will screw in the shower arm. Double-check that things are where they should be, and sweat the copper or clamp the PEX. Attach clamps as needed to keep the faucet and the showerhead very firm.

Tub and shower

The drainpipe for a tub must be correctly placed, so the tub's waste-and-overflow pipe will go into it. Consult your tub's installation literature to see how far away from the wall the waste-and-overflow will be. Often

the rough drainpipe is not cemented and is placed in a fairly large hole in the floor, so you can reach in and adjust its position before final cementing. The drainpipe should have a P trap, as shown below center.

Supply piping for a tub with a showerhead and a tub spout is much the same as for a shower-only setup, as shown on the facing page. However, most people prefer a tub faucet to be lower–12 in. to 18 in. above the rim of the bathtub. (Most modern tubs are about 16 in. tall, but some spa or claw-foot tubs may be 22 in. or even taller. Measure yours to be sure.)

➡ See "Installing a Bathtub," pp. 244–246.

>> >> >>

Tub supply piping usually consists of four pipes hooked to a faucet (valve): horizontal hot and cold water supplies going in, and vertical pipes for the spout and the showerhead going out. Be sure to include hammer arresters for both the supplies.

A tub's drainpipe should be the correct distance from the wall, and centered on the tub. If possible, do not cement the trap at this time; wait until just before you install the tub.

ACCESS PANELS

Wherever there is a valve, cleanout, or anything else that you may need to access later, frame out an access panel.

ROUGH PLUMBING CONFIGURATIONS (CONTINUED)

Toilet

A toilet requires only a single cold-water supply pipe. Most toilets are "12-in." models, meaning the drain is positioned 12 in. away from the wall framing, or 11½ in. away from the finished wall. A 10-in. toilet, unsurprisingly, has its drain 10 in. away from the wall framing.

➤ **See "Installing a Toilet," pp. 239–241.**

Bathroom sink

A bathroom sink requires hot- and cold-water supply pipes, plus a drainpipe with a trap adapter in the wall. Supplies are usually 20 in. to 24 in. above the floor, and the drain is usually 18 in. to 20 in. above the floor; check your sink's installation literature to be sure. For a pedestal sink with a wide pedestal, you may choose to put the supplies close together, so they will be hidden. For a pedestal sink, attach a 2x6 or 2x8 brace so you can connect mounting bolts to it.

➤ **See "Installing a Pedestal Sink," p. 243, and "Installing a Vanity Sink," p. 242.**

Toilet supply plumbing is simply a matter of one cold-water line, positioned behind the toilet to one side (not directly behind the bowl) and just high enough to avoid interfering with base molding.

Plumbing for a bathroom sink: supplies and a wall drain. Attach hammer arresters as well. Be sure the drain is adequately vented; you may need to use an AAV.

If you will install a pedestal sink, add a brace, so you can drive the mounting screws into it for a strong attachment.

Laundry room

A laundry room can be set up in a number of ways. One is to have a utility sink into which the washing machine will drain, as shown at right. Only one drainpipe with trap adapter is needed. You'll need hot- and cold-water supplies for the tub, positioned below the tub at 20 in. to 24 in. above the floor. Also install hot- and cold-water supplies for the washing machine, positioned at least 6 in. above the machine's control panel. A more compact option is to have a standpipe for the washing machine's drain hose instead of a sink. A popular way of doing this is with a washing machine outlet box, as shown below right.

Kitchen

Rough plumbing for a kitchen is surprisingly simple, because a dishwasher uses the same drain and supply pipes as the sink. (You can also add a hot-water dispenser, icemaker for a fridge, or a filtered water faucet using the same supply pipes.)

This laundry setup **includes supplies for a washer and a utility sink, as well as a single drain in the wall. Add hammer arresters for all the supplies.**

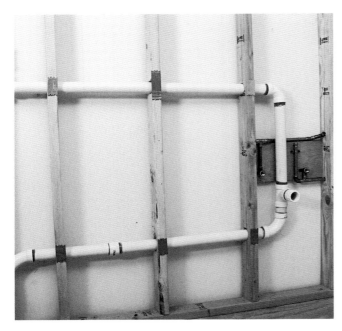

For a kitchen, **install a single drain (shown here with a revent pipe) and hot- and cold-water supplies.**

A washing machine **outlet box includes a shutoff unit with a single control for both hot and cold water, as well as an outlet for the washing machine drain hose. At left you see a gas pipe for a gas dryer.**

MAKING A CUSTOM SHOWER PAN

You can buy a ready-made formed shower pan of formed concrete, plastic, or another material, but you'll need to position the drainpipe precisely in order to install it. Here, I show making your own pan. This is not difficult using a plastic liner, but be sure to avoid nicking the liner with a knife or drill, or you'll end up with a persistent leak.

➡ See "Running Drainpipes under the Floor," p. 113.

Set a 1½-in. or 2-in. drainpipe in the floor, and pour a concrete slab around it. The slab should be good and level, or slightly sloped toward the drain. Install a drain flange. You may need to chip away the area around the drainpipe. Then use a cutoff (or oscillating) tool to cut the pipe flush with the concrete floor ❶. Clear away any burrs and apply primer to the pipe end and the flange. Then apply PVC cement and set the flange into the pipe, making sure it is level ❷. Lay the rubber liner in the opening and work to make it smooth on the bottom ❸. Carefully gather folds at the corners and attach them with screws driven several inches above the floor ❹. At the drain, make tiny slits so the screw heads can poke through, and carefully cut out the middle of the drain opening ❺. Take care not to make even a small miscut into the area around the inside of the drain. Remove the screws and use them to attach the drain's middle piece ❻ (p. 134).

>> >> >>

1 Chip away around the drainpipe and cut it flush with the floor.

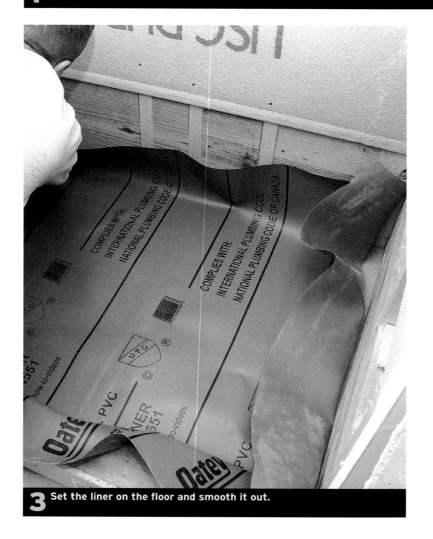

3 Set the liner on the floor and smooth it out.

2a Prime the drain flange, . . .

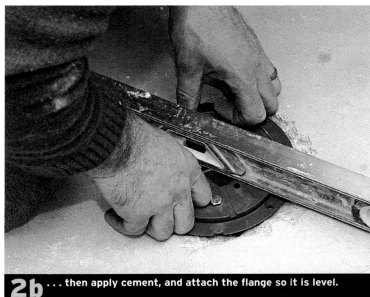

2b . . . then apply cement, and attach the flange so it is level.

4 Make folds at the corners and drive screws several inches above the floor to attach.

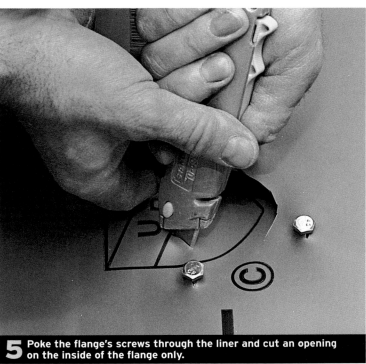

5 Poke the flange's screws through the liner and cut an opening on the inside of the flange only.

MAKING A CUSTOM SHOWER PAN (CONTINUED)

Attach pieces of backerboard that cover the liner on the sides. Do not drive screws lower than 3 in. or so above the floor. Also attach backerboard strips to the step ❼. Screw the drain cover in, so it is about 1½ in. above the liner. Mix batches of stiff concrete and pour into the area; spread with a wood or magnesium float. Periodically check with a level, to make sure the concrete is sloped toward the drain at a rate of at least ¼ in. per foot ❽. The concrete surface should be below the top of the flange cover by the thickness of the tiles you will install, plus ⅛ in. for the mortar. Finish the concrete with a magnesium float; aim for a very smooth surface and recheck for slope as you work ❾. Allow the concrete to cure and harden for at least a day. Lay out for tiling the floor; using a square flange minimizes cuts you will need to make ❿. Set the tiles in a bed of reinforced thinset mortar and allow to dry. Apply epoxy grout to finish the job.

➡ See "Laying Ceramic or Stone Tile," p. 197.

6 Attach the drain flange's middle piece by tightening the screws.

8 Mix, pour, and spread concrete, checking that it slopes toward the drain.

7a Attach backerboard pieces to the sides . . .

7b . . . and to the step.

9 Smooth the concrete, checking again for slope. It should be below the drain cover by the thickness of the tiles plus 1/8 in. for mortar.

10 Allow the concrete to set, and lay out for the tiles.

ROUGH WIRING

INSTALLING BOXES AND RUNNING ELEC-
trical cable or conduit for receptacles (outlets), switches, lights, small heating units,
and other fixtures generally happens after the
rough plumbing is finished, since cable is easy
to rout around pipes.

Once you have ensured that you are working
on only nonenergized wiring, then the installations are surprisingly easy to learn. Attaching
boxes, routing cable, and installing lights and
other fixtures often can be accomplished in
short order.

This chapter hits only the high points of
electrical work. For a greater understanding
of your electrical system, or to learn to
make more complicated installations, consult
Taunton's *Wiring Complete*. And if you are at all
unsure of how to install something correctly,
hire a professional electrician.

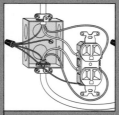

THE SERVICE PANEL

Understanding your electrical service begins with a look at the service panel. (You don't have to remove your service panel cover, but you will need to if you install new circuits for new service.) Unless you have an old house with outdated equipment, three thick wires enter your panel. One "neutral" wire connects to a strip of metal called a neutral or hot bus bar. The two "hot" wires connect to the two hot bus bars, which run down each side of the panel; individual breakers are connected to the bus bars.

Each breaker is connected to a hot wire that sends power to an individual or "branch" circuit. A breaker is a safety device that turns itself off when there is an overload, short, or other problem with the wiring. To restore power, some breakers turn back on with a single flip; others must be flipped one way, then the other.

Inside a service panel you will find a mass of wires. Hot wires, which are black, red, or another color, attach to breakers and carry power to electrical outlets throughout the home. Neutral wires, which are almost always white, carry power back from the outlets to the panel, where they hook to a neutral bus bar. Bare copper or green ground wires also lead back from the outlets to the panel, where they attach to the same bar as the neutrals or to a separate grounding bus bar.

If you have a fuse box instead of a panel with breakers, don't panic. It may work fine, as long as you don't have heavy electrical users. But if you will be adding service in your basement, you will need new electrical circuits. It's probably time to hire an electrician to install a new breaker panel with at least 100 amps—200 is even better.

When opening a service panel, be extra safety-conscious: Wear gym shoes or other rubber-soled footwear, and be sure to stay dry. And don't touch any bare wires in the panel.

Take extra precautions when opening a service panel. Most service panels are attached with four or six screws that are easily removed. You may need to lift the cover up, then out.

SAFETY ALERT

If you suspect any problem with the wires that run to your house, or to your electrical meter, do not touch anything; call your electrical utility to come out and assess the situation.

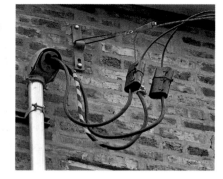

You'll find a lot of wires in a service panel—hot, neutral, and ground. Be sure you know what each wire is before working in a panel.

Volts, Amps, and Watts To put things as simply as possible, "volt" refers to the force with which power is pushed through wiring. Residential wires all carry between 115v and 125v, which is called 120v. Most devices and fixtures in a home use 120v, but some heavy users, such as air conditioners, electric stoves, or electric water heaters, use 240v. This amount of voltage is provided by two 120v wires.

Though voltage is the same throughout a house—120v per wire—the amount of power used varies quite a bit. This amount is measured in amperes, or amps. A light fixture—especially an LED—uses a tiny amount of amperage, while a window air conditioner or refrigerator can use a lot.

Most 120v circuits have breakers and wires that can handle either 15 amps or 20 amps. A 15-amp circuit uses #14 wire, while a 20-amp circuit uses thicker #12 wire. (These are also called 14-gauge and 12-gauge wires, or 14 awg and 12 awg.) It is important that a #14 wire not be attached to a 20-amp circuit, or it can overheat dangerously before the breaker shuts off.

Some very heavy 240v circuits use larger-amp breakers and correspondingly thicker wires. Thirty-amp circuits call for #10 wire, and 40-amp circuits require #8 wire.

Wattage (or "watts") is a measurement of the power used by fixtures or devices. It is calculated by measuring volts times amps. So for instance, a 15-amp/120-volt circuit has a cpacity of 1,800 watts. Codes require that it be loaded with no more than a "safe capacity" of 1,560 watts. And a 20-amp circuit should supply no more than 1,920 watts.

CIRCUIT WIRING

Older homes might have a fuse box instead of a panel. If this is the case and you are going to be upgrading your basement, it's a good idea to upgrade to a breaker panel.

Power passes from the hot bus bar to a breaker, and from there to a branch circuit via a hot wire. Each branch circuit supplies power to a number of outlets. Modern codes call for separate circuits (and separate breakers) for receptacles, for lights, for certain appliances, and so on. But in many homes, a single circuit may supply some receptacles, some lights, and maybe even an appliance as well.

In homes with well-organized circuitry, it is fairly easy to determine which users are controlled by which circuit: It may be a group of receptacles or lights, or it may be a certain room. However, don't be surprised if your circuits go all over the place and if a single circuit controls receptacles in one room, lights in another, and so on.

Contemporary electrical codes call for many more circuits than used to be required. For instance, in a kitchen you may need two circuits for countertop receptacles, as well as dedicated circuits for the refrigerator, the microwave, and an exhaust fan. And a bathroom's receptacle may need to be on its own circuit.

A duplex receptacle—the most common type, with two outlets—may be "split," so that the outlets are on separate circuits.

AVOIDING OVERLOADS

When adding new service in a basement, you may be able to extend an existing electrical circuit, but only if it has enough "room" for new users. If you add too much in the way of electrical users, you can overload the circuit, and the breaker will trip regularly. To determine if you can piggyback onto an existing circuit, add up the wattage or amps of the light bulbs, the plugged-in appliances, and the fixtures already being used, and add in the users that you plan to add. The result should be less than the "safe capacity" for the circuit.

For a 15-amp circuit, safe capacity is 12 amps or 1,440w. For a 20-amp circuit, safe capacity is 16 amps or 2,400w.

If usage will be over the safe capacity, then you need to install a new circuit. Check that your service panel has empty spaces where you can install new breakers; if not, you may need to hire an electrician to install a new panel.

➔ See "Running a New Circuit," p. 157.

Do You Need a New Service Panel?
Determining whether you need a new, larger service panel calls for some complicated calculations, which I cannot get into here. I can say this: If you have a 100-amp service panel, and the amperage of all your breakers adds up to more than 160 amps, you should consult with an electrician or your building department to see if you need a new 200-amp panel.

COMMON CODES

Electrical codes are constantly changing, usually in the direction of greater stringency. Here are some of the more common ones that you should be aware of. The following are based on the latest National Electrical Code® (NEC) regulations, but be sure to check with your local building department to be certain you comply with their regulations.

➔ See "Working with Your Building Department," p. 63.

- The service panel must have enough amperage. A 100-amp panel is usually sufficient for a medium-size home, but a 200-amp panel is preferred. Circuits should be labeled on the panel.
- Wire sizes must match the breakers: 14-gauge for a 15-amp breaker, and 12-gauge for a 20-amp breaker, for instance.
- Nonmetallic (NM) cable is allowed in most areas, but conduit or metal-clad cable is required in other locales. Where wiring is exposed rather than hidden in walls, it should run through conduit.
- Cable should be run in areas where drywall screws cannot reach it, or should be protected with metal nailing plates.
- There are specific rules for running NM cable. You may need to staple it within 8 in. or 12 in. of a box, depending on whether the box has a cable clamp.
- Electrical boxes must be within $1/8$ in. of flush with the surrounding drywall, tile, or other finished surface.
- Inside a box, there should be at least 6 in. of unsheathed wire. All splices must be made with wire nuts, not tape.
- Only one wire can be connected to a single terminal on a device or fixture.
- You may be required to wrap switches and receptacles with electrician's tape to protect wires and terminals.
- Install GFCI receptacles wherever the area may get damp.
- In most cases, there should be separate circuits for lights and receptacles.
- In a bathroom, there should be an exhaust fan. You may or may not be allowed to put a fan/light on the same circuit as a receptacle.
- Install at least one receptacle every 12 ft., and at least one receptacle on every wall that is at least 6 ft. long.

WIRING SUPPLIES AND TOOLS

In most areas, NM cable is allowed with either metal or plastic boxes. The supplies and tools shown here should handle most common wiring situations in a basement. If you live in an area where conduit is required, see pp. 151–153 for supplies and tools.

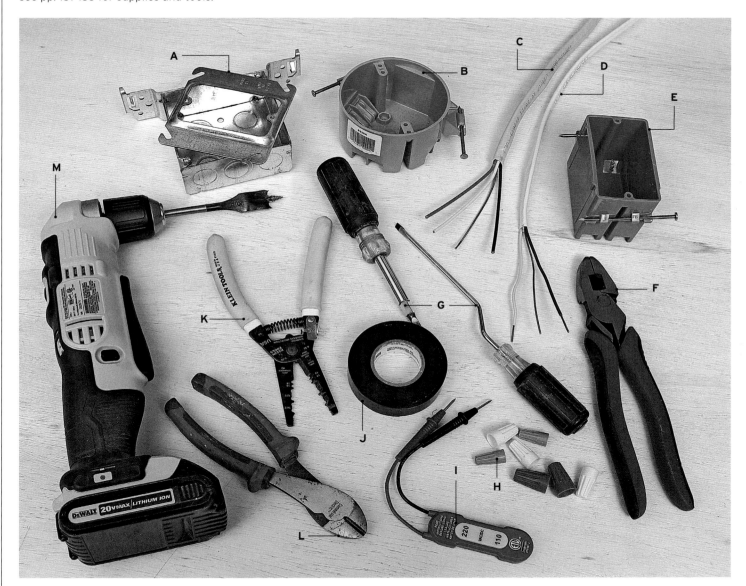

A Metal box with mud ring	**D** 14/2 cable	**H** Wire nuts	**K** Wire and cable strippers
B Plastic ceiling box	**E** Nail-on plastic box	**I** Voltage tester	**L** Diagonal cutters
C 12/3 cable	**F** Lineman's pliers	**J** Electrical tape	**M** Right-angle drill
	G Screwdrivers		

STRIPPING CABLE AND WIRES

Here I'll show stripping insulation, because it is often done at the rough wiring stage. Splicing and joining wires are operations that happen during the finish wiring stage, after drywall has been installed.

Like PVC pipe, NM cable (also called Romex) is easy to work with, but you still need to take care when stripping and joining. In particular, be sure not to nick the wire insulation when you strip the sheathing; bare wires could touch each other and cause a short.

This work is often done with a knife, but it pays to buy and use good tools, especially if you are a beginner. A number of good tools are on the market, but a pair of cable and wire strippers like the one shown on this page may be the best option. It will make quick and easy work of stripping without nicking wires. It has slots for stripping 12/2 and 14/2 cable, as well as holes for stripping 14- or 12-gauge wire. If you need to strip other sizes of cable or wire, go ahead and buy a tool for those sizes.

For clarity, I show these stripping operations being performed prior to running the cable through framing to the box. However, it is often easier to run unstripped cable to the box location and then do the stripping just prior to inserting into the box.

Measure to cut off a bit more than 6 in. of sheathing. To do this quickly, note where 6 in. comes on your tool, so you don't have to repeatedly use a tape measure ❶. Slip the cable into the slot for its size (here, 14/2), squeeze the handles together, and give it a twist as you squeeze. Then slide the sheathing off ❷. Pull any paper or plastic strips off the wires, and cut them near the cut end of the sheathing ❸. Or, it may be easier to simply tear off the paper. If you will strip the wires as well at this point (you may

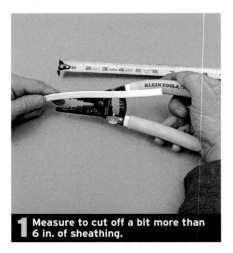

1 Measure to cut off a bit more than 6 in. of sheathing.

2 Use the correct slot on the strippers to remove the sheathing.

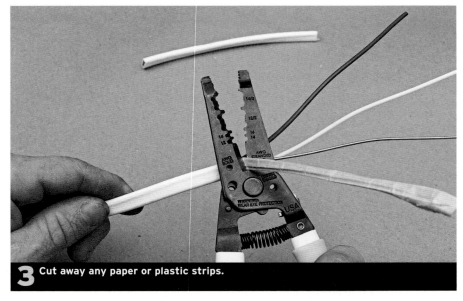

3 Cut away any paper or plastic strips.

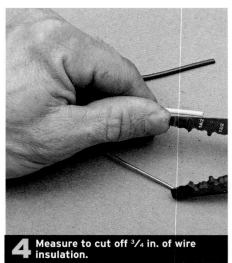

4 Measure to cut off ³/₄ in. of wire insulation.

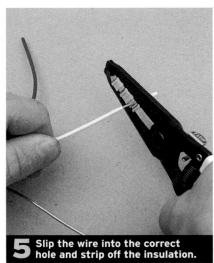

5 Slip the wire into the correct hole and strip off the insulation.

decide to do this later), measure 3/4 in. or so **4**. Slip the wire into the correct-size stripper hole, squeeze, twist, and pull the insulation off **5**.

If you feel skilled and want to try doing it the way many pros do, you can practice until you get good at stripping both cable and wire ends using a pair of lineman's pliers **6**. Once you are used to working this way, you can squeeze with just the right pressure so you quickly strip without nicking wires.

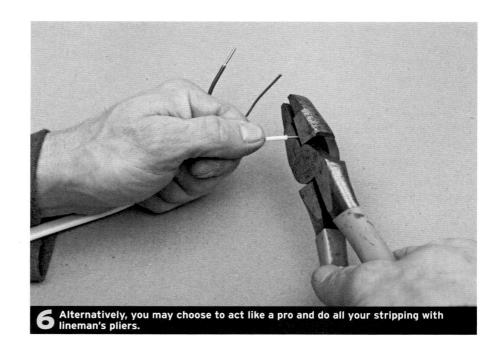

6 Alternatively, you may choose to act like a pro and do all your stripping with lineman's pliers.

SPLICING WIRES

Some people splice solid wires together simply by poking them into a wire nut and twisting, but you'll get a firmer connection by twisting them together first and then adding a wire nut. After stripping about 3/4 in. of insulation from two or more wires, hold them tightly side by side with their ends aligned **1**. Grab the wire ends with the tip of a pair of lineman's pliers and twist clockwise several times, to get a neat-looking, tight joint **2**. Pull on the wires to be sure the connection is tight; you should not be able to easily untwist. Snip the tip of the splice at an angle with the lineman's pliers or diagonal cutters **3**. >> >> >>

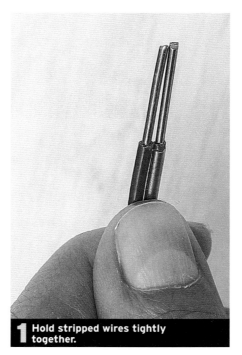

1 Hold stripped wires tightly together.

2 Twist together with lineman's pliers.

SPLICING WIRES (CONTINUED)

Insert the wires deep into a wire nut and twist clockwise to tighten ❹.

When joining a fixture's stranded "lead" wire to one or more solid wires, wrap the lead clockwise around the wire(s) so the lead extends about 1/8 in. past the solid wire. Insert the wires deep into a wire nut and twist clockwise until you achieve a firm connection.

3 Test that the splice is tight, then snip the end.

4 Firmly twist on a wire nut.

Wrap a stranded wire around one or more solid wires and tighten with a wire nut.

WRAPPING WITH TAPE

Wrapping the bottom of a wire nut and the wires with professional-quality electrical tape is not usually considered necessary, but doing this is a good idea. At the very least, make sure that no bare wire is exposed after the wire nut is attached.

CONNECTING WIRES TO TERMINALS

Many switches and receptacles have side-mounted terminals with screws. (They may have poke-in options as well, but most electricians don't trust them to make reliable connections.) To connect wires, strip off a full 1 in. instead of the 3/4 in. used for splicing. Use the tip of a pair of wire strippers (as shown) or longnose pliers to twist the stripped wire into a question-mark shape ❶. Loosen the terminal—brass for the hot wire and silver for the neutral—and slip the stripped end under the screw head. Squeeze the wire to tighten it around the terminal ❷. Tighten the screw firmly ❸. Also tighten any other terminal screws that are loose. Wrap the device with electrical tape, so all the bare wires and terminals are covered ❹.

Some high-quality devices have push-in terminals that get tightened after inserting the wire end. These make for reliable connections.

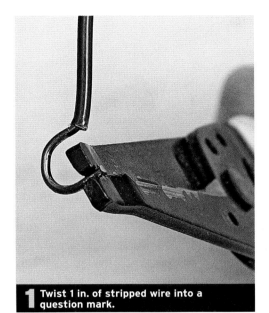

1 Twist 1 in. of stripped wire into a question mark.

2 Squeeze the wire around the terminal's shaft.

3 Tighten the terminal screw.

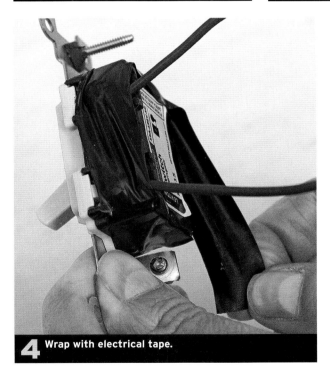

4 Wrap with electrical tape.

This type of push-in terminal **makes a solid connection.**

INSTALLING BOXES

Plastic boxes come in single-, double-, triple-, or even four-"gang" sizes, referring to the number of switches or receptacles you will install in them. They have integral screw holes for attaching devices.

Some metal boxes also come in different gang sizes. However, it is most common to install a "square" metal box whether you will install one or two devices. After cable is run into the box, you add a "mud ring" (also called a device extender ring) that is either one or two gang, so you can install one or two devices. This arrangement allows for plenty of room for wires.

Determine where you want your receptacles and switches. Receptacles should be no farther apart than 12 ft., and there should be at least one on every wall that is longer than 6 ft. Think through the placement; avoid putting receptacles where they will be hard to reach, and perhaps increase the number behind a desk and other places where you use lots of power.

Also think through switch placements. Avoid placing a switch where it will be hidden when a door is opened. Where a switch is near a door (as often happens), be sure it is not so close to the door as to interfere with the door molding. As a general rule, a switch box should be at least 3 in. away from the inside of the door's rough opening.

Plastic boxes are often installed with their bottoms 12 in. to 16 in. above the floor. Many electricians use this simple and quick technique for getting all the receptacles at the same height: Place the head of a hammer on the floor and set the box on top of the handle.

Plastic boxes have side indentations or other guides so you can easily install them with their front edges ½ in. out from the framing—so they will be flush with the wall surface once ½-in. drywall is installed.

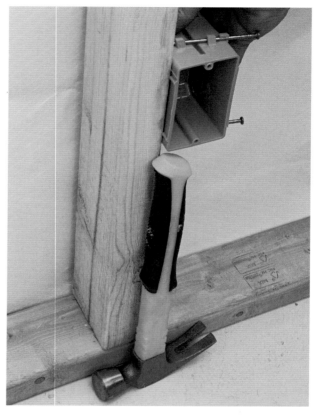

A hammer **makes for an easy and convenient height gauge for receptacle boxes.**

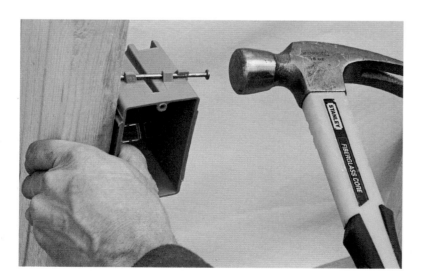

To attach this plastic box, simply position it using the guide, so it extends ½ in. out from the stud, and drive the nails.

PLASTIC AND METAL BOX SIZES

Plastic boxes are common, but in many areas, metal boxes are required.

Some metal boxes come in different gang sizes. However, it is most common to install a "square" metal box whether you will install one or two devices. After cable is run into the box, you add a "mud ring" (also called a device extender ring) that is either one or two gang, so you can install one or two devices. This arrangement allows for plenty of room for wires.

Many plastic boxes come with nails attached; simply drive the nails into the side of a wood stud to attach.

Metal boxes take just slightly more time to install than plastic boxes. There are several types, but for the most common type, use its guide to hold the front edge flush with the framing. The mud ring that gets installed later will bring it out ½ in. Drive two small tabs to hold the box in place temporarily, then drive a screw into each flange to secure the box to a wood stud.

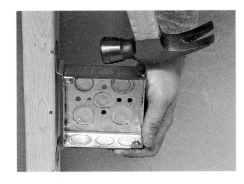

Hold this type of metal box **against the stud at the correct height, and tap in the little pointed tabs to temporarily hold the box in place.**

Drive at least two 1¼-in. screws **to hold the box firmly in place.**

WORKING WITH METAL STUDS

If you have metal studs, attach by driving self-tapping panhead screws.

Or, screw a block of wood **to the stud and attach the box to that.**

Metal studs have holes for running cable, but the holes have sharp edges. Buy bushings to fit the hole size, and snap them in before running cable.

RUNNING NM CABLE INTO PLASTIC BOXES

As shown in the top center photo on p. 148, cable is often run through holes drilled in the centers of studs where drywall screws cannot reach. (However, in the case of an outside wall where there is a space behind the framing, you can simply run the cable behind the framing.)

Drill ¾-in. or larger diameter holes through studs. They should be reasonably level with each other. A quick way to gauge this is to drill all the holes at hip height ❶. At a corner, drill holes through both studs, angling them slightly toward the inside corner. Bend the cable

>> >> >>

1 Drill holes for the cable at hip height.

RUNNING NM CABLE INTO PLASTIC BOXES (CONTINUED)

to roughly approximate the path it must take, and thread it through the two holes ❷. At a plastic box, strip the sheathing if you have not already done so. Poke the cable through the openings, which have flaps that keep them from backing out. The sheathing should show in the box just a bit—½ in. to 1 in. ❸. Staple the cables within 8 in. or so of the box and tuck the cable(s) into the box.

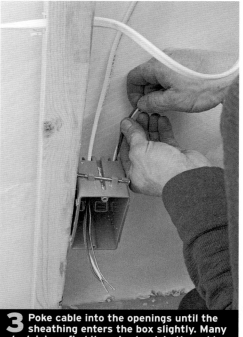

3 Poke cable into the openings until the sheathing enters the box slightly. Many electricians find it easier to strip the cable and wire ends at this point, rather than before running the cable.

2a At a corner, drill slightly angled holes in both directions.

2b Bend the cable, and thread through the holes.

HOOKING CABLE TO METAL BOXES

Metal boxes come with various means of clamping the cable, and here we show the three most common types. If the box has integral clamps, use a screwdriver to remove a tab for each cable ❹. Strip the sheathing, insert the cable(s) so the sheathing just shows beyond the clamp, and tighten the clamp ❸.

On a box without integral clamps, check with local codes to see if you need to use metal cable clamps, or if plastic clamps are allowed. Use a pair of lineman's pliers or a hammer and screwdriver to tap open a knockout slug and remove the slug by wiggling it out with the pliers ❻.

To use a metal clamp, unscrew its nut and slip it into the knockout hole ❹. With the screw heads facing you so you can tighten them later, screw on the clamp's nut. Use a screwdriver to tighten the nut ❺. Either push hard on the screwdriver or tap with a hammer until the nut is firmly connected. Slide the cable in so the sheathing is visible inside the box and tighten the clamp screws ❻.

If plastic clamps are allowed, things go faster. Poke the clamp up through the hole from the inside of the box ❻. You may need to tap it with a hammer. Slip the cable down through the clamp, taking care not to go too far; you cannot pull it back ❻.

A Remove knockout tabs from a box with integral clamps.

B Insert the cable and tighten the integral clamps.

C1 Poke open a knockout slug . . .

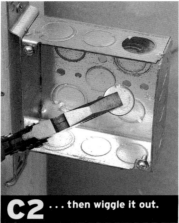

C2 . . . then wiggle it out.

D Insert a metal cable clamp and slip on the nut.

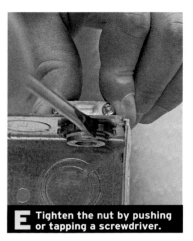

E Tighten the nut by pushing or tapping a screwdriver.

F Slip in the cable and tighten the screws to secure the cable.

G Push or tap a plastic clamp up through a knockout hole.

H Carefully poke cable into the box; be sure you don't push too far.

CEILING BOXES

Ceiling boxes may be plastic or metal, or they may be recessed canister bodies. In most respects, they attach to framing and receive cable in the same ways as wall boxes. If you will have a series of ceiling lights, take the time to measure carefully and string layout lines, so they will be evenly spaced and lined up in neat rows. Recessed canister lights often come with brackets that allow you to slide them from side to side, so you can fine-tune their positions.

A flush light with a metal box uses a mud ring like a wall box. To line it up with other ceiling lights, string lines in two directions. You'll likely need to install blocking pieces so you can locate the boxes precisely.

A round or octagonal box like this nails on easily but is difficult to position precisely. However, it can work well if a row of lights all align with the same joist.

INSTALLING A CANISTER LIGHT BODY

Canister lights, also called can or pot lights, have their own electrical boxes. Run cable to the area. Open the electrical box, which has a cover that may be attached with a clip or a screw. Strip the cable sheathing and wire ends, and clamp the cable in the box. Connect the ground, neutral, and hot leads to the cable wires and close the box **1**. (In this example, push-in connectors are provided with the unit.) Tuck the wires back into the box and replace the cover **2**. Attach the canister light by driving nails through the brackets into two joists; the bottom of the light housing should be 1/2 in. below the framing to allow for the drywall thickness **3**. Now you can slide the light to adjust its position **4**.

➡ **See "Splicing Wires," pp. 143-144, and "Connecting Wires to Terminals," pp. 144-145.**

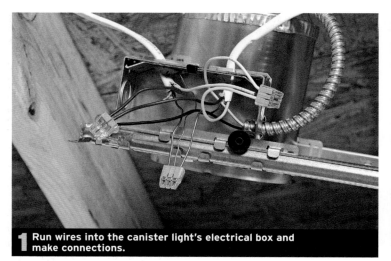

1 Run wires into the canister light's electrical box and make connections.

2 Tuck the wires into the box and replace the cover.

3 Drive nails to attach the light to the joists.

4 Slide the fixture to align it.

WIRING WITH CONDUIT

Conduit pipe, often referred to as EMT, is required for electrical work in some areas of the country. And if you will be installing wiring that is exposed, conduit is a very good idea, because it encases wires far more securely than NM cable. Joining conduit pipe to electrical boxes is not difficult, but bending it takes some skill, which you can learn with practice.

Make bends using a conduit bender of the right size for your conduit. Take some time to practice your technique, so you can make smooth, fairly accurate bends. Make your bends so that the conduit will end up a few inches longer than needed; you will cut it off later. Most bends are made on the floor: Insert the conduit, step on the footpad, and pull or push the bar to make the bend ❶. When making multiple turns, it may be easier to work with the bender upside down ❷. At the box, remove a knockout slug and insert a conduit clamp. Hold the conduit in place and mark for a cut ❸.

>> >> >>

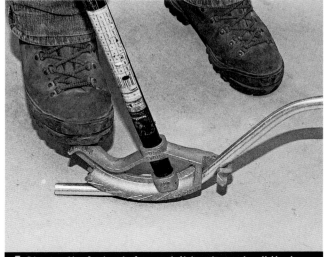

1 Step on the footpad of a conduit bender and pull the bar to make bends in conduit.

2 Multiple bends are sometimes easier to make with the bender positioned upside down.

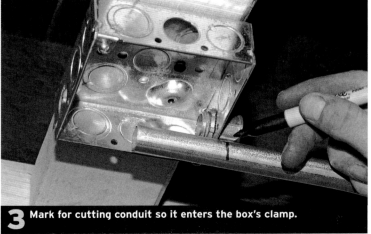

3 Mark for cutting conduit so it enters the box's clamp.

What Size Conduit?
The size of conduit you need depends on how many wires you pull through it, how many bends the conduit turns, and the length of the run. For most basement work, $1/2$-in. conduit is large enough; for instance, you can easily pull up to five 12-gauge or seven 14-gauge wires for a run that is 40 ft. long with four bends. However, if you worry that things may get tight, go ahead and buy $3/4$-in. conduit, which doesn't cost much more.

WIRING WITH CONDUIT (CONTINUED)

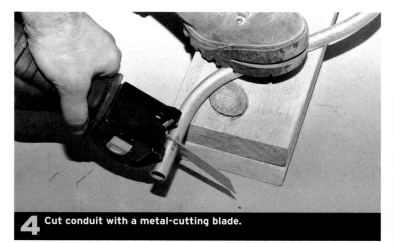

4 Cut conduit with a metal-cutting blade.

5 Be sure to remove all burrs with a reaming tool.

6 Insert the conduit and tighten the setscrew.

7a Push the fish tape . . .

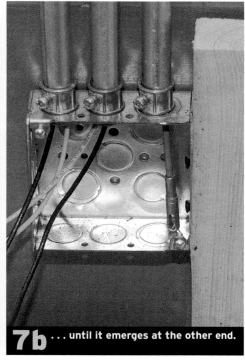

7b . . . until it emerges at the other end.

Secure the conduit, then cut with a hacksaw or a reciprocating saw equipped with a metal blade **4**. Then—and this is important—remove all burrs from inside the cut end. (Burrs will dig into the wire insulation and perhaps even strip it off.) Use a hand tool like lineman's pliers or a screwdriver, or—better—a reaming tool attached to a drill **5**. Slip the conduit end into the clamp and tighten the setscrew **6**.

Once all the pipes are attached to the boxes, it's time to fish wires. Insert a fish tape into one end of a run and push until it pokes out the other end **7**. Attach the wires to the end of the fish tape: Bend one of the wires over, then arrange the others in descending order, and wrap tightly with electrical tape **8**. Have one person gently push wires through while another person pulls with force at the other end **9**. If pulling gets tough, apply wire-pulling lubricant to the wires at the front end **10**. Once the wires are pulled through, cut them off **11**.

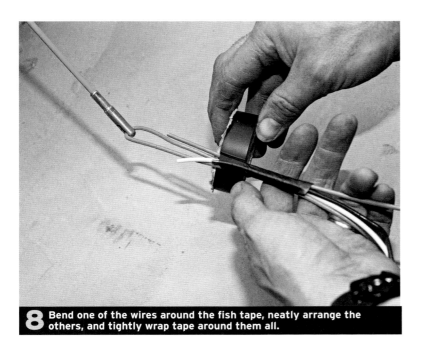

8 Bend one of the wires around the fish tape, neatly arrange the others, and tightly wrap tape around them all.

WIRE SPOOLER

A wire spooler like this makes it much easier to fish multiple wires through conduit. Make sure all the wires are long enough; it is against code to make any splices inside the conduit.

9 While one person pulls the tape, someone at the other end pushes wires gently.

10 Lubrication helps wires pull smoothly, especially if they must make multiple turns.

11 Once the wires are pulled through, cut them off.

— COMMON WIRING ARRANGEMENTS —

This book cannot cover all the wiring configurations you might need to use in a basement, but it will at least give you an idea of how two- and three-wire cable can be used to provide a wide variety of electrical services. Consult such books as Taunton's *Wiring Complete* for more possibilities.

Be sure that the new fixtures and receptacles will not overload a circuit; you may need to grab power by installing a new circuit. While in older homes power often runs first to the

fixture, in modern wiring power travels first to the switch, then to the fixtures.

➤ See "Avoiding Overloads," p. 140.

➤ See "Splicing Wires," pp. 143-144, and "Connecting Wires to Terminals," pp. 144-145.

TWO OR MORE FIXTURES CONTROLLED BY ONE SWITCH

Here, power enters the box (either from an existing electrical box, if that will not overload the circuit, or from a new circuit installed in the service panel). In the switch box, the hot wire is hooked to the two switch terminals, and white wires are spliced to travel through the box. In the first and any other intermediate fixture boxes, splice all the wires, and splice the fixture leads to the hot and neutral wires. At the final fixture, simply splice to the fixture leads.

SWITCH AND RECEPTACLE IN THE SAME BOX

A setup like this is often used in a bathroom, where the receptacle and light must be on a dedicated 20-amp circuit.

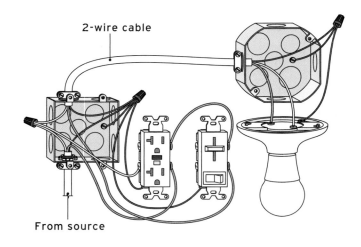

2-wire cable

From source

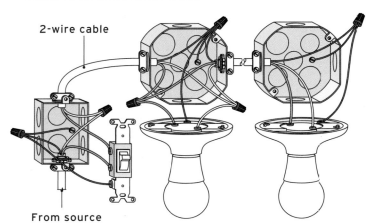

2-wire cable

From source

MULTIPLE RECEPTACLES

If you are installing a series of receptacles that are all on the same circuit, the wiring is straightforward. Hook wires to all four terminals for all the receptacles until you reach the last one, which gets only two wires.

From source

2-wire cable

2-wire cable

SPLIT-CIRCUIT RECEPTACLES

This arrangement is often used above a kitchen countertop or a workbench, because it allows you to plug two heavy-use appliances into the same receptacle without overloading a circuit. You'll need to run three-wire cable from a double-pole circuit breaker to all the boxes.

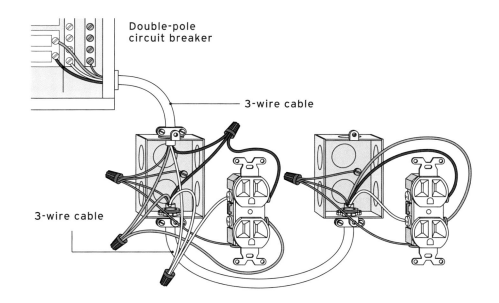

Double-pole circuit breaker

3-wire cable

3-wire cable

MULTIPLE LIGHTS AND SWITCHES

To control two or more lights with separate switches, install a multiple-gang box. The incoming hot wire is connected to one terminal of all three switches using pigtails. Another black wire leads from each of the other terminals to separate fixtures. All the white wires are spliced together in the switch box.

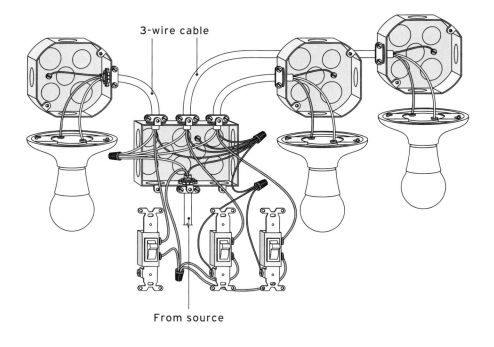

3-wire cable

From source

THREE-WAY SWITCHING

It's often convenient to control a fixture (or group of fixtures) from two different places with, for instance, one switch by a basement entry door and another at the top of the stairs leading to the first floor. Use special three-way switches, which have an extra "common" terminal. There are a number of ways to wire three-ways, but this is the most common.

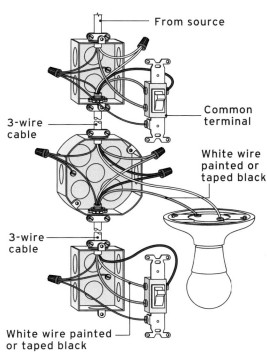

From source

Common terminal

3-wire cable

White wire painted or taped black

3-wire cable

White wire painted or taped black

TAPPING INTO AN EXISTING CIRCUIT

If a circuit has room for more amperage and your new service will not overload it, you can tap into the circuit. If there is a junction box (an electrical box with a blank cover), that is probably the easiest place to tap in. Otherwise, you will need to tap in at a receptacle box or a switch box. The illustrations below show how to wire the hookups. If the box is hidden behind drywall, you will need to cut around the box in order to run new cable into it; that is usually the most complicated part of the job.

TAPPING INTO POWER AT A RECEPTACLE OR SWITCH BOX

If a receptacle is at the end of the run and has two available terminals, you can simply hook the new wires to those terminals. If all terminals are engaged, use pigtails as shown here.

As long as power runs first to the switch box rather than to the fixture, you can grab power at the box using pigtails as shown.

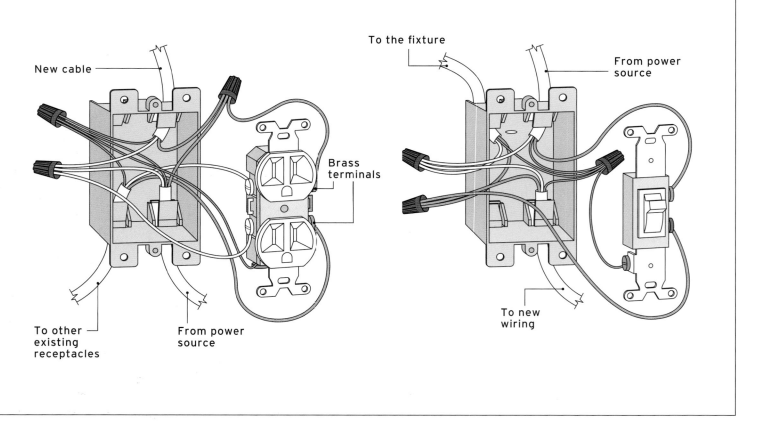

New cable

To the fixture

From power source

Brass terminals

To other existing receptacles

From power source

To new wiring

RUNNING A NEW CIRCUIT

Once you've determined that you have extra slots in your service panel and are certain there is room for extra amperage, hooking up new breakers for new circuits is actually pretty simple. Buy breakers made for your brand of panel. Use a 15-amp breaker for a circuit that uses 14-gauge wire, and a 20-amp breaker for 12-gauge wire.

Run cable from your new boxes in a "home run" to the service panel, leaving yourself a few feet of extra cable. Remove the cover to expose the wiring. Though many electricians work without doing so, you should shut off the main breaker that supplies power to the box. (Keep in mind that the wires leading to the main breaker will still be energized, so stay well away from them.)

Remove a knockout slug from a convenient place on the side or bottom of the service panel ❶. Install a cable clamp (of the same type as used for a metal box) in the knockout. Thread the cable through the clamp, allowing yourself lots of room for running wires around the box ❷. Carefully run wires around the perimeter of the panel to their locations. Insert the bare or green ground wire into an opening in the neutral/ground bar (unless yours has a separate bar for ground wires), and tighten the setscrew to secure it. Do the same for the neutral wire ❸.

Determine where the new breaker will be installed. Run the black or colored hot wire to that location and cut it, leaving yourself a few inches of slack. Strip the wire end, insert it into the breaker, and tighten the setscrew ❹. Snap the breaker into place on the bus bar. You will likely slide it into a holder on one side, then pivot down onto the bus bar ❺. Make sure the two metal parts of the breaker clasp the breaker bar tightly; the breaker should be at the same level as surrounding breakers.

Once you are certain all is secure and tight, turn the main breaker back on and test your new receptacles, lights, or appliances.

1 Shut off power at the main breaker. Remove a knockout slug at a convenient place.

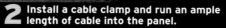

2 Install a cable clamp and run an ample length of cable into the panel.

3 Attach stripped ends of the white and the ground wire to a ground/neutral bar (which may be two separate bars).

4a Insert the stripped end of the hot wire into the breaker . . .

4b . . . then tighten the setscrew.

5 Snap the breaker into place. Restore power at the main breaker, and test.

WALLS AND CEILINGS

AFTER THE INNARDS OF THE WALLS and ceiling have been filled with drainpipes, supply pipes, ducts, electrical boxes, and electrical cable, it's time to cover up the framing and mechanicals, first with insulation and then most likely with drywall.

Although drywall is by far the most common surface for walls and ceilings, there are alternatives. Some manufacturers offer easy-to-install wall systems that combine insulation with the wall surface and are quick to finish. Over your head, you may decide to install a suspended (or drop) ceiling.

If using drywall, standard practice is to attach 1/2-in.-thick drywall with screws, cover joints with drywall tape, fill the joints and screw heads with several coats of joint compound, and sand everything smooth. Then you can apply primer and paint.

Drywalling is certainly a job you can do yourself with a helper, but consider subbing the job out to drywall specialists, if they offer to do it for a reasonable price. They will no doubt work much faster than you, and often produce very smooth surfaces. But with patience and attention to detail you can also make professional-looking wall and ceiling surfaces.

Some professionals install sheets of drywall by themselves, but most mere mortals benefit from enlisting an able-bodied helper for hanging the drywall.

Dust from sanding can be a big problem. You may want to buy a sanding unit that attaches to a vacuum or dust collector. It also helps to open windows and direct fans outward.

APPROACHES TO WALLS

HANGING DRYWALL

WALL SURFACE OPTIONS

Basements often feature walls with neatly smoothed drywall painted in light, neutral colors, because basements often have little natural light and need some brightening. There is certainly nothing wrong with that, especially if you hang artwork or displays of knickknacks. But luminous and cheery LED lights can really light up a space with a pleasant, natural effect, so you are free to color and texture walls in almost any way that feels good to you. Here are some possibilities. >> >> >>

These walls and doors feature wide strips of flat, simple trim reminiscent of the farmhouse style, adding traditional warmth to the basement entry.

A textured surface can stylishly mask a wall's imperfections. Here, a rustic adobe effect lends personality to this casual basement living room.

A hidden-door bookcase that opens via a hinge connected to the floor and upper door frame is a clever way to hide the unfinished section of the basement.

Older homes with unfinished basements often have concrete floors and brick walls. That combination has a certain harmony that never goes out of style. Wood trim and other design elements add dignified touches.

Wood paneling can quickly transform a basic wall into one with considerable design points. Lighter wood tones have an understated elegance in this spacious basement living area.

WALL SURFACE OPTIONS (CONTINUED)

Purchased systems

You can buy wall systems designed to be quickly installed on the outside walls of a basement. The product shown here, called SMARTWALL® by the DRIcore® Products Company, consists of panels with three laminated layers: a moisture shield laminated onto the back, foam insulation in the middle, and moisture-resistant drywall on the face. The panels fit together via vertical tongues and grooves and include channels through which you can run wiring. The joints between the panels are beveled and get filled with a proprietary patching compound that applies like standard joint compound but is more flexible, so there is no need to apply drywall tape.

This product is fairly expensive, but will save you a good deal of time versus the alternative: building framing, installing a moisture barrier and insulation, applying drywall, and applying several coats of joint compound. As shown here, the product is designed to be installed after a raised dry subfloor has been installed.

➜ See "Installing a Subfloor," pp. 188–194.

Start by installing a top track ❶. Attach a 2x2 against the wall, followed by a 1½-in.-wide strip of ¾-in. plywood or OSB. Secure the track with long screws driven up into joists. On a wall where the joists run parallel, you will need to install blocking. Then install the bottom track, which is offset from the top track by 2⅝ in. ❷.

Measure the height of the wall and cut the top—not the bottom—to fit. You can cut with a circular saw equipped with a fine-cutting blade or with a handsaw. If there will be a receptacle box, cut a hole for it as well. Attach the first panel to the top and bottom tracks with screws ❸. Cut subsequent panels to height, set them on the bottom track, and slide over until the tongues and grooves seat snugly ❹. You'll need to cut the tongue side of the last panel so it fits widthwise.

Run electrical cable through a channel provided in the panels. Pull the cables through the hole you cut, then thread them through an

1 Attach the top track to hold the panels away from the wall.

2 Attach the bottom track 2⅝ in. out from the top track.

3 Attach the panel with screws driven into the top and bottom tracks.

4 Slide the next panels so the tongues and grooves nest firmly, and screw to the tracks.

5a Feed electrical cable through channels in the panels . . .

5b . . . then install into boxes.

6 At an inside corner, cut the panel if needed. Run a bead of construction adhesive and slide the new panel into it.

7 Continue installing panels, measuring and cutting them to height as you go.

8 Apply a coat of patching compound and allow to dry; sand lightly and repeat with a second coat.

electrical box, and install the box ❺. When you turn an inside corner, slide the first panel of the next wall in place to see if it fits neatly; if not, scribe a line and cut the panel so it fits well. Apply a bead of construction adhesive along the first wall, then slide the first panel of the adjacent wall into the adhesive ❻. Continue installing panels all around the room; measure and cut each to height as you go ❼.

Once all the panels are installed, apply the filler compound to the joints; sand lightly to achieve a smooth surface and apply a second coat if needed ❽.

INSTALLING INSULATION BETWEEN STUDS

Even if you have installed rigid foam insulation against the concrete wall, you may want to add more insulation to keep your basement cozier and to reduce heating expense. Local codes may also require additional insulation. Fiberglass blanket insulation is the most common product used for this.

Because insulation is not a structural element, many people take its installation lightly. However, it's important to work carefully to achieve a precise fit and avoid gaps or squished insulation, which reduce efficiency.

Avoid the temptation to tightly shove extra insulation into narrow spaces. Insulation that is crammed is far less effective than insulation that is free to expand to its full thickness.

Wear gloves and long sleeves as you work, because fiberglass fibers will fly around a bit and can seriously irritate your skin. You may want to wear a disposable dust mask and protective eyewear as well. If possible, open a nearby window and direct a fan outward.

Prepare a large working area, so you can cut pieces to exact length. A sheet of plywood or OSB works fine for a cutting surface. Carefully position a tape measure hook at one end of the insulation—you can't pull on it—and use a felt-tipped pen to mark for cutting ❶. Position a framing square to make a square cut. With a knee on one end of the square, press down on the other end to compress the insulation tightly, and cut with a knife ❷.

Blankets are 14½ in. wide, to fit nicely between studs that are 16 in. on center. If the space is narrower or wider, cut or add insulation as needed. Press the insulation into place gently, so the insulation retains its fluff ❸. Fold out the tabs on the sides of the blankets and staple to the studs. Work to keep the blanket fairly taut at all points, with no large wrinkles ❹.

Where you meet electrical cable or pipes, take some trouble to maintain the fluff. Divide the insulation in half thickness-wise and slip the back thickness behind the cable ❺. Then staple the face as usual. To insulate a space narrower than 14½ in., there is no need to draw a long cut line. Instead, measure across the blanket and take note

>> >> >>

1 Precisely measure and mark for cutting a fiberglass blanket.

2 Compress the insulation and make a square cut.

3 Press the insulation in place between studs, maintaining the fluff.

4 Pull the tabs taut as you drive staples into studs.

5a At a cable, divide the insulation in half thickness . . .

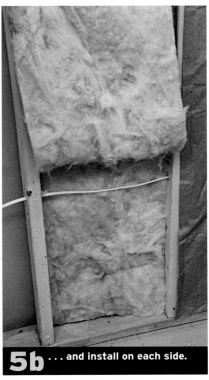

5b . . . and install on each side.

Gap between Blanket and Rigid Insulation

The R-13 insulation shown here is 3⁵/₈ in. thick. If you installed your framing 1¹/₂ in. out from the rigid insulation or the wall, that will leave an air gap between the fiberglass and the rigid insulation. If both types of insulation are tightly sealed, the air gap will actually have insulating properties as well.

INSTALLING INSULATION BETWEEN STUDS (CONTINUED)

of where the printing or lines on the paper align with your desired width. Set a level or other long straightedge along the printing, press down with your knee and hand, and make the long cut **6**.

At an electrical box, position the insulation and partly staple it in place. Carefully cut around the box **7**. Staple the blanket to the studs and very gently stuff any gaps with loose insulation: The insulation should be full thickness but should not be tightly crammed **8**.

You will likely have spaces above the stud framing where the rim joist needs insulating. Cut pieces precisely. In the example shown, notches were cut around pieces of blocking **9**.

After the fiberglass insulation is installed, take the time to seal any openings, such as the space around a window **10**.

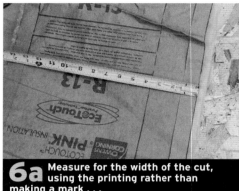

6a Measure for the width of the cut, using the printing rather than making a mark . . .

6b . . . then cut widthwise along the length.

7 Neatly cut around an electrical box.

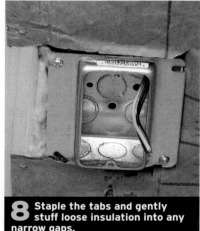

8 Staple the tabs and gently stuff loose insulation into any narrow gaps.

9 Precisely cut and gently press insulation in place above the stud wall.

10 Also apply foam or fiberglass insulation to any narrow gaps.

CHOOSING DRYWALL

Also known by the brand name Sheetrock®, drywall is the universal choice for covering up framing and producing smooth, straight ceilings and walls. Hanging drywall can be heavy work, so be sure to have a helper on hand. Drywall is easy to cut, but don't take the work lightly: If you make inaccurate cuts, the job of taping will be much more difficult and time-consuming.

Drywall comes in sheets 4 ft. wide. The most common length is 8 ft., but if you have walls or ceilings that are between 8 ft. and 12 ft. long, consider buying sheets that will span the entire distance. That will save you from taping butt joints, which is the most time-consuming aspect of taping. Of course, longer sheets are a good deal heavier, so you may want two helpers, and maybe also a drywall hoist, to install them.

➜ See "Finishing Drywall," pp. 173–181.

In addition to standard drywall, which is putty colored, you can choose moisture-resistant drywall, also called greenboard or blueboard for an obvious reason. Greenboard is a good choice where there will be slight moisture, such as the walls and ceiling of a bathroom. Where things will get downright wet—as in a tub surround or shower stall—install concrete backerboard, which holds firm even if it gets sopping wet.

Just getting the drywall into your basement can be a big task. You may want to pay extra to have it delivered to your home; you may also be able to pay someone to bring it down to the basement. Lean the sheets against a wall, setting them on top of two scrap boards; raising them up a bit off the floor makes cutting easier.

BUTT ENDS AND TAPERED SIDES

Drywall has sides that are tapered, so when two sheets are butted together, you can easily fill the resulting shallow valley with tape and joint compound. The ends, on the other hand, are not tapered, which makes creating a neat-looking butt joint something of a challenge.

CUTTING DRYWALL

Drywall is easy to cut. In most cases you need only a utility knife, a jab or other type of drywall saw, a drywall square, and a tape measure.

Cutting drywall to length

Measure for the cut at both sides of the sheet (that is, 4 ft. apart), to be sure that the sheet can be cut reasonably square. Hook a tape measure and slide a drywall square over until it aligns with the measurement **❶**. Jab your knife against the square into the drywall at some point so you will not accidentally bump the square out of position. Hold the square firmly at the top with your hand and wedge your foot against it at the bottom. Slice along the square all the way across the ⟫ ⟫ ⟫

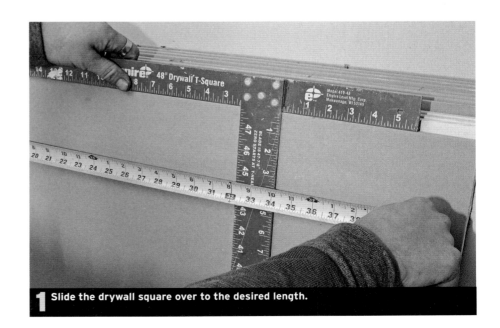

❶ Slide the drywall square over to the desired length.

CUTTING DRYWALL (CONTINUED)

2 Hold the square firmly with a hand and foot, and cut through the paper.

3 Snap the sheet along the cutline.

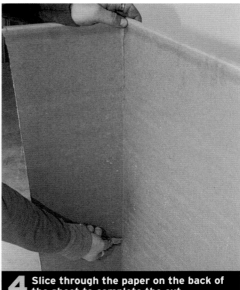

4 Slice through the paper on the back of the sheet to complete the cut.

⚠ WHAT CAN GO WRONG

Cut drywall has a slightly ragged edge and, since the world is an imperfect place, drywallers generally cut sheets 1/4 in. short of the measured distance to achieve a neat and snug joint. There's no sense trying to make a tight fit with drywall; if you do, you may end up cracking it, which will require extra taping.

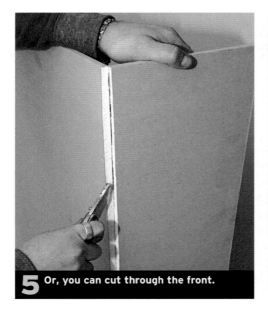

5 Or, you can cut through the front.

6 Scrape the ragged cut until smooth.

sheet **2**. (You may find it easier to slice down most of the way, then up for the bottom foot or so.) Pull the drywall out a foot or more, hold the keeper side with one hand, and push to snap the waste side **3**. For the cleanest cut, slice through the paper on the back of the sheet; with the cutoff held at an angle, this is easy to do **4**. The cut is now complete. If reaching the back of the sheet is difficult, slice through the front **5**. This creates a somewhat more ragged cut, so you may need to scrape along the edge of the cut with your knife **6**.

Rip cutting to width

To make a rip cut that is parallel to a sheet's edge, mark a spot indicating the desired width of the cut. Using your "good" hand, clasp the knife blade against the blade of the tape measure. With the other hand, hold the tape so that your hand rests on the edge of the drywall while the knife blade is on the cutline. Holding firmly with both hands, dig the knife blade into the drywall, rest the knuckles of your "bad" hand on the edge of the sheet, and slide them both along ❶. This produces a surprisingly straight rip cut.

If the rip cut is not parallel to the edge of the drywall, measure and mark each end to width and snap a chalkline between them. Cut freehand with a knife, taking care not to wander more than 1/4 in. or so from the chalkline ❷.

1 Make a straight rip cut using one hand as a guide while the other hand cuts with a knife clasped to the tape measure's blade.

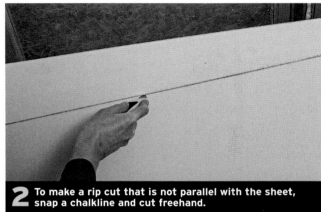

2 To make a rip cut that is not parallel with the sheet, snap a chalkline and cut freehand.

Making a large cutout (notch)

If you need to cut a notch, use a pencil, tape measure, handsaw, and utility knife. Mark the sheet for the cutout and draw an X indicating the waste. Cut along the shorter leg of the cutout using a drywall saw ❶. Here, we show a jab-type drywall saw, but you could also use a saw with a wider blade. Next, slice through the paper along the longer leg of the cutout. Here, I'm using a tape measure as a guide: Hold the tape with one hand along the side of the sheet, clasp the knife to the hook end of the tape, and slide them together to make the cut ❷. Snap the waste portion back as you would for a full-width cut, and cut through the back paper, either from the back or from the front ❸.

>> >> >>

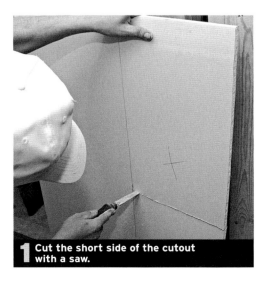

1 Cut the short side of the cutout with a saw.

2 Cut through the paper only along the longer side.

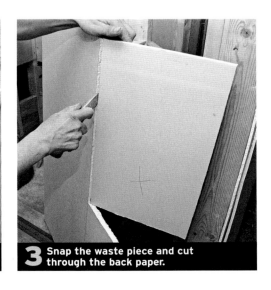

3 Snap the waste piece and cut through the back paper.

CUTTING DRYWALL (CONTINUED)

Cutting a rectangular hole

For electrical boxes and other small obstructions, you will need to cut a square or rectangular hole. Measure from the wall to the two width sides of the box (or in this case, the mud ring); plan for a hole that is ¼ in. larger than the box opening in both directions. Make the same measurements for height. Use a pencil and a drywall square to draw the opening ❶. Slice through the face paper on all four sides, then use your knife to poke through the drywall at all four corners ❷. From the back side, cut lines that run from knife poke to knife poke ❸. Knock out the waste with a hammer ❹. Alternatively, slice the front paper with a knife, then cut the hole using a jab saw, holding the blade to the inside of the knife cuts for a clean cut ❺.

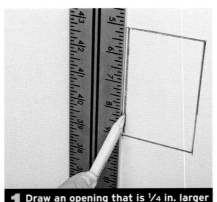

1 Draw an opening that is ¼ in. larger than the box in both directions.

2 Slice the paper and poke through to mark the four corners.

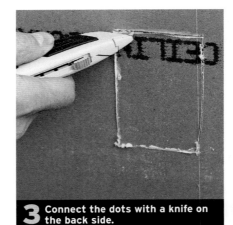

3 Connect the dots with a knife on the back side.

4 Knock out the waste.

5 Or, cut the hole using a jab saw.

TRADE SECRET

You can draw a circle and then cut it with a jab saw, but this adjustable hole saw with a dust collector makes neater and quicker work and is a good idea, especially if you need lots of holes for canister lights. Adjust the cutter's blade for diameter, and make test cuts on scrap pieces of drywall to be sure you've got it right. Mark the center of the hole and poke the tool's guide bit into that spot. When you cut, the plastic tray collects the dust, which otherwise would fly all over the place.

CUTTING BACKERBOARD

Though you can buy a special backerboard knife, you can also cut concrete backerboard using a utility knife. Because backerboard sheets are only 3 ft. wide, it is not as easy to use a drywall square when cutting. (For more on cutting backerboard, see pp. 190–191.) To cut a hole for a pipe, use a masonry-cutting hole saw, or, as shown, ream the hole with a jab saw. Fasten with special backerboard screws, not drywall screws.

HANGING DRYWALL

Drywall is usually installed first on the ceiling, then on the upper wall, then on the lower wall. That way, the upper-wall sheets butt against the ceiling sheets and the lower-wall sheets meet the upper-wall sheets in a tapered joint that is easy to tape.

Working with a helper or two, you can raise the sheets into position by hand. For greater ease of installation, rent a drywall lift, also called a hoist.

Driving screws

It used to be common to attach drywall with nails, but nowadays most drywallers use screws, which are easy to drive using a drill. However, be aware that drywall screws must be driven to an exact depth: If you drive one too far, it will rip the paper and thereby lose most of its holding power. And if you don't drive it far enough, the head will protrude and make it impossible to apply joint compound and achieve a smooth surface.

You can achieve just the right depth using a simple screwdriver bit, but you would have to work very carefully. Fortunately, there is a tool that comes to the rescue: a drywall screw bit, also called a screw setter, which makes it impossible to drive too far. It also produces an indentation as it drives the screw, so the head rests in a neat dimple that is easy to fill with joint compound. There is one caveat: you must drive the screws straight into the drywall, not at an angle.

>> >> >>

A drywall bit like this dimples the wall and prevents you from driving too deep, so it's easy to achieve perfect results.

Aim to drive screws **straight into the drywall, so the screw heads will not protrude.**

A well-driven drywall screw is slightly indented but does not tear the paper.

HANGING DRYWALL (CONTINUED)

Marking to hit studs and joists

Few things in life are more heartbreaking than when you muscle up a sheet of drywall, struggle to get it correctly aligned, drive a screw—and miss the joist or stud. Not only does it mean extra work hanging, but later you'll have to tape and smooth out the places where you misdrove the screws.

Avoid this fate by clearly marking the positions of framing members. Before installing a sheet on the ceiling, measure and mark the sheet for the centers of the joists. It's actually worth the trouble to use a drywall square to draw lines across the sheets. Before installing the upper wall sheets, mark the ceiling drywall with the positions of studs. And before installing the lower wall sheets, mark stud positions on the floor.

Fastening methods

For drywall to be firmly attached, these spacings are recommended: On joists or studs in the middle of the sheet and at inside corners, drive at least one screw every 12 in. At butt joints, drive at least one screw every 6 in. If you apply construction adhesive to the joists, you can use fewer fasteners.

Installing around openings

At a large opening, it is common practice to attach sheets that hang over the opening. Then use a drywall saw or a small router equipped with a cutting tool to cut out the pieces using the framing as a guide for the cutting tool.

At tricky spots like this, you will need to improvise and perhaps use small pieces. Use construction adhesive where you cannot drive screws.

At a doorway or other opening, pros often attach drywall so it overhangs the opening. Then they use a router with a cutting bit to cut around the opening.

FINISHING DRYWALL

With all the drywall fastened to walls and ceilings, install any outside corner bead and then get ready for "taping." This step is a bit of a misnomer because you will spend far more time applying and sanding joint compound than you will applying tape.

Installing outside corner beads

At outside corners, apply corner bead to create a straight and strong corner. Several types are available, including plastic and types with rounded-over edges, but the most common corner bead is the metal type shown here. Cut the bead to length with a pair of tin snips ❶. It need not reach all the way down to the floor, but should butt up against the ceiling. Press the bead with medium pressure—not too hard—in place and centered, so that the bead will be a bit proud of the wall on each side, and drive fasteners ❷. You can use drywall screws, but be careful to keep their heads from sticking out too far; finish-head screws are a bit better. A power stapler is the ideal tool. Run a taping knife along the bead as shown, to be sure nothing protrudes and you can fill the void with joint compound ❸. You may need to remove a screw and drive it in a different place. Or, if the corner bead's flange is protruding, you will need to remove the bead and try again.

>> >> >>

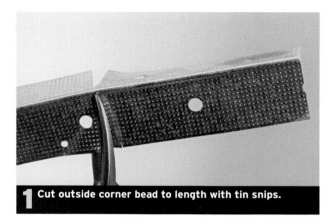

1 Cut outside corner bead to length with tin snips.

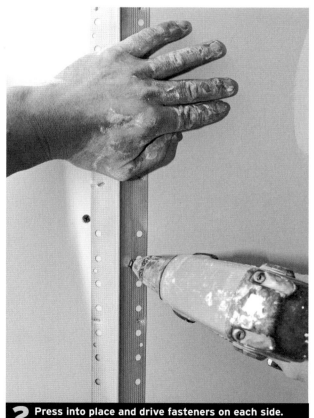

2 Press into place and drive fasteners on each side.

3 Test that nothing will stick out when you fill with joint compound.

FINISHING DRYWALL (CONTINUED)

TAPE TYPES

Here are three of the most common types of drywall tape. From the bottom: **Fiberglass mesh tape** is ideal for flat joints, because it is self-sticking, easy to apply, and very thin. **Standard paper tape** is typically used at inside corners, because it can be folded to help define an inside corner. **Rigid paper tape** (known by the brand name Strait-Flex®) works even better to create a crisp, straight inside corner line and is worth the extra cost. (The ovate holes along each edge hold plenty of joint compound and so help keep it from sliding out of alignment.)

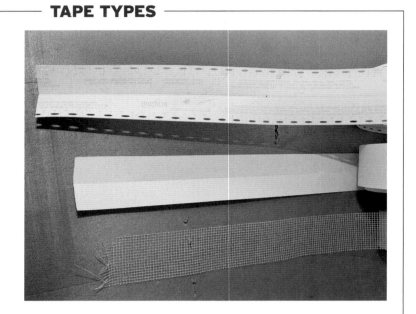

Mixing and transporting joint compound

If you use setting-type joint compound, pour an inch or so of water into a very clean bucket, then add the dry powder. (Take care not to mix more than you can use in the allotted time.) Mix a small amount using a margin trowel, but for larger amounts use a mixing paddle attached to a drill ❶. If you are using ready-mix compound, it's a good idea to scoop out a few inches of compound into another container, then add a cup or so of water and mix. This will produce a creamier compound that is easier to work with. Once you have made a smooth mix with no lumps, scoop the compound into a mud pan (a.k.a. joint compound tray) ❷. Cover the bucket to keep from getting crumbs in it.

1 Whether mixing setting-type powder or adding water to ready-mix, use a mixing paddle attached to a drill to stir the compound until it is smooth and creamy.

2 A mud pan makes it convenient to transport and apply joint compound.

Taping flat joints and screw holes

It is common to use fiberglass mesh tape at flat joints. Cut the mesh with a knife and press it into the joints; it will stick by itself **❶**. Keep the tape smooth, with no folds or bubbles. To tape across a tapered joint, first use a 6-in. or 8-in. taping knife to apply an ample amount of compound to the joint **❷**. Then hold a 12-in.

>> >> >>

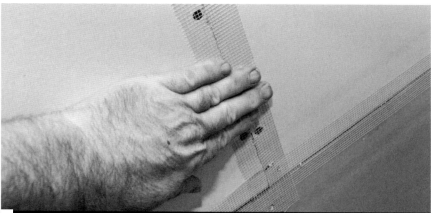

❶ Apply self-sticking fiberglass mesh to tapered and butt joints.

❷ Fill a tapered joint with a good amount of compound.

JOINT COMPOUNDS

Setting-type joint compound comes in bags of powder that you mix with water. These are often given the numbers 5, 20, 45, or 90; the numbers roughly refer to the number of minutes you can work with the compound until it starts to harden.

Standard setting-type compound is very strong and also very difficult to sand, so many installers use it for the first coat only.

"Easy-sand" setting-type joint compound mixes and dries in the same way, but is less strong and, of course, easier to sand.

Ready-mix compounds can be used right out of the bucket, though some installers prefer to mix with a bit of water first. They take a good deal longer to set and dry, and are easy to sand.

Topping compound is not strong and is also very easy to sand, and so is often used for the top coat only. It typically comes in a cream or other color, so you can more easily identify spots that need filling or sanding.

If you want to sponge rather than sand your joints in order to keep the dust down (this will result in less smooth walls, but not too bad), be aware that only ready-mix compound can be finished this way; moisture does not affect it, and it must be sanded smooth.

FINISHING DRYWALL (CONTINUED)

knife so it spans across both tapers and scrape to create a smooth joint ❸. Apply only medium pressure, so you don't bend the blade inward and make a concave surface.

At a butt joint, apply joint compound to each side of the tape ❹. Use an 8-in. blade to feather out on one side, then the other ❺. The tape should be at least mostly covered with compound. Don't worry too much about the middle, which you will fill in later.

To fill in screw holes, first spread compound across the area with a 6-in. knife ❻. Then scrape across it with the same knife to remove nearly all the compound from the surrounding area while filling in the hole ❼.

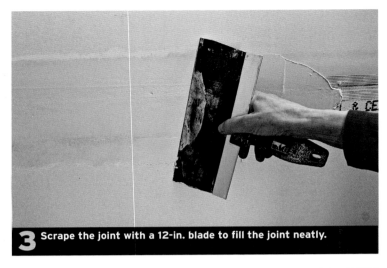

3 Scrape the joint with a 12-in. blade to fill the joint neatly.

4 Apply compound to both sides of a butt joint.

5 Feather out both sides of a butt joint.

6 Apply mud to screw holes.

7 Scrape away compound on the wall while filling in the hole.

Taping inside corners

Paper tape is not self-stick, so you must first apply joint compound, then set the tape in it. Apply a good amount of compound to both sides of the corner ❶. There should be no voids, so the paper sticks to the compound at all points. Cut the tape to length; it's OK if it over- laps another piece of tape on the wall. You can cut with a utility knife or tear it off neatly using a taping knife ❷. Fold the paper and run

>> >> >>

FILLING OUTSIDE CORNERS

The sides of an outside corner bead can consume quite a bit of compound. Spread plenty in there, then use a 12-in. blade to start making a smooth surface from the bead to the wall. It will likely take several passes before you fill in all the voids.

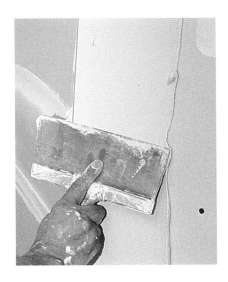

1 Make a bed of compound.

2 Cut paper tape to length.

FINISHING DRYWALL (CONTINUED)

your fingers along it to make a firm V shape ❸. Gently press the tape into the compound, working to make a straight line with no creases ❹. Carefully scrape each side with a knife to fully embed the tape ❺. Once the corner is nice and straight, apply another layer of compound to each side ❻.

Applying second and third coats

Pros typically apply a first coat, let it dry, then scrape or lightly sand, and then apply a second coat of the same compound and do the same. When the walls are very close to smooth and filled, the topping can be applied. However, a beginner will likely need to apply more coats. For each coat, scrape first and then sand only where needed. Work to feather edges, so they make a smooth transition to the drywall surface, and fill in voids.

>> >> >>

3 Crease the tape all along its length.

4 Gently press the tape and form a straight line.

5 Scrape with a knife to fully embed the tape.

6 Apply another coat of compound on top of the tape.

APPLYING TOPPING

Most professionals use topping that comes in a bag and is mixed with water, but you can also buy topping ready-mixed in a bucket. It is smoother and easier to sand than the other coats, and often of a different color so you can clearly see where it has been applied. Rent a topping applicator from a home center. Mix the topping and use a pump to fill the applicator. Press firmly as you apply the topping to the wall or ceiling, feathering edges and filling voids.

FINISHING DRYWALL (CONTINUED)

Sanding

Final sanding will produce a good deal of dust, so open windows and point fans outward, and tape doorways to other rooms. Use a pole sander for almost all the sanding; it is easier to use and works better than a handheld sander. Often sanding is done with a type of sandpaper that folds over the sander at the edges, but that can actually cause unwanted indentations at inside corners. Instead, use a sanding block that uses a simple straight piece of sandpaper that does not fold over ❶. Attach the sander to a pole and sand with long, sweeping strokes ❷. Use light pressure and work the sander in several directions. Avoid short, digging strokes. At tricky or hard-to-reach places, use a foam sanding block ❸. In very tight places, you may need to scrape the wall smooth ❹. As a final test of smoothness, don't trust your eyes alone. Run your hand across the surface to see if you detect any bumps or voids ❺.

1 This type of sanding block, with paper that does not fold over, works best.

FINAL FINAL

Even the pros end up with imperfections that they don't notice until after painting. To achieve perfection, draw circles around these areas, straighten them out with topping and sanding, and reapply primer and paint.

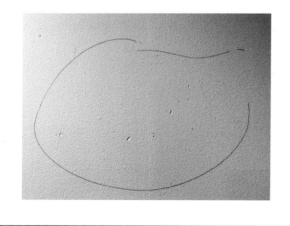

2 Sand with gentle, long strokes.

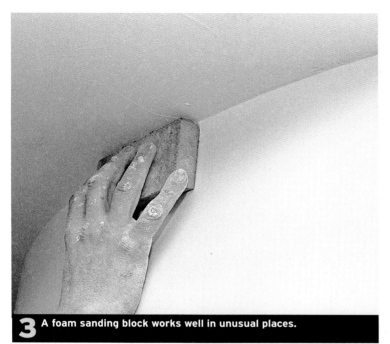

3 A foam sanding block works well in unusual places.

4 Where you don't sand, scrape.

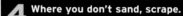

5 Make a final test by feel.

FLOORING

YOU CAN INSTALL ANY TYPE OF flooring in a basement, but if flooding is a possibility, consider types that will not get damaged by prolonged contact with moisture.

Before any finish flooring can be installed, however, you'll need to prep the concrete floor. You may need to do some patching—how smooth the patches need to be depends on the type of flooring you will install. Also, install a subfloor that is appropriate for your basement situation and finished flooring. This may be as simple as a plastic sheet or two to act as a moisture barrier, or you may need to install something more substantial. Air-gap floor insulation is often a reliable option.

If you want the floor to be nice and warm, consider installing radiant heat when the concrete substrate is poured, as shown on pp. 56-57. Otherwise, installing rigid insulation and/or a plywood subfloor will at least make the floor less cold.

FLOORING OPTIONS

Common Types of Flooring, p. 182

REPAIRS

Patching and Repairing a Concrete Floor, p. 186

FLOOR SUBSTRATES

Installing a Subfloor, p. 188

FINISH FLOORING

Laying Out the Finished Floor p. 195

Laying Ceramic or Stone Tile, p. 197

Installing a Floating Floor, p. 203

Installing Carpeting, p. 208

Installing Carpet Tiles, p. 210

Acid Staining the Floor, p. 212

COMMON TYPES OF FLOORING

Hardwood strip flooring has a classy appearance and will last a lifetime.

For the most part, you can choose the same flooring for a basement that you would choose for any other living space in your home. This is not the case, of course, if your basement is wet or if you haven't taken steps to ensure water will not seep through the concrete walls or floor.

Here are some of the most common types of flooring. Before you make your choice, read the section in this chapter on installing it, to be sure it will be possible in your situation.

Economical vinyl flooring is a good option for a room that will see a lot of wear and tear.

Hardwood

Standard hardwood flooring is beautiful, can be stained to any color you like, and can be sanded and refinished several times over the years, so it typically lasts up to a century. However, installation is a bit of a pain. After attaching the strips, the entire floor must be sanded, a job best left to professionals. Then coats of stain and polyurethane finish must be applied. As a result, you typically cannot walk on it for a week or so. Because it is so difficult to install, we recommend you either hire a pro for a "real" hardwood floor or install engineered wood flooring.

Engineered wood flooring

One of the most popular types of flooring these days, engineered wood flooring has a hardwood veneer, often 1/4 in. thick, laminated onto a body of plywood. Strips may be 2 1/4 in. to 4 in. wide. As opposed to solid hardwood flooring, it is ready to use as soon as laid, because it does not need to be sanded and already has a polyurethane finish. (However, you may want to apply another coat of finish.) Disadvantages: It forms a surface that is not perfectly smooth (though it comes close), and it cannot be sanded and refinished after years of use.

Natural stone can provide a high-end look to your basement floor, with color and pattern choices ranging from subdued to dramatic.

"Luxury vinyl" strip flooring offers the look of hardwood without the cost or installation requirements.

Stain-resistant carpeting is a good choice in a basement. If the floor floods, it can be removed and replaced.

Vinyl

Many older styles of vinyl sheet flooring had garish designs, but many of today's sheets effectively mimic the look of hardwood flooring or ceramic or stone tile. They are easy to wipe clean and rarely need a new application of finish. And vinyl is inexpensive and quick to install. It's not a good choice if you expect heavy-duty scratching from playing children or dogs. But under a normal level of wear, it can last a very long time; and if you want to change it out, you can easily install a new sheet over it.

Vinyl also comes in strip form (often called "luxury vinyl") and is easily glued down. Like vinyl sheet flooring, it is relatively inexpensive, quick to install, and easy to keep clean. Many types are designed to give the appearance of a natural wood floor.

Acid stain

If your concrete floor is in pretty good shape and fairly uniform in appearance, you may choose to apply an acid stain, as shown on pp. 212-213.

Ceramic tile

Ceramic tiles come in a huge variety of colors and patterns. Glazed tiles have a shiny surface that resists staining and is easy to clean; quarry tile and other types are porous and need sealing. The grout you choose will affect the appearance of the floor as well. Porcelain tiles are especially strong and durable.

Stone tile

Natural stone is a beautiful choice, and there are many types. Granite tiles resist staining, but other types of stone tile—such as marble, travertine, agglomerated, and slate—need a solid coating of finish to make them easy to keep clean.

Carpet

High-quality stain-resistant carpeting can be an excellent choice in a basement. Carpet should be laid by professionals, who have special tools and can often get materials for a lower price than you can.

PATCHING AND REPAIRING A CONCRETE FLOOR

Before you can install your new floor, you'll need to examine your concrete basement floor to ensure it meets the finished floor's installation requirements. Any basement floor should be free of cracks and holes, and it should be level. If a concrete floor has a crack but the area is firm, you can repair it with epoxy injection as for a wall. But if the damage covers a fairly large area, chip it out and pour concrete, as shown. If your floor feels wobbly when you walk on it, call in a pro for evaluation; you may need to tear out and repour, regardless of what finished floor you're going to lay down. You can also fix a floor that's not level.

➡ See "Sealing Cracks with Epoxy Injection," pp. 36–37.

Chipping and filling a damaged area

To repair a damaged, raised, or otherwise unsuitable area for the flooring you want to install, you could use a masonry saw to cut an outline that is about 2 in. deep. Or, use a rented electric jackhammer to chip the area out, taking care not to dig too deep ❶. (Most basement floors are 4 in. to 6 in. deep, but in an older home it may be only 3 in. deep.) To keep the dust down, have a helper hold a vacuum hose near the chipping blade. Remove all material to a depth of at least 1½ in. below the surrounding surface. Vacuum the area and slightly dampen it. Mix batches of high-strength concrete and pour into the area ❷. Use a board that spans across the patch to roughly "screed the concrete": drag it across, then use a sawing motion to push the stones down ❸. Smooth the surface to suit your needs. Use a wood or magnesium float, then a steel trowel, to bring the liquid to the surface and to feather out the patch where it meets the surrounding floor ❹. The slower the concrete cures the stronger it will be, so cover with plastic or spray with a mist every 8 hours or so to slow down the curing.

1 Chip out the damaged area to a depth of at least 1½ in.

2 Mix and pour batches of high-strength concrete.

3 Roughly screed the patch with a 2x4.

4 Smooth the patch with a magnesium float, then a steel trowel.

Leveling with self-leveling compound

If an area of the floor dips down more than ¼ in., it will adversely affect most any kind of flooring. Check your floor by dragging an 8-ft. level or a long, perfectly straight board across it in two directions at all points ❶. Where you see a significant rise, just chip it away if you can; otherwise, follow the steps on the previous page for chipping and filling. Where you see a dip, fill it with "self-leveling compound."

This product does not quite live up to its name—you can't just pour it and walk away—but it is easy to level and feather out. Mix a batch according to directions, so it is pourable, and pour into the area ❷.

Smooth it with a trowel ❸. Take care to feather the edges as finely as possible. Avoid overworking the surface; more than a few strokes will bring too much fine material to the surface, weakening it. Check with a straightedge to make sure you are filling the indentation but not raising the patch above the floor surface ❹.

1 Use a long straightedge to check the floor for indentations.

2 Mix a soupy batch of self-leveling compound and pour into the area.

3 Smooth with a trowel.

4 Check that the new patch is level with the surrounding surface.

INSTALLING A SUBFLOOR

The type of subfloor you choose depends on moisture conditions and the flooring you will install. Once you have the moisture issue figured out, prepare a subsurface suited to your flooring material.

- If you will install carpeting or carpet tile, the subsurface need not be very smooth or very firm. You may need only to patch large cracks or holes in concrete, or you can install onto a plywood subsurface. Small imperfections will not show through noticeably.

- If you want to install resilient flooring like sheet goods or vinyl tiles, the subsurface must be very smooth, but it need not be extremely firm. Use the existing concrete floor only if it is very smooth; the material will telegraph every dip and bump. It can be very difficult to patch a damaged concrete surface to this level of evenness, so you may need to apply a layer of concrete backerboard (pp. 189–190) or a plywood subfloor (pp. 192–194).

- For ceramic or stone tile, the subsurface does not need to be very smooth, but it must be very firm. The thinset mortar that you set the tiles in will fill imperfections, but if the surface on which the tiles are set flexes at all, the tiles or grout joints could crack. Usually, these tiles are set onto the concrete surface or onto a layer of concrete backerboard applied directly to the concrete. If you need to install a new subsurface that is insulated because the concrete gets moist, then you will need to install first a sheet of air-gap underlayment, then a layer of ³/₄-in. plywood, and then top it with a layer of ¹/₂-in. concrete backerboard.

Removing and cutting trim

Butting new flooring up against existing wall trim will certainly lead to a sloppy-looking result. Before you install any substrate and finish floor material, clear the walls of base trim and other obstacles.

If your baseboard has a base shoe at the bottom, you could just remove that and replace it after the floor is installed. However, that

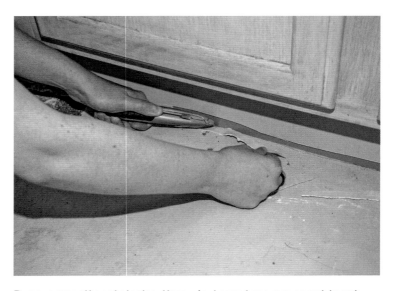

Remove any other obstacles. Here, vinyl cove base curves out to get in the way. The bottom portion is being cut away; new molding will cover the rest of the base cove.

Cut the bottom of door casings so that the substrate and the finish flooring can slip underneath. Here, for example, the height guide is made with a sheet of backerboard, thin shims to represent the thickness of the mortar in which the tiles will be installed, and a tile. Cut with a special saw made for the purpose, or as shown here, with a Japanese pull saw.

Don't Feed the Mold To grow, mold needs not only moisture but also anything organic. It's not picky, and will thrive on things like glue, wood, and drywall paper (as well as soap residue left on the surface of grout). So if your concrete is certain to get moist on a regular basis, avoid applying anything that mold likes to munch on. That includes mastic adhesive (often called "organic mastic"). Concrete backerboard is free of organic mastic, as is thinset mortar.

could make the baseboard look a good deal narrower, depending on your installation. If you will reuse the existing baseboard, use two taping knives and a flat pry bar to keep from damaging the trim. If the trim doesn't look great, it will look out of place next to your new floor, so plan to replace it with new trim.

Applying concrete backerboard

Applying concrete backerboard to a basement floor smooths out imperfections and helps consolidate the floor; it also offers a certain amount of protection against moisture infiltration. It's a good first step if you will install resilient flooring, and it is often done in preparation for ceramic or stone tile as well. Simply applying directly onto the concrete means you will raise the height of the floor ½ in., which may be a consideration if your ceilings are low.

Plan the layout. Chisel away any protrusions and sweep the floor thoroughly. Measure the room's width and length, and plan for an installation that avoids any strips of backerboard narrower than 6 in. or so. If the room includes cabinetry, measure to avoid narrow strips there as well ❶.

Mix a batch of thinset mortar (p. 198). Use a notched trowel to apply an even coat to the floor ❷. You can take this opportunity to fill in small holes. Use long, sweeping strokes to form an even surface. Lower the first sheet into the adhesive ❸. If the wall it snugs up against is less than straight, you may need to adjust its position slightly so its outer edge forms a straight line. Position two or more sheets in the thinset, check for alignment and nudge them into position if needed, and then drive screws.

>> >> >>

Measure to avoid ending up with narrow strips along walls and along cabinetry.

WHICH SIDE UP?

With this type of backerboard, apply with the rough side up for thinset mortar and ceramic tiles; apply with the smooth side up if you will install thin resilient tiles or sheet goods.

2 Spread thinset mortar with a notched trowel.

3 Set backerboard sheets in the thinset.

INSTALLING A SUBFLOOR (CONTINUED)

4 Drill pilot holes. Keep a glass of water handy to help keep the drill bit cool.

5 Drive masonry screws so their heads are slightly below flush with the backerboard.

The thinset will provide most of the holding power, but you need to drive screws to ensure the sheets lie flat. Using a masonry bit sized to match the masonry screws you will use, drill a series of holes spaced 16 in. apart or so **4**. Drill additional holes where the sheet needs to be held down. The holes should be about ¼ in. deeper than the length of the masonry screws you will drive; wrap a piece of tape around the bit to use as a depth guide. Periodically dip the bit in water to keep it from overheating. If the bit starts to smoke, take a break to let it cool down. Drive masonry screws into the holes so their heads are slightly below flush with the surrounding surface **5**.

Wherever possible, position a sheet against an obstruction to mark for cutting. Elsewhere, use a tape measure. Here, a straightedge is used to mark for a notch cut **6**. As much as possible, avoid small pieces, which can make the surface less than even.

WHAT CAN GO WRONG
Don't try to make backerboard fit tightly. Make your cuts about ¼ in. short, so the pieces will fit easily.

6 Wherever possible, position pieces to mark for cutting, rather than using a tape measure.

7 To cut backerboard, first slice through the mesh on one side.

8 Then snap the piece back and slice through the mesh on the other side.

To cut backerboard, you will need to slice deep enough to cut through the embedded mesh **7**. Then bend the piece back and finally cut through the mesh on the other side. Make at least some of the cuts with the sheet lying on the floor, so you can press hard. On a cutout like the one at left, you will need to cut with several passes on the short side until you slice all the way through; then cut along the long side. After bending the cutout back, slice through the mesh on the other side **8** or cut from the front.

>> >> >>

TRADE SECRET

If you have a lot of backerboard to cut, consider buying a special backerboard cutting knife, which cuts deeply with ease. However, if you have a dozen or fewer sheets to cut, a knife works fine. This work dulls blades quickly, so replace the blade often.

GAPS THAT CAN BE FILLED WITH MORTAR

In small areas where a subfloor slopes up or has other problems, it is often best not to cover with backerboard; this area can be filled with mortar, either now or when you set the tiles.

INSTALLING A SUBFLOOR (CONTINUED)

Installing plywood or OSB subfloors

In order to install nailed down tongue-and-groove strip flooring, sheet goods, or resilient tiles, it is often best to install a plywood (or OSB) subfloor. It is possible to simply attach plywood (preferably pressure-treated) directly to the floor, but that invites moisture damage, and attaching to concrete is a difficult undertaking. It's better to install a subfloor along with an air-gap underlayment. This can be done by first laying out the membrane and setting plywood on top, or by purchasing 2-ft.-square OSB tiles that have a similar membrane affixed to their undersides.

Air-gap underlayment

This type of dimpled underlayment comes in large rolls that cover over 150 sq. ft. The type shown here has a top layer of foam; other types are hard plastic on both sides. It is roughly $5/8$ in. thick and has insulating properties. Buy the special tape meant for the rolls. To install, roll out the sheets and place them side by side. Make any cuts with a utility knife. Cutting does not need to be precise; within $1/2$ in. of the wall is close enough ❶. Fasten sheets together first with 12-in.-long pieces of tape across the seam every 24 in. ❷. The sheets may not lie flat at first. Push gently with your knees as you apply tape along the seam to seal the sheets together ❸. Be sure to press the tape firmly, so it forms a moisture-tight seal; otherwise, vapor could damage the plywood underlayment you will put on top. To further encourage the underlayment to lie flat, slide

Air-gap underlayment comes in large rolls.

a fairly heavy board along the surface ❹. Engineered hardwood, laminate, or other floating-type floors can be installed directly on top of this product. If you want to install flooring that gets nailed down, install an OSB or double-plywood subfloor first for a nail surface. >> >> >>

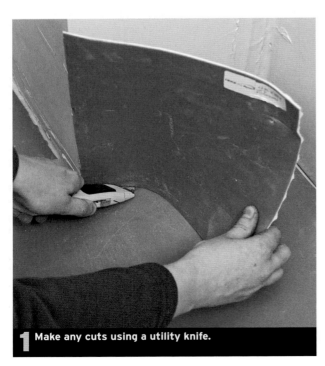

1 Make any cuts using a utility knife.

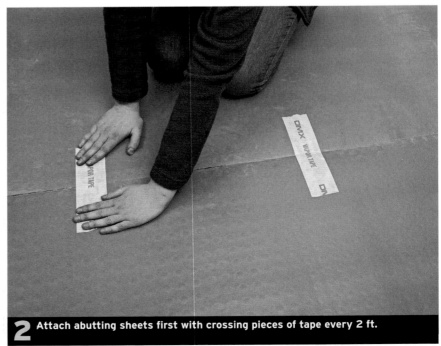

2 Attach abutting sheets first with crossing pieces of tape every 2 ft.

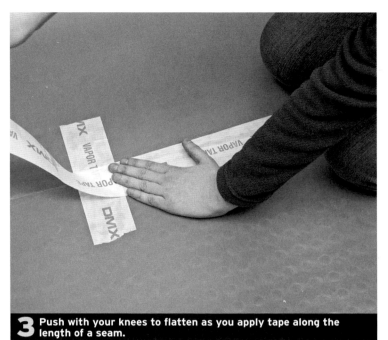

3 Push with your knees to flatten as you apply tape along the length of a seam.

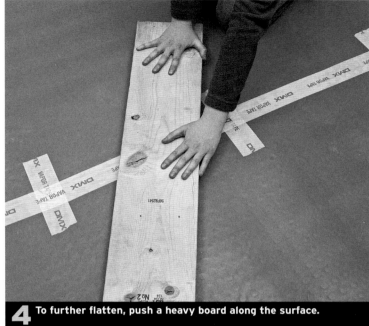

4 To further flatten, push a heavy board along the surface.

"Floating" floors can be installed directly on top of the underlayment.

OSB ON TOP OF AIR-GAP UNDERLAYMENT

To install OSB or plywood underlayment on top of the air-gap underlayment, cut 3/4-in. sheets so their seams are offset by at least 2 in. The sheets should basically lie flat, but you will need to drive occasional screws at places where the sheets rise up. Drill masonry holes using a bit of the right size for your screws, then drive screws long enough to penetrate the concrete by at least 1 1/2 in.

INSTALLING A SUBFLOOR (CONTINUED)

Position two layers of plywood with offset seams.

Drive occasional short screws to keep the sheets from separating.

Doubled plywood

If you will drive staples or nails to attach flooring, $3/4$ in. of nailing thickness may not be enough—and you don't want your staples to penetrate the subflooring. First lay air-gap underlayment. (Here we show a black version.) Lay one layer of $1/2$-in. plywood on top of the underlayment with joints offset. Then lay another layer of $1/2$-in. plywood with joints offset from each other and from the layer below. You will need to drive occasional $3/4$-in.-long screws to keep the sheets from rising up here and there.

INTERLOCKING UNDERLAYMENT PANELS

An alternative to the rolled underlayment sheets is to install tongue-and-groove underlayment panels that have a layer of air-gap underlayment laminated to their undersides. Attach together by slipping tongues into grooves and cut using a circular saw.

PLASTIC SHEETING

If you are confident that your floor will only occasionally have minor moisture, here's a minimalist approach that has worked for many people over the years: Simply apply a double layer of 5-mil or thicker plastic sheeting to the floor. If you snap clear layout lines on the concrete, you can see them through the plastic.

LAYING OUT THE FINISHED FLOOR

Before you start installing your finish flooring, measure and plan the job. Careful planning is especially important for ceramic, stone, or vinyl tiles, but it is a good exercise for other types of flooring, too. Plan with these considerations:

- Avoid ending up with thin slivers of tile or strips, which look sloppy.

- If both sides of a room will be visible, plan so that the tiles on each side are close to the same width, for a symmetrical appearance.

- If one wall is not parallel with a nearby wall, or if the walls are significantly out of square with each other, you will end up with a row of flooring that grows progressively narrower along its length. Make this row as wide as possible, so the imperfections will be less noticeable.

- Sometimes you can't avoid having a row of narrow or sloping tiles or strips. In that case, try to position them where they will be covered with a couch or other large piece of furniture.

Often you need to make layout compromises. In the basement shown below (bottom left), for example, it would be ideal to have tiles or strips of equal width at each of the walls, for symmetry. But if that leads to a very narrow row against the cabinet, you may need to adjust the layout. Starting with full-size tiles at the left will lead to 5-in.-wide tiles against the cabinet and 7-in.-wide tiles against the right wall—perfectly acceptable. But you may want to cut off 2 in. or so from the left-side tiles for an even better look.

Layout stick

With ceramic or stone tiles that have grout joints, it can be a bit confusing to get the measurements right. So make a layout stick: Lay a row of tiles on the floor, separated by the spacers you will use. Set a board next to the tiles and make a mark in the center of each grout line. This layout stick will help you visualize how the tiles will be arranged when you lay them.

>> >> >>

This floor **presents what would be serious layout challenges—a good number of places where you could end up with narrow slivers— if you are installing square tiles. Strip flooring reduces the challenges, because narrow strips are not unsightly.**

Measure and plan **so the tiles abutting both walls and cabinetry will be of a pleasingly substantial width.**

To make a layout stick, **set the tiles on the floor with spacers and mark the centers of the joints.**

LAYING OUT THE FINISHED FLOOR (CONTINUED)

Marking layout lines at a right angle

If you will install tiles, you'll need to start with layout lines at a perfect 90° angle. Use the 3-4-5 method. Start by snapping a chalkline (or drawing a pencil line using a long straightedge) that is two or three tiles away from a wall **❶**. Make sure you will be able to kneel on one side of the line and install tiles up to the wall. Make a short mark on the chalkline indicating where you want a tile to end in the other direction. Measure 3 ft. along the chalkline and make another short mark. Mark a line 4 ft. away from the chalkline, estimating to be at a right angle to the first short mark **❷**. Then measure carefully and mark the place that crosses the third line precisely 5 ft. away from the second line. Chalk a line between the first mark and the intersection of the last two marks. The two chalklines will be exactly square to each other **❸**.

1 Chalk a line indicating where one row of tiles will go, and also mark where you want a tile to end.

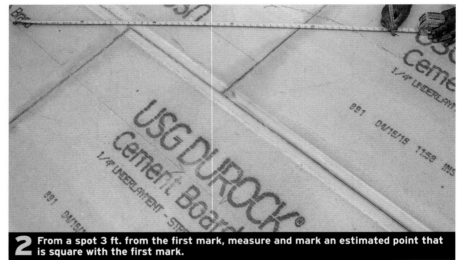

2 From a spot 3 ft. from the first mark, measure and mark an estimated point that is square with the first mark.

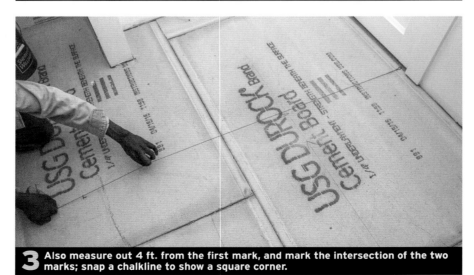

3 Also measure out 4 ft. from the first mark, and mark the intersection of the two marks; snap a chalkline to show a square corner.

LAYING CERAMIC OR STONE TILE

Be sure to choose tiles made for flooring; wall tiles will almost certainly crack. Choose your cutting method: Ceramic and porcelain tiles can be straight-cut using a snap cutter; for cutouts, you will need a grinder (or a circular saw) equipped with a masonry or diamond blade, or a wet tile saw. Natural stone tile should be cut with a wet tile saw, which you can rent.

The surface you are tiling over must be very firm: When a large adult jumps on it, you should feel no flex. This is usually not a problem with a concrete basement floor, but if the subfloor is plywood, it should be firmed up with a layer of concrete backerboard. Set the tiles in polymer- or latex-reinforced thinset mortar.

You can use standard sanded grout to fill the joints. In the example shown on pp. 198–200, I used epoxy grout, which is a bit more difficult to install (you'll need to wipe it more often and more thoroughly), but it forms a stain- and mold-resistant surface that is easier to clean. Buy plastic tile spacers that produce the grout width you desire. I used $3/16$-in. spacers, a common choice.

Sweep or vacuum the subfloor thoroughly. If it is dusty, give it a quick damp mop to ensure that the mortar will stick to it.

>> >> >>

Although some maintenance is required, ceramic tiles make a durable, beautiful floor.

USE THE RIGHT TOOLS AND MATERIALS

The right tools and materials are key. Ask your tile dealer which notched trowel is best to use. For most tiles, $1/4$-in.-deep notches work best; for thicker tiles, use a trowel with $3/8$-in.-deep notches.

Fortified or reinforced mortar gets mixed with water only. If the mortar is not fortified, manufacturer's directions may tell you to mix with latex liquid. If you mix this type of mortar with water only, it will not be strong enough and tiles will come loose.

LAYING CERAMIC OR STONE TILE (CONTINUED)

Fasten a temporary straightedge to guide your first row of tiles.

2 Mix a batch of reinforced thinset mortar.

3 With the flat side of the trowel, push and spread the thinset.

KEEP THINGS CLEAN

Work clean; squeezed-up mortar is easier to remove before it dries. You may need to regularly wash your hands and your tools.

then spread with the smooth side of the notched trowel ❸. (Many installers skip this step, but it ensures that the mortar sticks to the floor.) Then comb the surface with the notched side of the trowel. Use long, sweeping strokes, aiming at an even surface with no large blobs ❹. The trowel should graze the subfloor only gently if at all. Take care not to cover any layout lines.

Lower the tiles into position. Avoid sliding them more than a half inch or so ❺. After several tiles are set, insert plastic spacers to produce straight grout joints. In the center of four tiles lay the spacer flat, so it spaces all four tiles. Where only two tiles meet, set the spacer on end ❻. Once you install adjoining tiles, you will pull out and lay most of these spacers flat as well. Once in a while pick up a tile and look at its back, to be sure

It's important to start nice and straight. Temporarily attach a long straightedge to the floor, aligned with your layout mark. Here we use the factory edge of a sheet of drywall, but you can use plywood as well ❶.

Pour a couple of inches or so of water into a 5-gal. bucket. Add powdered polymer-reinforced thinset mortar. Using a drill with a mixing paddle, start with short bursts, then

run the drill steadily to produce a smooth mix ❷. You will need to add water or powder as you go. The final mix should be the consistency of mayonnaise—plenty wet, but firm enough so ridges produced by a notched trowel (next step) hold their shape.

Work in small sections at a time; you should be able to finish a section in 10 minutes. Drop dollops of mortar onto the area, it is resting in thinset over at least 75% of the surface ❼. If not, you may need to press the tiles or lay mortar with greater thickness.

Run a short straightedge, like the board shown, over the surface to check for any high or low tiles. These can often be leveled out by laying a board on tiles and tapping with a hammer ❽. In some cases, you may need to pick up a tile and either add or scrape away some mortar, then reset the tile.

After a number of rows, the tile lines may start to get a little wavy, especially along a line that will be highly visible. Press a straightedge against the line to fine-tune the positions ❾.

>> >> >>

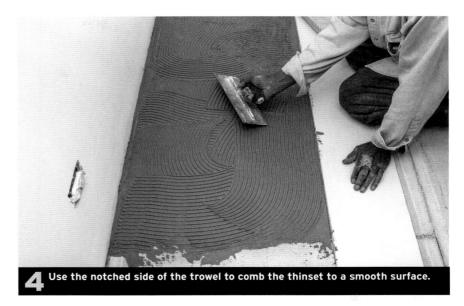

4 Use the notched side of the trowel to comb the thinset to a smooth surface.

5 Lower tiles onto the thinset so you don't need to slide them very much.

6 Slip in plastic spacers to maintain consistent and straight grout lines.

7 Periodically check the back sides to be sure tiles bed in the mortar.

8 Use a flat board to check that the surface is even, and tap where needed.

9 Every six or seven rows, align tiles with a straightedge.

LAYING CERAMIC OR STONE TILE (CONTINUED)

10 Mix a batch of epoxy grout according to the manufacturer's directions.

11 Hold the grout float flat and press grout into the joints.

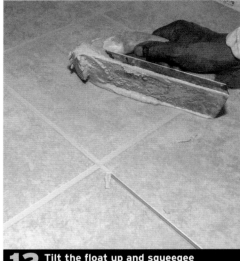

12 Tilt the float up and squeegee away most of the excess grout.

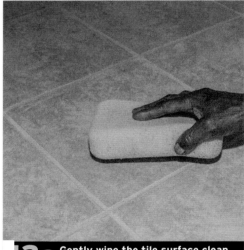

13a Gently wipe the tile surface clean of grout . . .

13b . . . and rinse the sponge often.

14 Use the sponge to form grout lines that are consistent in depth.

Allow the mortar to dry for at least a day. Probe gently with a screwdriver to see that the mortar is dry. Mix a batch of sanded grout according to the package directions. Here we mix epoxy grout, which has an epoxy additive **10**.

Drop dollops of grout onto the floor. Use a laminated grout float to first press the grout into the joints **11**. Press firmly with the float held nearly flat, and sweep the float in at least two directions at all points, to be sure

there will be no voids. Then tilt the float up and use it like a squeegee to scrape away most of the excess grout **12**. Always scrape at an angle to the grout lines, or the float will dig into the joints.

Fill a bucket with clean water. After you have grouted for 15 minutes or so, start wiping with a large damp sponge. Press gently and use long, sweeping strokes. You will need to turn the sponge over, then rinse repeatedly **13**. Clean several times. When

the water gets dirty, replace it with clean water. As you clean the tiles, also use the sponge to create consistent grout joints **14**. This is sometimes best with the sponge bunched up. When grout dries on the tile surface and produces a haze, wipe it gently away with a damp sponge. The next day there will still be some haze. Buff it with a dry or slightly dampened towel.

>> >> >>

CUTTING TILE

To make straight cuts on ceramic or porcelain tile, position the tile against the fence of a snap cutter ❶ so the cutting wheel aligns with the cut mark. Lower the wheel onto the tile and press down with medium pressure as you slide the cutter to score a line all along the length of the tile. Lift up on the handle, then press down to snap the cut. To make a number of same-size cuts, position and tighten the tool's guide. If you have an angled cut to make, position the tile so the cut marks are both over the center strip, and score a line in the same way ❷. You may need to use a nibbling tool to complete the cut.

A nibbling tool, also called tile nippers, can often be used to make rough cutouts or small cuts—which may be accurate enough if they will be covered with wall trim ❸. If you need to cut a narrow sliver, first score a line with a snap cutter, then use a nibbling tool to complete the cut ❹.

A wet saw makes neat cuts and is the best tool to use when cutting stone tile. You can also make occasional cuts using a grinder with a diamond or masonry cutting blade ❺. This produces clouds of dust, so do it outdoors.

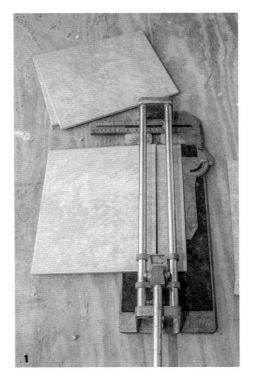

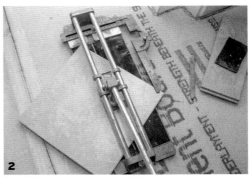

Scrape before Grouting
Before you start grouting, wash the tiled surface clean of any mortar smears. Check the joints to see if mortar has squeezed up near the tile surface. If so, scrape it away with a screwdriver. Otherwise, the mortar will show through the grout.

A FAN CAN HELP

On a basement floor, and especially if the room is humid, it may take more than a day for the mortar to dry before you can apply grout. To speed up drying, direct a fan to gently move air around the room.

LAYING CERAMIC OR STONE TILE (CONTINUED)

MOSAIC TILES

Mosaic tiles come on sheets of individual tiles attached to a mesh backing. You can cut out whole tiles easily, by slicing through the backing ❶. To cut through individual tiles, use a wet saw. Or, for ceramic tiles (but not stone tiles), score cut lines with a snap cutter ❷ and finish the cuts using a nibbling tool ❸. When you wipe up the grout, don't try to tool individual grout lines; just wipe gently and repeatedly with a damp sponge.

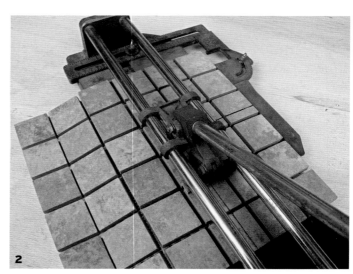

INSTALLING A FLOATING FLOOR

Many types of tongue-and-groove flooring are designed to "float," meaning they are not nailed to a subsurface. Planks or strips fasten together via tongues and grooves on all four sides. Some of these "click" together to automatically join as designed when you lift one plank, slide into the next, and snap down. However, click-type flooring, while pretty much idiotproof, does not form as tight a seal as when you carefully install flooring that slides together. That's the type shown here.

These techniques apply to all sorts of floating products, including cork, laminate, and engineered flooring.

The product on this page has a cork surface and is made by the WE Cork Company. It comes prefinished, and the joints, if installed correctly, are tight enough that there is no need to apply a finish after installation. Cork is a surprisingly durable product that also offers a comfy bit of "give" when you walk on it.

These are large planks, each covering about 2 sq. ft., and most take less than a minute to install, so the entire installation can proceed very quickly. However, you must work carefully and methodically: Each and every plank must be installed tightly at both seams—you cannot go back later and tighten any loose spots.

This floating cork flooring has a layer of cork on both sides. The cork layer on the bottom has very good moisture-resistant properties.

Plastic sheet underlayment

For this installation on a very dry floor, two sheets of plastic form the underlayment. The plastic extends up onto the wall, where it will be covered later with base molding. For greater protection against moisture, install air-gap underlayment. One width of sheeting is rolled out, planks are installed on top, then the next sheeting width is taped when the first is nearly covered; this prevents wrinkles and bubbles that can occur if you try to cover the whole floor with plastic before installing the flooring.

→ See "Air-Gap Underlayment," pp. 192-193.

>> >> >>

When applying plastic sheet underlayment, lay one sheet then apply flooring until it's time to lay the next sheet.

TAP WITHOUT DAMAGING

The tongues and grooves of laminated flooring planks are easily damaged if you tap on them directly with a hammer. Instead, place a 3-in.-wide scrap of the flooring against the plank being tapped so it nestles neatly. Then place a scrap piece of lumber against the scrap and tap away.

INSTALLING A FLOATING FLOOR (CONTINUED)

Because the planks are wide, you can measure across the room and plan the layout. If starting with full-width planks on one side will result in a narrow sliver on the other side, rip-cut the planks for the first side so those on the other side can be at least 3 in. wide.

Install the planks with the tongues facing outward. The planks should be offset so their ends are staggered. Install a full-length plank for the first board of the first row, a $2/3$-length plank for the first board of the second row, and a $1/3$-length plank for the first plank of the third row. Install the first row $3/8$ in. away from the wall, to allow for expansion due to changes in humidity **1**.

To attach a plank to others, tip it up slightly and push its lengthwise groove into the tongue of the abutting plank **2**. Rest it on the floor and push into the lengthwise board **3**. Using scrap pieces against the plank, tap the plank until it seats firmly against the abutting one **4**. Check out the lengthwise joint, and if it is not perfectly tight, tap it as well **5**.

As shown here, you can cut planks with a jigsaw, which produces little sawdust and can often be used without getting up and down. Cuts rarely need to be perfectly straight, because they will get covered with base molding. You can also use a circular saw, a power miter saw, or a table saw. To cut at an angle, measure and mark both sides of the plank, draw a line between the two marks, and cut with the saw **6**.

>> >> >>

1 Install the first rows with staggered joints $3/8$ in. away from the wall.

2 Tip slightly as you insert a plank's groove into the abutting plank's tongue.

3 Press the plank down and slide it over to fit into the next piece lengthwise.

4 Using scrap pieces to keep from damaging the plank's end, tap it tight.

5 If the long joint is not perfectly tight, tap in that direction as well.

6a When meeting an angled wall, measure and mark for the length on both sides.

6b Draw a line to connect them, and cut.

NICE AND TIGHT

A high-quality product like this, when installed correctly, has joints that are barely visible. In this photo, three pieces intersect; you may have to squint to see the joint lines.

INSTALLING A FLOATING FLOOR (CONTINUED)

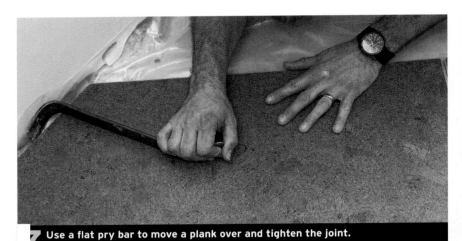

7 Use a flat pry bar to move a plank over and tighten the joint.

8 Where you meet the wall lengthwise, cut planks ³/₈ in. short of the wall.

9 Use a pulling tool and hammer to achieve a tight joint.

10 Near an end wall, use a pulling tool and press down on the other end.

Use a flat prybar to move the plank over and tighten the joint **7**.

When you reach the other wall widthwise, measure and cut planks to fit, again with a ³/₈-in. gap **8**. The gap will allow you to easily insert the cut piece. To pull for a tight fit, use a pulling tool and hammer **9**. If you don't have that tool, use a flat pry bar. When you near the other wall lengthwise, the pulling tool comes in handy, since you won't have room to swing a hammer. Use the pulling tool and hammer, and press down on the other end with your foot (or have a helper press down) as you tap into position **10**.

At a doorway, cut the stop molding (the small piece that the door butts against when it closes) and the casing molding so the flooring can slip under them. Carefully cut a notch so the piece will be snug against the jamb in both directions, and slide the plank in **11**. You may need to bend the plank so it can be inserted at the other end. Or, partially cut a tongue.

To cut around a curved obstacle, position the plank against the object, aligned with the other planks. Adjust a compass to the distance that the plank needs to move over **12**. (Since this gap will be not be covered with base molding, I allow for a gap of only ¹/₈ in.) Tighten the compass so it will not go out of adjustment as you work. Position it against the object, and keep the pencil at full distance from the object as you draw a curved cutline **13**. Cut with a jigsaw. Install the plank and check the fit; you may have to fine-tune it if it will be visible **14**.

11 At a doorway, undercut the stop and casing molding, and cut the plank to fit neatly around the jamb.

12 To cut around a pipe, position the board against the obstacle and adjust a compass for the depth of the cut.

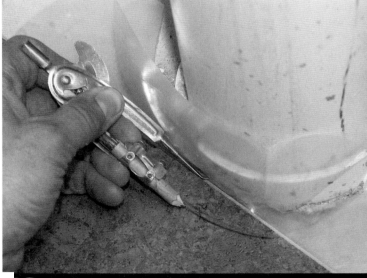

13 Keep the compass correctly adjusted as you mark for the cut.

14 Test the fit and make adjustments as needed.

INSTALLING CARPETING

Wall-to-wall carpeting may sound like an odd choice, but it's actually one of the most popular basement floorings. Padding is often installed on the concrete floor, which needs to be only reasonably–not perfectly–flat. It can also be installed onto a wood subfloor. Padding provides a small amount of insulation; combined with a fairly thick carpet, the resulting floor can be quite comfortable. Of course, this is a practical solution only if you trust your concrete floor to stay dry. If there is moisture, mold can develop in and under the padding. If there is a flood, you will need to pull up the carpet and padding–a messy job, but not nearly as difficult as removing other types of flooring.

Unless you have experience, you're better off hiring professionals to install carpeting. They have the tools and experience to do it far more quickly and neatly than you can.

Padding is rolled out and stapled or taped down. A good padding is important; some experts say that on a budget you should pay more for a good padding and scrimp on the carpeting.

Tack strips around the perimeter of the room will hold the carpeting in place. Tack strips are available for wood or concrete floors.

A super-long stretcher is one of the special tools pros use to make the carpet smooth and taut.

As a final step, a knee kicker is used to press the carpeting firmly onto the tack strips.

INSTALLING CARPET TILES

Carpet tiles have a slip-resistant backing, so you might be able to get away with just setting them in place, with no adhesive.

Carpet tiles are easy to apply and easy to pull up in case of flooding. You can install them all of the same color, or, as shown here, make a patterned floor using a number of different-colored tiles. If you do that, be sure to choose tiles that are all of the same thickness.

Choose tiles that have a non-slip backing. If your floor is dust-free, you can just lay them in place, with no adhesives. The floor certainly need not be perfectly smooth, but fill in any holes larger than 1/2 in., and scrape or chisel away protrusions that can telegraph through the carpeting ❶.

Arrange the tiles in a pattern of your choice ❷. Here, tiles of three different colors are used, and each color will march in a diagonal line. Set the tiles so they abut snugly, but not so tightly that they may bunch up. Walk on the surface to check the fit.

If the carpets slide a bit, you'll want to adhere at least some of them—perhaps just one edge of some of the tiles around the perimeter—to the floor with double-sided carpet tape, which has a paper backing on one side. Turn a tile upside down and press the nonpapered side onto the tile so that half its width overhangs the tile ❸. Turn the tile right side up and position it where it will go. Pull away the paper backing from underneath the tape ❹. Take care not to move the tile as you do this. Carefully lay an abutting tile onto the revealed tape ❺. Once you are sure of its position, press and slide your hands to firmly affix the tiles to the floor ❻.

To cut around a pipe, hold the tile in position and use a knife or tin snips to start making a cut at the center of the pipe ❼. Make the cut about 1/4 in. longer than the distance of the pipe. Press the tile into position and use a utility knife to cut around the pipe ❽. Hold the blade against the pipe as you cut. Press the carpet down around the pipe; it should fit snugly, but be loose enough not to raise up ❾. If it is too tight, shave off portions with a knife or snips.

1 Scrape or chip away any bumps and fill in any holes larger than 1/2 in.

4 Position the tile and remove the tape's paper backing.

7 Make a cut in the center of a carpet tile, extending it 1/4 in. past the pipe.

2 Arrange the tiles in a pattern if you like. Be sure seams fit snugly together.

3 To adhere with double-sided tape, press the sticky side onto the underside of a tile, allowing it to overhang.

5 Gently set the next tile in place.

6 Once you are sure of the fit, press the tiles down to fasten securely to the floor.

8 Position the tile and cut around the pipe with a utility knife.

9 See that the fit is just snug, and not too tight.

ACID STAINING THE FLOOR

This lightly mottled gray floor blends with the painted walls, letting the bar area take center stage.

If your concrete floor is reasonably consistent in color and texture—or if the inconsistencies are visually appealing—acid staining is a quick and easy way to achieve a surface that is both artistic and durable. Stains come in a wide variety of colors, and the effects you get are limitless, depending on how heavily and consistently you apply the stain. You can even use two or more colors if you like. If possible, experiment with staining—clean, apply a stain, and apply sealer—in an area that will not be visible to see the final look.

Start by cleaning the floor thoroughly. Scrape away any obvious raised spots and splotches with a flooring scraper ❶ and scrub with a degreasing cleaner or trisodium phosphate (TSP). Rinse thoroughly and let dry completely. Cover walls with plastic, because the stain will spatter ❷. Spray the acid stain onto the floor using a pump sprayer ❸. Aim for fairly even coverage. Use a mop or other tool to dab at or swirl the stain, to create the look you like ❹. Allow to dry completely, and perhaps apply a second color, with less complete coverage than the first color. Apply a coating of clear sealer for the final look ❺.

1 Scrape the floor so it is smooth and wash away stains.

2 Protect walls and other surfaces from stain spatter.

3 Spray acid onto the floor.

4 Dab or brush with a mop to create a pleasing pattern.

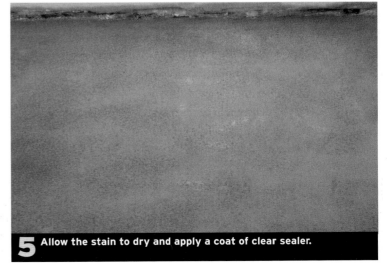

5 Allow the stain to dry and apply a coat of clear sealer.

WINDOWS, DOORS, AND TRIM

THIS CHAPTER IS ABOUT TRIM carpentry, which calls for good accurate tools, some patience, and attention to detail. We will cover the basics, but you will no doubt run into situations where you have to improvise solutions. You may be getting antsy to finish your basement at this point, but take a deep breath, collect tools and materials, and work carefully.

Trim carpentry can be done before you paint the walls and ceiling, especially if you will paint the trim as well. If you will install stained windows, doors, and trim, you are probably better off installing them after the walls are painted.

For more information and more trim possibilities, see Taunton's *Stanley Trim: A Homeowner's Guide* or a similar book.

INSTALLING A WINDOW

A window needs to be kept square while installing so it will slide smoothly. The frame into which it is installed should be 3/8 in. or so wider and taller than the window, which allows you to comfortably shim it while installing. Here we show installing new windows into existing openings (called replacement windows when you go to order them). If you want a new opening, it's probably best to hire a pro to cut your concrete or masonry wall.

Your concrete or masonry wall, plus the interior insulation, framing, and drywall, will add up to a very thick wall. Depending on light conditions and other factors, you may choose to position your window near the outside (so you end up with a wide sill), near the interior wall (so the sill is narrow), or somewhere in the middle. Note that the correct term here is really "stool," but most people think of it as a "sill."

Replacement windows are simple to install once the framing is done. When you remove an existing window, check the "buck"—the thick wood jamb (frame) that attaches to the masonry opening. Poke it with a screwdriver to see if there are rotten places. If there are only a few bad spots, you can chip away the rot and fill with two-part epoxy wood filler, which makes for a permanent fix. If the bottom piece is rotted, it will need replacing.

If most of the buck is in bad shape, install a new one. You can simply cut pieces of 2-by pressure-treated lumber or use treated decking, which is 1 in. thick. Check window availability first: If there is a standard size that will save you money, you may be able to use thicker or narrower lumber so it will fit. Some windows install using screws driven through the sides, and some have nailing flanges. If your window has flanges, be sure the buck is thick enough to accommodate them.

Or, remove a buck (if there is one) and attach the window directly to the masonry opening. Surround the window with rigid insulation, and squirt in foam adhesive after you've installed, to fill all the voids.

Measure to learn the thickness of the window buck pieces. Here, the window will rest on a piece of rigid insulation, for a bit less heat loss. Install to produce an opening that is square at the corners and about 3/8 in. narrower and shorter than the window.

This old buck (and its outside trim) was in basically good shape, but the bottom pieces had some rot and so were replaced.

Some windows have special clips that provide extra rigidity. They should be inserted so that you will drive the mounting screws through them.

When installing a window, check for square and plumb or level. Drive mounting screws into the wood buck. Or, if there is no buck, drill holes into the concrete or masonry, and drive masonry screws that penetrate at least 1 1/2 in.

INSTALLING AN EGRESS WINDOW

This egress window has a single large pane that opens on a hinge. Outside, there is both a ladder and a set of steep steps, for easy egress and access.

An egress window provides a place to exit a basement. If your basement has a bedroom, an egress window will likely be required by codes. The same is true if your basement does not have an exit door. Codes call for a large opening and a set of easy-to-negotiate steps, so that a person can escape easily from inside and rescue personnel with bulky equipment can also enter from the outside.

Many types of windows are acceptable, but check local codes carefully to be sure yours will be. In general, the opening—not the size of the entire window, but the size of the opening when a sash is lifted or slid to the side—must be at least 24 in. tall and 20 in. wide.

The outside egress well and its steps also must conform to codes. The size of the opening depends on how deep the hole is—the more steps, the larger the opening. >> >> >>

Here, a sash can be slid to the side to provide access to a set of steps. This unit has no cover, but has an ample drain that is covered with loose gravel, so rainwater does not remain in the opening.

INSTALLING AN EGRESS WINDOW (CONTINUED)

First, a large hole must be dug next to the house. Large machinery makes quick work of digging, but care must be taken not to damage the concrete wall or the footing. The excavating company must first check to make sure they do their work away from any water, gas, or electrical lines.

WATCH THE LOT AND SETBACK LINES

If the egress window will be near your side property line, check carefully to see that it will not cross into your neighbor's property or extend beyond the required setback line. If yours crosses a legal line, see if you can get a variance (which may be allowed for safety considerations), or if your neighbor will grant you an exception. If not, perhaps you can be permitted to install an egress window in the front or back. In a worst case, you may need to hire a contractor to excavate and install a new doorway in the back or front.

I recommend that you hire professionals for this job. They have the digging machinery, masonry cutting tools, and expertise to handle a job that is beyond the capabilities of a do-it-yourselfer. And pros can probably navigate the codes and deal with inspectors, so you won't get into trouble with your building department. The photos on the following pages show what you can expect a construction company to do.

An opening in the concrete wall is cut using a large wet-cutting masonry saw. As the cutting proceeds, the area above the opening—which in this case is brick rather than concrete—may need to be temporarily supported.

The finished opening is neatly cut and ready for the window. At the top, you can see that a metal lintel has been inserted to support the brick.

Drainage should be provided in the bottom of the hole, so rainwater will not collect. A preformed egress window well may be made of galvanized steel, heavy-duty fiberglass, or another product. It is attached to the side of the basement wall with a watertight seal.

Once the well is installed, the hole is backfilled with gravel. The top 4 in. or so also may be filled with gravel or with topsoil and sod.

The simplest of wells features a set of ladder-like steps.

A variety of easily removable covers is available to keep snow and rain out of the well. Most are simply removable and not hinged, since it is not expected that they will be used very often.

INSTALLING AN INTERIOR PREHUNG DOOR

Prehung doors cost a bit more than separately buying a slab door, the hinges, and jamb material, but they save plenty of time and aggravation, and produce clean lines and a perfect fit that you would have difficulty imitating.

Check across the doorway for level **❶**. If one end is more than ¼ in. higher than the other, cut its jamb shorter than the other, or the gap at the bottom of the door will be noticeably skewed. Measure for the jamb height on each side **❷**. If the uncut frame will fit, there is no need to cut it. If the door frame's lintel is out of level or if the door's top jamb is less than 2 in. shorter than the frame, that will not be a problem; It will be covered by casing molding.

Some folks install prehungs with the doors still attached, but I recommend removing the door for part of the installation. Tap out the hinge pins with a hammer; you may need to tap with a nail from below as shown, or just use a screwdriver to tap up the hinge pin's head. Put the hinge pins where you won't lose them **❸**. Carefully move the jamb assembly (two sides and a top) and support the raised side jamb so you can work on it. If your jamb assembly is inadequately fastened with staples, drill pilot holes and drive screws to reinforce the joints **❹**. Measure and mark a jamb side, draw a square line, and cut with a circular saw **❺**.

1 Check the floor for level, and cut the jamb sides accordingly.

2 Measure for the height of the jambs.

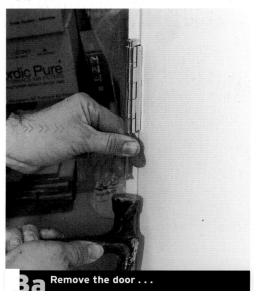

3a Remove the door . . .

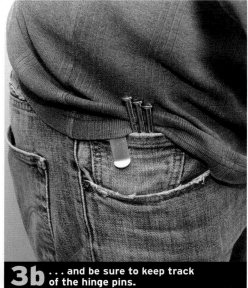

3b . . . and be sure to keep track of the hinge pins.

TRADE SECRET
If you have a low ceiling you may need to cut off more than ³⁄₄ in. from the bottom of doors. That will be difficult with hollow-core doors, because you will expose the hollow center and have to fill it in. Rather than going to that trouble, buy solid doors in this case, which cost a bit more but will save you serious hassles.

Also cut the other side, if needed. Set the jamb in the opening; make sure the hinges are on the correct side **6**. Check that the head (top) jamb is level **7**. If not, you could shim up one of the side jambs, as long as the flooring you will install will cover the gap at the floor; if not, cut the jamb on the high side.

Shim the hinge-side jamb so it is plumb and straight; check with a level as you work. To shim, push in a shim from each side **8**; if you shim from only one side, the jamb will be twisted. Install a pair of shims in the middle and one near the bottom, checking for plumb as you go. Check that the jamb edge is flush with the drywall surface and drive a pair of finish nails near—but not through—each pair of shims **9**.

Reinstall the door: Slip the hinge halves together, push in the pins, and tap them all the way down **10**. To make the hinge jamb strong, at each hinge remove one of the screws going into the jamb, and

>> >> >>

4 If your jamb is flimsy, reinforce it with screws.

5 Cut side jambs as needed.

6 Carry and insert the jamb assembly into the framed opening.

7 Check the head jamb for level.

8 Shim the hinge-side jamb with pairs of shims.

9 Drive pairs of finish nails near the shims.

INSTALLING AN INTERIOR PREHUNG DOOR (CONTINUED)

10 Reinstall the door.

11 At each hinge, remove a jamb screw and replace with a long screw.

12 Also shim the latch-side jamb.

13 Check for an even ⅛-in. gap all round, and install a pair of shims at the head jamb.

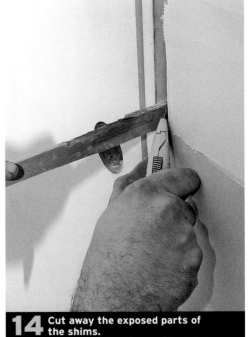

14 Cut away the exposed parts of the shims.

replace it with a long screw that penetrates the framing by at least 1½ in. **11**. Push in a pair of shims on the latch-side jamb near the hole for the handle, make sure the gap between door and jamb is ⅛ in. and that the jamb edge is flush with the drywall surface, and drive a finish nail to hold it in place **12**. Continue adding shims as needed to the latch-side jamb, working carefully to maintain a consistent ⅛-in. gap. Also add a pair of shims at the head jamb **13**. Finally, use a knife to cut away and break off the shims flush with the drywall and jamb **14**.

CHOOSING TRIM MATERIALS

You can cut with a hand miter saw, but a power miter saw (a.k.a. chopsaw) makes accurate, clean cuts with ease. Make some test cuts, and adjust the saw if it doesn't make perfect 90° and 45° cuts. If cuts show some splintering, change the blade. Set the saw on a table, and set things up so you can easily rest trim boards flat on the saw's base.

Wood trim, either painted or stained, is the finishing touch for your walls, windows, and doors. The following photos show the basics for installation; for more detailed instructions, as well as a wide variety of possible trim designs, see Taunton's *Stanley Trim*.

Things to consider when choosing trim materials:

- If you will paint your trim, be aware that priming and painting can take longer than installation. Consider buying primed trim, which needs only a quick coat of finish paint.

- Medium-density fiberboard (MDF) trim is an inexpensive option that resists denting. However, it will swell up if it gets even a little wet, so use it only where you expect things to stay dry.

- You may be tempted to buy faux-finished trim boards that are very lightweight; they are made of polystyrene. I do not recommend this product, because it is easily dented, and even minor imperfections cannot be filled in attractively.

- Unfinished softwood (usually pine) is a very common choice. It's easy to work with and can be either primed and painted, or stained. However, it is somewhat susceptible to denting, and if stained will not have the rich look of hardwood.

- Oak or other hardwood will set you back in the bucks department. With a power miter saw and a power nailer it is no more difficult to cut and install than the other types. It resists dents and is easily stained for a very handsome look.

➡ See "Trimming a Window on the Inside," pp. 226–229.

TRIMMING A DOOR

Once a door is installed, the gap between jamb and wall needs to be covered with casing. Installing casing is pretty much the same for doors as for windows. Here, I show installing plain casing with backband; for mitered casing and casing with plinth blocks, see the section on trimming a window.

The molding here is simple primed 1x4, rip-cut to a width of $2^7/8$ in. so it will look less massive ❶. You can also purchase "plain" casing. If you add backband as I do (steps 8 and 9), be sure it will match up with the casing's thickness.

Check the area around the door opening and scrape away any protrusions, so the casing can lie flat against the wall and jamb edge ❷. If the jamb edge protrudes a bit past the wall surface, plane or sand it flush.

Use a sliding square and pencil to draw a line all around the jamb edge showing the "reveal"—the portion of the jamb edge that will be exposed after the casing is installed ❸. Measure the height of the side casing pieces—from the floor to the reveal line on the head jamb. Cut the side pieces and install them along the reveal lines—or so they just barely cover the lines. Start at the bottom and drive pairs of nails every 16 in. or so as you go up ❹. You'll probably need to bend the casing slightly to keep it aligned with the line. If you are driving hand nails, use small brad nails to drive into the jamb and 6d nails for attaching to the wall framing. If you have a power nailer, 2-in. finish nails work fine for both, but angle the nails slightly back when driving into the jamb, so the nails don't poke through the face of the jamb.

Measure across the side casing pieces for the size of the head casing ❺. Hold the top casing in place; if it angles outward, you may need to slice the drywall paper around the outline and tap the wall in with a hammer and flat tool ❻.

>> >> >>

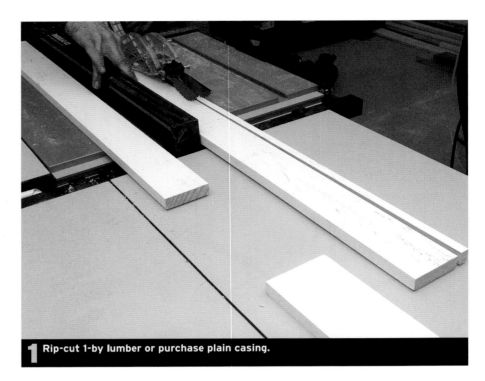

1 Rip-cut 1-by lumber or purchase plain casing.

5 Measure and cut the head casing.

2 Scrape away any protrusions on the wall or jamb.

3 Mark the reveal on the jamb edges.

4 Cut side casing to height and install with pairs of nails along the reveal line.

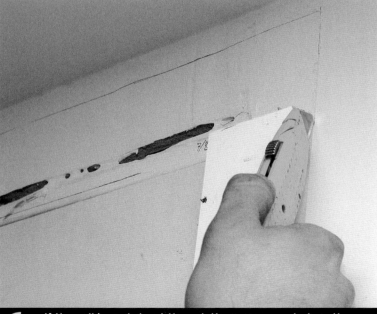

6a If the wall is angled, cut through the paper around where the casing will go . . .

6b . . . then tap the wall in.

TRIMMING A DOOR (CONTINUED)

Install the head casing with nails driven into the casing and the framing, and at an angle through the side casing **❼**.

Measure for cutting the backband, mark the inside where it will meet the corners of the plain casing, and cut at a 45° bevel **❽**. Hold the backband pieces so they form tight miter joints and drive small finish nails to attach to the plain casing **❾**.

7a Attach the head casing with nails driven into the jamb and framing . . .

7b . . . and through the side casing.

8 Mark the backband with the cutline where it will meet the corner and cut at a 45° bevel.

9 Attach the backband with small nails.

TRIMMING A WINDOW ON THE INSIDE

While casing for a window is much the same as for a door, the horizontal elements below the window are different. In most cases, you need to install a stool (often called a sill), jambs, and an apron as well.

If the window is set deep in the wall, you will end up with a stool that is also a deep shelf, which may be made of hardwood plywood, solid-surface countertop, or another material. The sequence here shows a window set about 5 in. back from the drywall.

Start with the stool. The board you use should be wide enough to extend in front of the drywall by at least ³/₄ in.; 1 in. or 1¹/₂ in. is common. First, figure the total length of the stool; this does not have to be precise, since it will run past the casing on each side by an inch or so. Position a scrap piece of the casing

1 Use a scrap piece of casing and a square to determine where the stool will end.

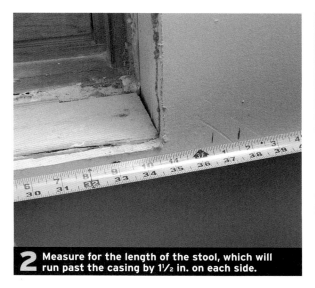

2 Measure for the length of the stool, which will run past the casing by 1½ in. on each side.

3 Mark for the width of the notch cuts.

you will install where it will end up: Take into account the thickness of the jamb as well as the reveals on the window frame and the jamb **1**. Look at the steps ahead to help visualize this. Then make a mark about 1½-in. past the casing. Do the same on the other side, and measure between the outside marks to find the stool's total length **2**.

Next, mark for cutting notches on each side of the stool. Use a square to mark for the width of the notch; allow yourself a gap of ¼ in. or so, where it will be covered by the jamb later **3**. To determine the depth of the notch, use a compass, as shown. If the depth is too deep, measure and mark with a tape measure and square. Find the depth and transfer that measurement to the stool **4**. Do the same on the other side and cut with a miter saw and/or a jigsaw **5**.

>> >> >>

4a Use a compass or another tool to measure the depth of the notch . . .

4a . . . and transfer the measurement to the stool.

5 Cut notches with a jigsaw.

TRIMMING A WINDOW (CONTINUED)

6 Install the stool so it is level and leaves the desired reveal on the window frame.

7 Install the apron.

8 Install jamb pieces to produce the desired reveal on the door frame.

Place the stool in the opening, shim as needed to keep it level and even with the window frame **6**, and drive finish nails. Cut a length of casing or other trim material for the apron and install it against the wall under the stool, checking the stool for level **7**. Cut side jambs to run from the stool to the reveal mark on the window frame and install with shims to keep them square. Install the head jamb as well **8**.

To install mitered casing, mark a reveal line on the jamb. Cut two scraps of casing at 45° miters and hold them in position against the jamb to test for a tight miter fit **9**. If the joint is wider at one side, slightly adjust your saw and test again until you achieve a great-looking joint. Miter-cut the side casing pieces so the short side of the cut reaches the reveal line, and partially hand-drive a few nails to temporarily hold them in place **10**. Measure across the top and cut the head casing. Position it; you may need to remove the temporary nails in the side casing to adjust for tight miter fits **11**. Finish attaching the casing with 2-in. power-driven nails, or with wire brads driven into the door frame and 6d nails driven into the wall framing **12**.

9 Test your casing cuts, and adjust your saw if needed for tight fits.

10 Cut and attach the side casing pieces with temporary nails.

11 Add the head casing and adjust the casing pieces for snug fits.

12 Drive nails to attach the casing.

MORE CASING POSSIBILITIES

Here are some more possibilities for casing windows and doors. All use trim pieces commonly available at lumberyards and home centers, and none call for making miter cuts. And for all, you can choose stained wood or painted trim.

To install this "traditional" style of casing, attach plain casing (also called sanitary casing) to the sides. Top them with a "fillet" of 1⅛-in. casing stop or a similar small piece. Then add a head casing of 1x4, and top that with another fillet, this time one that is a bit thicker.

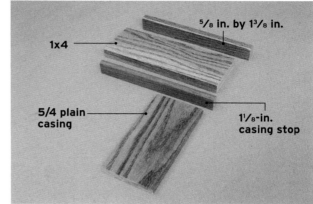

1x4
5/8 in. by 1³/8 in.
5/4 plain casing
1⅛-in. casing stop

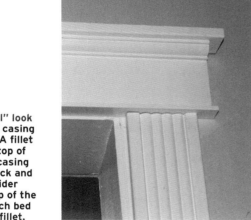

A distinctive "classical" look is achieved with fluted casing attached to the sides. A fillet of lattice is placed on top of that, and then a head casing that is about ⅝ in. thick and 3½ in. wide. Place a wider and thicker fillet on top of the head casing, then attach bed molding below the top fillet.

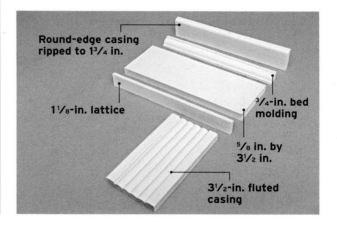

Round-edge casing ripped to 1³/4 in.
1⅛-in. lattice
³/4-in. bed molding
⅝ in. by 3½ in.
3½-in. fluted casing

This one is simplicity itself and can look either rustic or modern, depending on the materials you use. On the sides, install plain ("sanitary") casing, then install a head casing of 1x4 (which is ³/4 in. thick). Install the head casing so it overhangs the side pieces by ³/4 in. on each side.

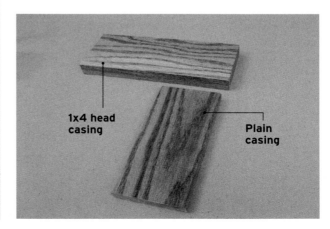

1x4 head casing
Plain casing

TRIMMING A WINDOW ON THE OUTSIDE

Brick molding, as shown here, is the most popular choice for outside window and door trim. Here, I use PVC vinyl brick molding, which will never need painting, lasts forever, and is easy to work with.

Measure the opening. If there are any masonry or old caulk protrusions, chip them away or plan for a trim size that takes them into account. (You can always install a thick bead of caulk around the molding, so there's no need to try for a tight fit.) Measure the diagonals ❶. If they are equal, the window is square; if not, remove the fasteners and use shims to bring the window square. You can draw a reveal line, or just plan on making the inside of the trim ½ in. wider and taller than the inside of the window frame, for a ¼-in. reveal all around. Also measure for the width of the molding all around. In this case, the bottom trim will need to be narrowed with a rip cut ❷.

➡ **For a reveal line, see step 3 of "Trimming a Door," p. 224.**

Miter-cut trim pieces, with the short side of the miters running from reveal to reveal. You can't hook your tape measure to a miter-cut end, so "burn an inch": Hold the tape at the 1-in. mark and make the cut mark at a point that shows 1 in. longer than the desired length ❸.

The bottom piece rests on a sill that is sloped down away from the house. So the piece will follow that line, rip-cut with a table saw or a circular saw set to a slight angle ❹. Working on a flat surface, assemble all four pieces of trim with four finish nails driven into each corner ❺. Where the bottom piece was rip-cut, you will need to cut off a little nub ❻. Set the trim assembly in place and nail or screw in place, taking care not to drive fasteners where they will interfere with the operation of the window ❼. Paint the trim. Finish with a bead of high-quality caulk. If a gap is wider than ¼ in., first push in some foam backer rod ❽.

1 Check that the window is square and make adjustments if needed.

2 Measure for the width of the trim all around.

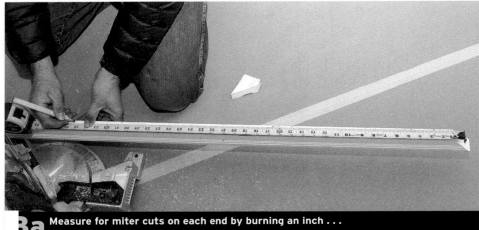

3a Measure for miter cuts on each end by burning an inch . . .

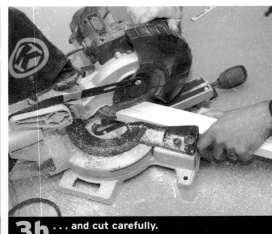

3b . . . and cut carefully.

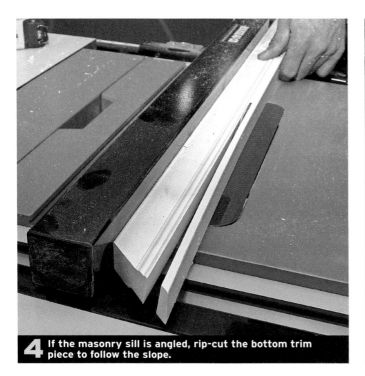

4 If the masonry sill is angled, rip-cut the bottom trim piece to follow the slope.

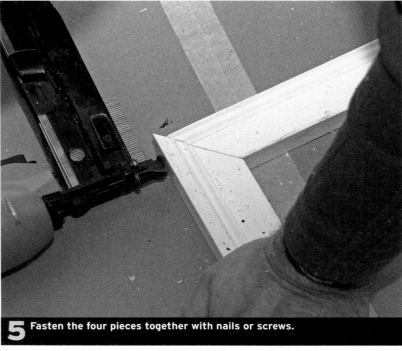

5 Fasten the four pieces together with nails or screws.

6 If one piece was rip-cut, use a handsaw to cut off the resulting protrusion.

7 Slip the assembly in place and fasten.

8 Push foam backer rod into the gap, then finish with a healthy bead of caulk.

INSTALLING BASEBOARD TRIM

Installing baseboard is much easier than window and door trim. The only significant wrinkle comes if you need to make a coped cut, but even that is easier than it may appear. As much as possible, buy trim boards long enough to span all the walls. Where boards cannot reach all the way, simply butt two neatly cut pieces together.

Measure for the length of a cut with a tape measure ❶. Where the tape curves upward, estimate the precise measurement and add ⅛ in. or ¹⁄₁₆ in. You can always cut the board if it's too long, and it's usually possible to bend long boards to fit.

A magnetic stud/screw finder, like the one shown, quickly finds fastener heads and stays stuck to the wall while you work. If you don't have one, look for fastener heads before applying the trim, and make light pencil marks on the wall or place pieces of tape on the floor to indicate where the studs are. In this case, it is certain that the studs are 16 in. on center, so the tape is placed with a red stud-space arrow at the known stud; all the other studs will be at the other red arrows ❷. For a simple base like this, drive two nails into each stud ❸. At a corner, a simple butt joint ❹ is more attractive than a more difficult mitered joint.

1 Measure for the cuts, adding ¼ in. for long runs, so you can bend the board in.

2 Locate the studs.

3 Drive two nails every 16 in. or so.

4 For simple moldings, butt-joint the corners.

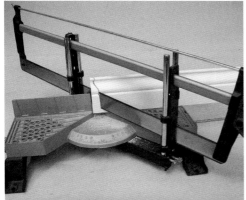
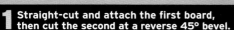

1 Straight-cut and attach the first board, then cut the second at a reverse 45° bevel.

2 Use a coping saw to cut along the revealed profile.

3 The cope-cut piece should fit snugly.

4 Test outside corner cuts with scrap pieces and adjust the saw if needed.

5 Use a well-placed shim to slightly adjust the angle of a bevel cut.

6 Base shoe can be simply cut at 45° bevels.

Making coped and miter cuts

More traditional base molding uses coped cuts at the corners of the trim and bevel cuts (often called miter cuts) for the base shoe. A beveled joint—with each piece cut at a 45° bevel—may seem the right choice for the base shoe as well, but it often results in a sloppy joint because walls are rarely perfectly square. A coped joint covers those sins.

Straight-cut the first board and attach it to the wall. The second board should be longer than needed; you will cut it to length later. With a miter saw, position the exposed edge of the cut board facing outward and cut at a reverse 45° bevel. (Here, I show a hand miter saw, but of course a power miter saw also works.) **1** Use a coping saw (or a jigsaw with a scrolling blade) to cut back along the profile that is revealed by the bevel cut **2**. Hold the saw so you back-cut at more than a 90° angle to the face of the board. The cope-cut end should fit snugly against the first piece **3**, though you may need to use a rasp or the saw to make minor adjustments. Hold the cope-cut piece in place and mark for cutting the other end to length.

At an outside corner, cut two pieces to 45° bevels and test the fit **4**. If the joint is not tight (as is often the case when the corner is not square), adjust your cuts and retest until you achieve the desired result. To adjust a cut, you could make tiny adjustments to a power miter saw. Or, place a shim against the miter saw's fence to make the bevel larger or smaller **5**. Base shoe is narrow and will usually look fine when simply cut at 45° bevels at a corner **6**.

FINISH PLUMBING AND WIRING

PLUMBING AND WIRING FIXTURES ARE usually installed last. Don't lose patience; take your time with these final installations, which if done right will elevate the look and feel of your new basement. Most of these projects are simple but need to be done carefully for a clean look and to be sure the systems will operate safely and effectively.

It's time to work clean. Wash your hands, cover floors, and keep the tools in your belt on a safe surface, so you do not mar the paint or dent walls as you work. Take steps to ensure that you don't nick chrome or brushed-nickel plumbing parts as you tighten them. Handle light fixtures gingerly, so you don't dent or scratch them. Take particular care with porcelain plumbing parts, which are strong and durable but can break if you are careless.

This is the good stuff, the final flourishes that will make your basement a place you can be proud of. Go ahead and bask in the compliments you will receive; you deserve them.

INSTALLING STOP VALVES

Install stop valves for the sink and toilet. You could install stop valves that are soldered onto copper pipe, but valves with compression fittings are easier to install, and you won't smudge your nice walls. The same type of fitting is used for PEX pipe. For good looks, install valves to completely cover the pipes.

Make sure the water is shut off. Hold the valve and the flange in place and mark for where you will cut the pipe. You can use a felt-tipped marker, but just holding your thumb in place works fine ❶. Cut the pipe with a tubing cutter or a PEX cutter ❷. Sand or wire-brush the cut end to get rid of any burrs. To install a compression-type valve, slide the copper or plastic ferrule onto the pipe, then slide onto the valve. Hold the valve in position, with the outlet pointing where you want it to point, and tighten the compression nut ❸.

CHOOSING STOP VALVES

Not all stop valves are created equal. Very inexpensive gate valves, called multi-turn valves for obvious reasons, are notoriously unreliable. Often, after some years they will fail to completely shut water off, which can be very annoying when working on plumbing. Better-quality and more reliable valves are usually of the ball type, meaning that you make a quarter turn to shut water off or turn it on.

1 Measure for cutting the pipe so the valve will hide it.

2 Cut the pipes with a tubing cutter.

3 Hold the valve still and tighten the compression nut.

INSTALLING TUB AND SHOWER FIXTURES

As long as the rough plumbing was done correctly and the outlets and tub/shower valve were installed firmly and in the correct positions, attaching the finish parts is pretty much a breeze. Still, take the time to read and follow the manufacturer's instructions. Here, I will show some of the most common procedures.

Wrap both ends of the shower arm with Teflon tape, which may be blue or white ❶. This ensures a tight seal and makes screwing things in place go more smoothly. Screw the arm in as tightly as you can by hand. If you are fairly strong, that will be tight enough; otherwise, wrap a cloth around the arm and tighten with a wrench. Add the showerhead and tighten with a crescent wrench ❷.

At the faucet (the valve), remove screws and pull out the temporary plastic guide ❸. Follow the manufacturer's instructions to assemble a mounting plate and screw it to the valve, then snap the escutcheon onto the mounting plate ❹. (Some models do not have a plate like this; the escutcheon mounts directly to the faucet with screws.) Screw on a handle assembly, then attach the

1 Wrap Teflon tape clockwise around both threaded ends of the shower arm.

2 Tighten the shower arm, then the showerhead.

3 Remove the faucet's plastic guide.

4a Mount the escutcheon. Here, a plastic plate is screwed on . . .

4b . . . then the escutcheon is snapped into place.

INSTALLING TUB AND SHOWER FIXTURES (CONTINUED)

handle to it; here, it attaches via a hex-head screw hidden under the handle **5**.

Spouts attach in various ways. For the model shown, buy a threaded nipple (short pipe) of the required length. Or, solder threaded male fittings onto both ends of a copper pipe. Wrap Teflon tape clockwise around both threaded ends **6**. Screw the pipe into the outlet in the wall and tighten with a pair of channel-type pliers. Hand-tighten the spout to the pipe and finish tightening by wrapping the spout with a protective cloth and turning with pliers or a pipe wrench **7**. (For a slip-on spout, you install a copper pipe with no threads, slip the spout onto it, and tighten a setscrew from below.)

5a Install the faucet's handle assembly . . .

5b . . . then attach the handle.

6 Wrap both ends of a pipe with Teflon tape and screw into the outlet in the wall.

7 Protect the spout from scratches and tighten with a wrench.

INSTALLING A TOILET

The toilet's drainpipe should be either 12 in. or 10 in. from the wall, depending on the toilet. (To be precise, 11½ in. or 9½ in., for a snug fit.) Cut off the pipe close to floor level using a reciprocating saw or handsaw. Then use a drill-mounted cutting tool to cut the pipe slightly below the floor level **❶**. Test-fit a toilet drain flange (also called a closet flange) by inserting it into the pipe; it should slide down all the way to the floor. If not, cut the pipe deeper or chip away any protrusions on the floor. Apply primer to the outside of the flange and to the inside of the pipe. Then apply PVC cement and push the flange down into place **❷**. Be sure to align the flange so you will be able to position the mounting bolts on the sides of the flange (see step 6). Drill pilot holes with the correct-size masonry bit and drive masonry screws to anchor the flange to the floor **❸**.

>> >> >>

For a snug fit, the toilet drainpipe should be ½ in. shy of either 12 in. or 10 in.

1 Cut the drainpipe slightly below floor level.

2a Dry-test the fit. Apply primer and cement . . .

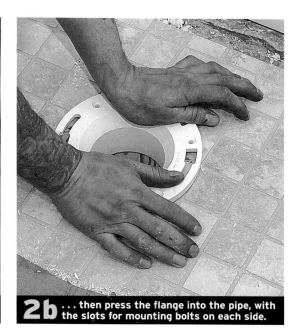

2b . . . then press the flange into the pipe, with the slots for mounting bolts on each side.

INSTALLING A TOILET (CONTINUED)

Assemble the toilet, following the manufacturer's instructions. On the tank, slip on a large rubber spud gasket and attach two or three mounting bolts ❹. Attach the tank to the bowl by tightening nuts from below as you hold the mounting bolts still from inside the tank ❺.

On the flange, slip on bowl mounting bolts so they are parallel to the rear wall and pointing up. Special plastic washers help hold them in position. Press a flanged wax ring onto the flange ❻. Lift the toilet, waddle over to the flange, and carefully lower it so the mounting bolts thread through the holes in the bowl ❼. Press down hard to see that the bowl rests firmly on the floor. You may need to slip in plastic shims if the floor is not level ❽. Slip on and tighten the mounting bolts ❾. If the bolt threads stick up too far, you will need to cut them with a hacksaw. Fill the decorative caps with plumbers putty and snap in place to cover the bolts ❿. Attach a supply tube running from the stop valve to the toilet's inlet, located under the tank.

3 Drill pilot holes and drive masonry screws to anchor the flange to the floor.

4 Prepare the tank for mounting onto the bowl.

5a Mount the tank onto the bowl by tightening mounting nuts.

5b From inside the tank, hold the bolt still as you tighten the nut from below.

6 Position upward-pointing mounting bolts and a flanged wax ring onto the toilet flange.

7 Lower the toilet so the mounting bolts thread through the holes in the bowl.

8 Push to see that the bowl rests firmly. Install plastic shims if needed.

9 Tighten the mounting bolts and cut them to height if needed.

10 Fill the plastic caps with putty and snap them over the mounting bolts.

INSTALLING A VANITY SINK

Most vanities have open backs, so it's easy to run the plumbing. If yours has a closed back, you will have to cut holes for the drain and supply pipes. (Or, remove the back.)

Install stop valves (p. 236). Slip the trap arm into the trap adapter in the wall, and just start to tighten the nut, so you can slide the arm as needed. Set the cabinet in place and check that it will fit nicely against the wall and will be at least reasonably level ❶. You may need to shim the bottom of the cabinet or cut base molding so the cabinet can go flush to the wall.

Install the faucet onto the sink top, following manufacturer's instructions. This model goes into a single hole; others use three holes ❷. Install the sink's tailpiece, which has an arm for the pop-up assembly. Attach the faucet's clevis strap to the pop-up arm and test that you will be able to raise and lower the stopper from above ❸. Set the sink top in place on the cabinet. From below, connect the trap to the tailpiece as shown. Slip on plastic or rubber washers for each joint and tighten the nuts with a wrench ❹. (If the nuts are designed to be tightened by hand, there is no need to use a wrench.) Check that the sink top is centered over the cabinet. Add any needed knobs or hardware and check again that you can easily raise and lower the stopper. Run a bead of caulk under the sink top to attach it to the cabinet ❺.

1 Check the fit of the cabinet against the wall.

2 Install the faucet.

3 Install the tailpiece and popup assembly.

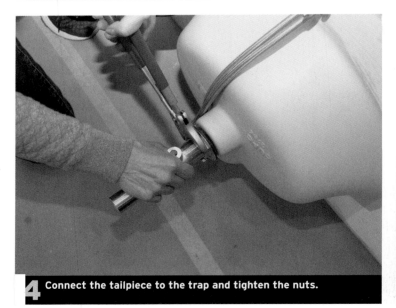

4 Connect the tailpiece to the trap and tighten the nuts.

5 Run a bead of caulk under the sink to attach to the cabinet.

INSTALLING A PEDESTAL SINK

You install a pedestal sink in some of the same ways as a vanity, except that the sink rests on a narrow pedestal rather than a cabinet, so it must be supported with screw/bolts driven into a framing member in the wall.

Set the pedestal in position and rest the sink on top so it abuts the wall. Check for level and draw a line around the top of the base on the bottom of the sink. Also insert your pencil into the fastener holes, to mark where the screw/bolts will go ❶. Remove the sink and drill pilot holes through the marks on the wall. If the wall is tiled, drill wider holes through the tiles with a tile or glass bit, taking care not to crack the tiles ❷. Install the faucet and tailpiece onto the sink ❸ and hook up the pop-up assembly as shown in the instructions for the vanity sink on the facing page.

Tap the bolts, which have a threaded and a machine end, into the holes so they engage with the wood framing. Thread two nuts onto the bolt and use a wrench to tighten the screw/bolt ❹. See that the bolts extend far enough out from the wall so they can be used to fasten the sink. Reposition the sink in place, threading the bolts through the mounting holes. Add a washer and nut, and tighten just enough to make the sink feel firm. If the pedestal feels wobbly because the floor is uneven, insert a plastic shim where needed ❺. Hook up the trap and the supply tubes for the faucet. You may choose to run a bead of silicone caulk where the sink meets the wall.

1 Position the sink and mark for the screw holes.

2 Drill pilot holes. If the wall is tiled, drill a larger hole through the tiles.

3a Install the faucet . . .

3b . . . then install the tailpiece.

4 Tighten bolts with a wrench, being careful you don't ding the tile.

5 If the pedestal wobbles, use a plastic shim to firm it up.

INSTALLING A BATHTUB

This is the most complicated and difficult of the finish plumbing installations, and you may consider hiring a pro for it. If the tub is cast iron, it will weigh 400 lb. or more, and you will have to move it back and forth while figuring the drain connection. The main trick: getting the tub's waste-and-overflow assembly to insert into the drainpipe in the floor—a particularly difficult task in a basement, where you don't have good access to the drainpipes.

Install a tub before installing backerboard and tile or another finished surface, so that the finished surface can overhang the tub's rim and splashed water will run into the tub. Most tubs are 60 in. long; some are 66 in. Check the manufacturer's instructions, but usually the opening should be about 1/2 in. longer than the tub. The framing should be precise and accurate, and there should be no obstacles (such as door jambs) in the way of getting the tub in place.

The literature will tell you exactly where the drainpipe (which leads directly into a P trap) should end up: how far away from the plumbing wall, how far away from the side wall, and how far below the floor level. Provide yourself with access, so you can reach in and connect the waste-and-overflow assembly with the drainpipe after the tub is in place ❶. Work carefully to install the pipe and trap with precision ❷.

Assemble a waste-and-overflow unit that is made for your tub ❸. There are a good number of possible sizes, so test the fit after assembly to be sure. Do not attach the assembly at this time. Working with helpers, carry the tub into the room and either slide it into place on top of strips of wood or tilt one up, position it, and drop it into place ❹. Check that the tub is level in both directions and shim as needed to make it level. ❺. Also check that it is at least close to being tight against the framing all around and adjust its position as needed ❻.   >> >> >>

1 Cut away framing and concrete so you can reach in to make connections.

2 Connect the drainpipe to a P trap and position it according to the manufacturer's instructions.

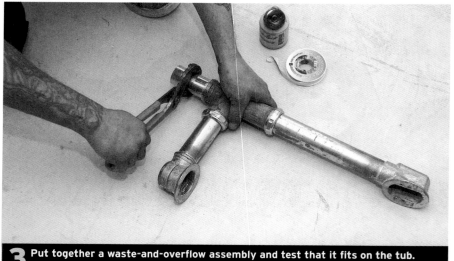

3 Put together a waste-and-overflow assembly and test that it fits on the tub.

4a Wrestle the tub into the room . . .

4b . . . and slide and/or tilt it into position.

5 See that the tub is level in both directions.

6 Adjust its position so it is snug along the framing.

INSTALLING A BATHTUB (CONTINUED)

Slip the waste-and-overflow assembly down into the drainpipe. Have a helper look from inside the tub to see that the connections match up with the overflow and drain holes on the tub, and partially tighten the assembly so it stays in place as you work **7**. Position a gasket and drive machine screws to attach the overflow **8**. Apply a rope of putty under the drain flange and screw the flange into the waste-and-overflow **9**. Tighten all the plumbing connections. Run water into the tub to test that there are no leaks.

If the tub is not stable, insert plastic shims to stabilize it. Attach concrete backerboard to the sides and apply tile or another surface; caulk the joint **10**.

7 Slip the waste-and-overflow's bottom pipe into the drainpipe and temporarily tighten the nut to hold it in place.

8 Attach the waste-and-overflow at the top, with a gasket behind the tub.

9 Place a rope of putty under the drain flange and screw it into the waste-and-overflow.

10 Install backerboard and tile or other finish material.

INSTALLING DEVICES AND FIXTURES

With the boxes in place and the wiring run, installing switches, receptacles, lights, and other features is usually a simple matter of following manufacturers' instructions and joining wires–either splicing them together with wire nuts or joining to terminals. Install all electrical cover plates after the walls and ceilings are painted; don't try to paint around them, or the result will be sloppy.

And, of course, be sure to shut off power at the service panel, and test to be sure that power is off before doing any work with wires.

➡ See "Stripping Cable and Wires," p. 142.

INSTALLING SWITCHES AND RECEPTACLES

Here, I show installing basic devices. If you have a split receptacle, a 240v receptacle, a three-way switch, or another out-of-the-ordinary installation, consult a book like Taunton's *Wiring Complete*.

Be sure to comply with local codes when you connect the ground wires for devices and fixtures. In most cases, if you have a metal box you need to use grounding pigtails (short sections of wire) that connect to both the device and the box. If you have plastic boxes, you need only connect to the device.

Installing receptacles

If one cable enters a receptacle box, strip and connect the hot (black or colored) wire to a brass terminal, and the neutral (white) wire to the silver terminal. Also connect the ground wire to the ground terminal. If two cables enter (as shown at right), splice the grounds together and run a pigtail to the grounding screw on the receptacle. If the box is metal (as shown below right), connect another pigtail to the box. Connect the two hots to the brass terminals and the two neutrals to the silver terminals.

Switches

In most cases, one cable brings power into a switch box and another cable carries it out to the fixture. Connect the grounds to the switch's ground terminal–and to the box as well if it is metal. Splice the neutrals together. Hook the two black wires to the switch's two terminals.

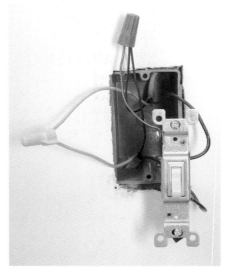

If two cables enter a switch box, connect the grounds, splice the neutrals, and connect hot wires to terminals.

To wire a receptacle, connect grounds together, then to the ground terminal. Connect hots to the brass terminals and neutrals to the silver terminals.

COOL TOOLS

Installing devices and a cover plate goes faster if you have one of these swiveling screwdrivers. If a cover plate does not cover all wall imperfections, try an oversize cover plate.

WHAT CAN GO WRONG

WORK SAFELY, WITH THE POWER OFF. Before you work on any wiring project, be sure to shut off power at the service panel and test to verify that power is off.

INSTALLING LIGHTS

Light fixtures come with attaching hardware and wire nuts or push-in connectors. Most attach to the ceiling box via a strap with two mounting screws or a center stud.

Start by connecting the fixture's ground wire, which may be green or bare, to the house ground wire. Or, in the case of conduit wiring, connect the ground to a grounding screw ❶. Attach the strap with two mounting screws ❷. Some straps are rectangular and run across the box; this one is round. Connect the hot house wire to the fixture's black lead and the neutral wire to the white lead. This fixture has a push-in connector ❸. Carefully fold the wires up into the box, so they cannot be damaged when you attach the fixture ❹. Attach the globe or lens with the hardware provided ❺.

1 Connect the ground wire to a metal box or to the house's ground wire.

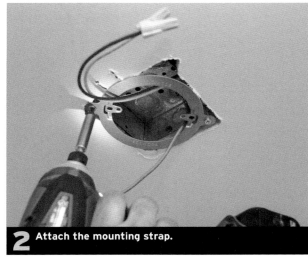

2 Attach the mounting strap.

3 Connect the white lead to the neutral wire and the black lead to the hot wire.

4 Fold the wires up into the box.

5 Attach the lens or globe.

CENTER STUD HARDWARE

If a fixture attaches using a center stud, attach the strap to the box and screw in the center stud. After connecting the wires, slide the fixture up through the stud and screw on a nut to fasten to the ceiling.

RECESSED CAN TRIMS

These are usually simple to install, though the wire mounts can be a bit balky. Simply clip the fixture's light socket to the trim. Squeeze the wire pairs together, slip them into slots in the fixture, and push up. A variety of trims are available, including the rotatable eyeball below.

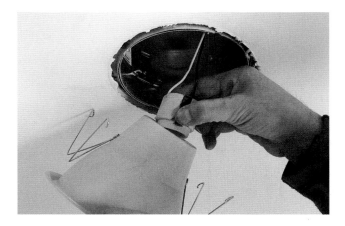

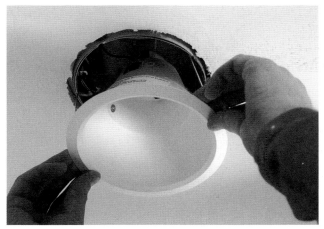

SIMPLE ACCESS COVERS

Access covers for plumbing require some framing, but these are small and can be simply slipped over a hole cut in the drywall.

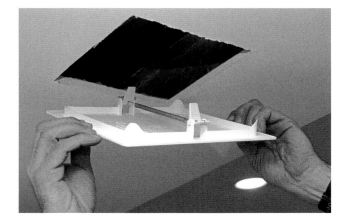

INDEX